HOW TO MAINTAIN & ENJOY YOUR
COLLECTOR CAR

Josh Malks

Motorbooks International
Publishers & Wholesalers ®

To my wife Betty
who winces at my greasy fingernails
and listens to my enthusiast's prattle
and loves me anyway
this book is dedicated.

First published in 1995 by Motorbooks International Publishers & Wholesalers, 729 Prospect Avenue, PO Box 1, Osceola, WI 54020-0001 USA

Motorbooks International books are also available at discounts in bulk quantity for industrial or sales-promotional use. For details write to Special Sales Manager at the Publisher's address

Library of Congress Cataloging-in-Publication Data

Malks, Josh B.
    How to maintain & enjoy your collector car / Josh Malks.
        p.   cm.
    Includes index.
    ISBN 0-7603-0056-9 (pbk.)
    1. Antique and classic cars--Maintenance and repair. I. Title.
TL 152.M234   1995   95-38151
629.28'72--dc20

On the front cover: Pontiac's sportiest offering for 1956 was the convertible Star Chief. A 317ci, 227hp Strato Streak V-8 provides the urge for Dennis DuBrow's red beauty, and Ronny's Automotive in Altadena, California, provides the period backdrop. *Dennis Adler*

Printed and bound in the United States of America

Contents

Acknowledgments

Sections of this book were written with the help of some extraordinary professionals and talented hobbyists. Some are retired, others currently active in their fields. All have graciously offered their knowledge to help other enthusiasts preserve their precious vehicles. In addition to their other accomplishments, most of them love and maintain old cars, boats, and planes. I list them here in alphabetical order, with their credentials.

Bill Cannon is founder and Technical Editor of *Skinned Knuckles* magazine, whose sub-title speaks volumes: *Written by Restorers, for Restorers.* I've tried to learn from Bill's meticulous documentation of the opinions he expresses.

Carl Cedarstrand is a physicist, retired from Beckman Instruments. He spent four decades in the design of mechanical, electromechanical, and optical devices, and the development of materials necessary to make them work. He drives an MG-TD, and has an avid interest in the failure mechanisms of mechanical parts.

Corky Coker is president of the Coker Tire Company, a leading supplier of tires for collector cars. He is chairman of the Automotive Restoration Market Organization (ARMO), a group which has aided hobbyists in fighting clunker laws and restrictive licensing agreements. He's a life member of the Antique Automobile Club of America.

Jeff Dreibus is "The Old Carb Doc." He shared his wealth of experience in carburetion, fuel delivery systems, and the effect of the new fuels on older car parts.

Douglas Godfrey began his career in tribology at the NASA laboratory in Cleveland. He later joined Chevron Research, retiring in 1983. He has written fifty-five papers on tribology and has been honored by the Society of Tribologists and Lubricating Engineers. He has continued consulting since his retirement.

Bruce Hamilton is an analytical chemist who lives in New Zealand. He's worked for General Motors and for British Petroleum. His current position involves him with emissions analysis and with the evaluation of alternative automotive fuels.

Matt Joseph is best-known for his articles in *Skinned Knuckles* and *Cars and Parts*. I thank him for his willingness to share his breadth of knowledge of matters automotive.

Robert C. Joseph, Ph.D., is the author of the definitive history of the Ethyl Corporation.

Gordon Millar is a consulting engineer. Before he retired he was a vice president of the Ethyl Corporation. His love is antique boats, and he writes extensively for boating magazines.

Thomas S. Pendergast is a mechanical engineer. He's retired from a career that included work with aircraft electrical systems and with aeronautical and industrial gas turbines. He drives and restores classic and collector cars and flies an antique plane.

Fred Rau is the editor of *Motorcycle Consumer News*, a fast-growing non-advertising magazine that tests and rates motorcycle industry products. An electrical engineer, he operated a power plant for a major utility for twenty years. In 1986, he turned his full-time attention to his true love, motorcycling. He's edited *MCN* since 1990.

John and Betty Schoepke first developed the concept of "bag" storage of collector cars in 1985. They've been active since in researching methods and materials for safe storage of valuable vehicles.

A. Grayson Walker III is a Florida management consultant. He's an avid enthusiast, with a particular interest in Ferrari. His experiences with his 1984 308 Spyder find voice in his writings on exterior and interior detailing.

Robert E. Wallace, is a vice-president of J.C. Taylor, Inc. They are one of the leading agencies providing collector car insurance coverage.

Mark D. Warden, Ph.D., is president of COVA, the Council of Vehicle Associations. The organization has been in the forefront of educating hobbyists in appropriate responses to government actions that affect our hobby. He writes extensively for current magazines.

My thanks also to the Eastwood Company, The Gates Rubber Company, Griot's Garage, Herguth Laboratories, Hunter Engineering Company, Pall Industrial Hydraulics Corporation and Wix Filters for the use of photographs and drawings, and other courtesies extended to me. Special thanks to my friend Hans Halberstadt for his sage counsel.

Introduction

When many of us bought our first car, it was often a vehicle between ten and fifteen years of age. It had usually seen better days, which was why we could afford it. We lavished months of effort on "fixing it up." (Who knew then that this was called restoration?) We often attempted to improve on the original, mechanically and visually. We went on dates in it, hung around it, worked underneath it, told lies about it, loved it . . . and drove it. After all, that's what it was for. And it ran and ran.

Decades later, that same car has become "collectible." The time and the money that a new owner puts into returning it to original appearance and condition are usually multiples of the purchase price when the car was new. In the fifties and sixties, collectible cars were often the grand classics of an earlier era. Today's popular collectibles are more likely to be cars originally intended for stylish everyday transportation.

And what happens after these cars are restored? Lewis Carroll would have loved it. In a development worthy of *Alice In Wonderland*, Americans spend millions of dollars each year buying and restoring machinery whose intended purpose was transportation, then consign that machinery to suspended animation under a car cover. Ironically, this is done in the interests of preserving these artifacts of another era. In practice, it's destroying them.

Idle mechanical devices deteriorate. Seals dry up, brake fluid congeals, rust begins. Cars that are started and idled only occasionally suffer the additional damage of acid corrosion.

Given reasonable care, the best thing you can do to preserve your collectible car is to drive it. The wear it will receive is far less damaging than the results of vegetating. How to keep your car driveable is what this book is about. At least once a week, my mid-1930s classic car goes out for exercise. Sometimes, on my way home, I stop to pick up something in the supermarket, or pause to fill the gas tank. Admiring passers-by often ask "Aren't you afraid to drive it?" Nope. As a matter of fact, I'd be afraid *not* to.

Even more important than the effect on the car is the effect on the driver. If your newly restored collectible wears out, it can be restored again. But you, the driver, can't. Every year in which you miss the fun of driving your prize is a year less in which to do it.

Driving is good for the spirit, too. Drivers and passengers in other cars smile, wave, and applaud. Children stare at your rolling history lesson, and actually engage their parents in conversation.

There's a cloud gathering over that happy scene, though. It's true that our collector cars are still viewed positively by most of the population. To remain so, they must be driven responsibly, with concern for the environment. Collectors themselves must participate in what has become a national debate on the place of the automobile in our society. To help our cause, we must become familiar with the facts and not rely on the platitudes of yesteryear. Make no mistake. The concept of the collector car as a benign artifact is under attack and must be wisely defended if it is to survive.

The purpose of this book is to help you maintain your car as a driving vehicle. I'll share with you some of the knowledge of experts in a variety of disciplines that affect our car hobby. You won't find specific "how-tos" on subjects common to all cars, like tune-ups or paint touch-up. Neither will you find instructions for repairs or restoration. There are already many good sources for such information. I do suggest some places to look.

In some of the discussions in this book I mention proprietary products and some sources. I have no financial interest in any of these products or sources and report only on my own experience with them.

Some of the concerns I raise regarding the protection of your car from the assaults of corrosion, abrasion, and other ills may seem extreme. Remember, though, that you may plan to keep your collector car for a much longer time than your every-day machine. Also, modern metallurgy and technology are incorporated in the new cars that we drive daily. These protect them from some of the ills that can beset our older treasures. To similarly protect our older cars, we need to work a bit harder. I've tried to provide the background that led to each of my recommendations. So pick and choose among my proposals, but at least consider them.

A decision you'll have to make before following some of the suggestions in this book has to do with how *you* dear reader, use *your* collector car. While I hope that all readers are drivers, the ratio of driving-to-show-going will vary dramatically from car to car. Californians may drive more than New Englanders, and lucky owners of several collectibles may drive some and show others. As I define it, "Show Trim" is the way you want your car to look when the car is exhibited or judged at a car show. "Tour Trim" describes the modifications you may make to insure reliability on the road, for trips and tours. If most of your use is for judged shows, you'll want to maintain your car in Show Trim. You'll convert to Tour Trim for occasional long trips. If driving your collector car is your major pleasure, then maintain it in Tour Trim. Convert to Show Trim for the occasional show.

Tour Trim may alter the appearance of some parts of your car. Ideally, visible modifications should be of a bolt-on nature, so they can be quickly replaced by original components when you exhibit your car. Some improvements are permanent, but with ingenuity you can often render them near-invisible. You'll need to provide access to those components that may need service. Advance thought given to these issues will make the conversion from Tour to Show Trim easier and more satisfying.

On a side street in London once, I watched a magnificent old Daimler limousine pull up in front of a small hand laundry. The uniformed chauffeur was alone in the car. He got out, went in, and emerged carrying a paper-wrapped package of shirts. Back behind the wheel and the gorgeous vehicle purred off. A classic worth a fortune had gone on a prosaic errand. Did that demean the Daimler? I don't think so; I think it elevated the laundry!

Driving your pride and joy is good for you and good for the car. Let's do it.

—*Josh B. Malks, fall 1995*

CHAPTER ONE

Wear and Lubricants

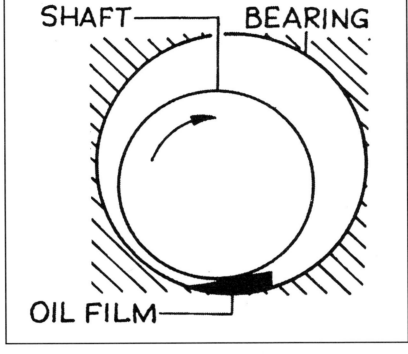

The wedge of oil created by HDL lifts the journal off the bearing.

A restorer friend recently showed me a project he was working on. A fine classic of the 1930s had been purchased at a respected auction. This particular make had a reputation for excellent driving characteristics. The new owner found it otherwise, and sought help. My friend found some mechanical problems, which he repaired. What was most startling, however, was that, except for the engine, transmission and rear end, there was not a drop of lubricant anywhere on the car! Door strikers and dovetails were chromed and polished. Hood and trunk props were literally squeaky clean. Steering linkage and tie rod ends, when dismantled, were actually rusty! This car gave new meaning to the word "clean." It was also well on its way to self-destruction by wear.

The study of the causes and effects of friction, lubrication, and wear is called Tribology. An automobile is a big tribological device. Friction, lubrication and wear abound. Many parts of a car couldn't work without friction. Friction holds a nut on a bolt. Friction is required for a clutch to work, and for brakes to stop the car. Moving parts of the car, on the other hand, must be lubricated to reduce friction and prevent wear. Because lubrication is sometimes imperfect, some wear can still take place.

There's no need for you to become a lubrication engineer or a tribologist to keep your collector car running for decades more than its builders anticipated. This chapter will look at the causes of wear, what makes up modern motor oils and other lubricants, and how to match them to the needs of your collector car. It'll be a simplified exposition of a complex subject. But an understanding of the causes of wear and how lubrication works will put you in a better position to make decisions on which products to use, procedures to follow, and driving techniques to practice.

Kinds of Wear

To the unaided eye, polished metal surfaces look mirror-smooth. Crankshaft and connecting rod bearings, and the journals that turn in them, are examples. Under high magnification, though, these smooth-appearing metal surfaces

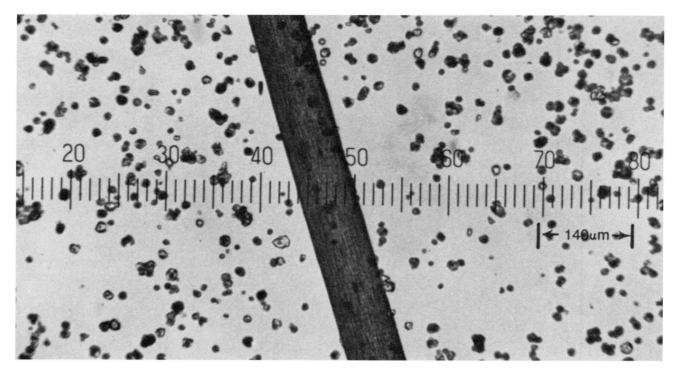

The human hair shown in this photograph is about 70 microns wide. The particles, any of which could damage a car's engine, are about 10 microns in size.

actually show impressive projections called asperities. It's these asperities whose contact with each other we're trying to eliminate. If contact occurs, wear occurs. Oil prevents metal-to-metal contact by keeping parts floating on a film of oil most of the time. Different operating conditions call upon different physical and chemical characteristics of the oil. The oil you use and the way you drive determines the lubricant's ability to protect your engine and drive train from damage.

All circulating used engine oil carries solid particles. Some dirt enters the engine through the carburetor and some through crankcase breathers. Dirt in the fuel eventually makes its way into the oil. So do abrasives from an often-overlooked source: dirt and metal chips left behind during engine overhauls. Other particles are the results of the wear of engine components.

While there are at least ten different kinds of wear that can occur in the moving parts of our cars, some of them are immune to any corrective action we can practically take. Happily, three of the worst car-destroyers can be controlled, if not completely eliminated, by proper maintenance and operating practices.

Abrasion is the gouging of metal surfaces by hard particles that are too large to pass freely through the clearance between a bearing and its journal. When your engine is running, a jour-

nal doesn't ride centered in the bearing. Most of the clearance is on the top; only a fraction is at the bottom. (Actually, the position of the clearances change as the load changes direction, but "top" and "bottom" are easy to visualize.) An oil film separates the surfaces. Film thicknesses are measured in thousandths of a millimeter, commonly called microns. (A micron is about 0.00004in.) So oil film thickness may range between 0.5 and 20 microns.

Particles of grit circulating in the oil will eventually attempt to pass through the bearings. They'll cut their way through the soft babbitt surface of the bearing, or embed themselves in it. The Cummins Engine Company has done extensive testing of the relationship of the size of grit particles to engine damage by abrasion. While the tests were conducted on diesel engines, the principles hold true for our gasoline engines as well. What Cummins found was that the most wear was caused by the smallest particles. Particles that were much larger than the bearing's dynamic clearance couldn't enter the bearing at all.

Exactly the same results were found to apply to the cylinder walls. Most of the grit in this case enters with carburetor air. Findings were similar for cam lobes, cam followers, and the bushings used on the camshaft.

The meaning is inescapable. Cleanliness—clean oil, clean air, clean fuel—is a vital factor in achieving long life for all parts of your car and its engine. Achieving that cleanliness is a function of filtration, the topic of a later chapter.

Adhesion describes what can happen when actual metal-to-metal contact occurs in your engine. As we've seen, even the smoothest, most finely-machined metal surfaces are rough, when viewed microscopically. Because of this, when two metal surfaces are pushed together, the "high spots" begin to touch. The more the surfaces are squeezed together or loaded, the more of the high spots that touch. If the surfaces are sliding against each other, microscopic welds occur. As the welds are torn apart, metal is transferred from one surface to the other in a disorderly manner. The surface becomes increasingly rough and even more likely to weld together. We see the result as scuffing.

Adhesion is prevented by keeping the surfaces from touching. Accomplishing this means using the proper oils and greases.

Acid corrosion occurs on damp surfaces exposed to exhaust gases. While that seems to only describe the inside of your exhaust system, it applies equally to the cylinders of your engine. About a gallon of water is formed in your exhaust for every gallon of gasoline burned. Exhaust gases contain sulfur, among other things; the combination of these produces sulfuric acid. Any acid that is permitted to condense on cylinder walls begins a corrosive attack on that wall.

You can minimize acid corrosion by choosing a motor oil with additives that neutralize acid. You can stop acid condensation, and the damage it causes, by proper starting, driving, and stopping techniques. We'll discuss these in the chapter on touring.

How Lubrication Works.

To lubricate our collector cars properly, and to avoid the problems described above, its helpful to understand how lubricants protect moving parts. The engine, the most complex mechanism in your collector car, benefits from three "regimes" of lubrication.

HDL

When your engine is running at a constant speed, under moderate load and at moderate temperature, crankshaft and rod journals in their bearings act somewhat like pumps to produce a wedge-shaped film of oil on which the journal actually rides without touching the shaft. This is hydrodynamic lubrication, or HDL. It's the best kind of lubrication; it results in low friction and extremely low wear. Note that the desirable wedge of oil that is characteristic of HDL is generated by hydraulic pressure developed by the rotation of the shaft. It is not solely a result of engine oil pressure, which by itself is insufficient to completely separate the moving metal parts. We've all experienced HDL at work in the frightening phenomenon of hydroplaning. In this case, rainwater is the lubricant, and the smooth tires and highway represent the surfaces of bearings and shaft. No outside hydraulic pressure is applied. With the brakes locked, the sliding tire generates the wedge of water all by itself and lifts the tire off the road.

In the best circumstances, other internal parts of your engine operate with HDL, too. These include camshaft bushings, piston rings against the cylinder wall (except at top and bottom dead center), the valve lifter, the part of the cam lobe that's circular, and the valve stems in their guides.

BL

In earlier years, motor oil was essentially a refined petroleum with undesirable components like wax removed. These "base stocks" met automotive lubrication needs if oil was changed often enough. Engine life in the 1930s and 1940s rarely reached 100,000 miles, and then only with valve and ring jobs along the way. Striving to do better, chemists and engineers added small amounts of oil-soluble chemicals to base stocks. These additives have played a major role in the increased longevity of modern engines. They can play a similar role in the long life of your collector car. One important additive function comes into play when a part of your engine isn't operating in the HDL regime.

When you accelerate suddenly, the relative speed of the crankshaft journals and their bearings increases rapidly. But the load on those bearings increases even more rapidly. The oil film is ruptured momentarily. Actual metal-to-metal contact may occur. Into the breach to prevent catastrophic failure springs boundary lubrication, or BL. It's called that because the "boundaries" or surfaces of the metals are involved. BL occurs between surfaces sliding at relatively slow speeds under high temperatures and high loads. The burden for providing BL falls mostly to additives dissolved in the oil by the refiner. These "anti-wear agents" react chemically with the metal surfaces, just when temperatures rise due to initial metal-to-metal contact. They form thin, inorganic films with a high melting point.

Think back to sliding along in your stocking feet on a bare wood floor. Now recollect the sensation on a waxed floor, and you can visualize the action of the films formed by the anti-wear additives.

The most widely used anti-wear additive is a form of zinc dialkyldithiophosphate. ("Zinc" is good enough for future mentions.) The films formed on the metal surfaces are sacrificial—they are worn away as they protect. When fresh metal appears again, the zinc causes new films to form. This vital oil additive is used up as it performs its function. This is one of the reasons to replace motor oil regularly.

Some parts of the engine never experience conditions for HDL. These include the piston ring-cylinder wall contact at top and bottom dead center. As the piston slows, then stops, the oil wedge is lost. ("Slow" is a relative term in engine work; that piston may be slowing, stopping, and restarting forty times a second!) The only lubrication here is BL. If you've ever dismantled or rebuilt an engine, you've noticed that cylinder wear is greatest at the top of the piston travel. This is one of the reasons. Wear with BL is many times greater than under HDL conditions.

EHL

When hard metals contact each other at concentrated spots under great pressure, an extremely thin film of oil prevents actual contact. Pressures like these actually cause the metal parts to deform where they touch. You've seen strobe pictures of a golf ball flattening when the club hits. The elasticity of the material permits it to regain its original shape as soon as the pressure relaxes. Hard steel is also elastic, and ball and roller bearings deform in exactly this way. So do gear teeth. In an engine, so do the cam lobes and the lifters on which they push. The flat area is extremely small and the oil film extremely thin. Under these enormous pressures the oil actually turns to a very viscous material almost like nylon. It liquefies again when the pressure is removed. This kind of lubrication is elastohydrodynamic lubrication, or EHL.

The lubricating regimes described above do occur in your engine and other parts of your car. Mixed HDL, BL, and EHL conditions also occur. Some components operate in mixed regimes, and some go quickly from one to another.

You may find this discussion of tribology either interesting or boring. The important knowledge for us as car owners is that the survival of our machinery depends on our providing lubricants that are capable of maintaining the lubrication patterns described above, and in treating the machinery in a manner that interferes as little as possible with the conditions of good lubrication.

Remember too that the oil washing the bearings does more than keep metal surfaces from touching. It carries away any wear particles, so they may be trapped by the oil filter and removed from circulation. Even more vital, it plays an important role in carrying away heat from the bearings and journals. The hot oil returns to the oil pan, where it gives off some heat through the walls of the pan. Highly stressed engines may use aluminum oil pans, often with fins, to improve heat transfer. Racing engines use small oil radiators, called oil coolers, to remove even more heat from the oil before it recirculates.

About Motor Oil

The simple quart of oil that you put in your collector car's engine is far more than just refined petroleum. It's a complex chemical combination designed to provide the three types of lubrication required by different conditions, and in different combinations. Before considering the additives, it's useful to understand the most important consideration in choosing a motor oil—its viscosity.

Viscosity is the property that primarily governs the thickness of the oil film in HDL. It's a measure of an oil's resistance to flow. "Thicker" oils have a higher viscosity, "thinner" oils lower. Viscosity is measured in units of Centipoise, Centistokes, or Saybolt Universal Seconds. None of these laboratory measurements is used to identify the motor oil that you buy for your car. The Society of Automotive Engineers (SAE) has set up a numbering system that's more familiar. It's commonly referred to as "weight;" engineers prefer the term "grade." For automotive purposes, SAE grades range from five to fifty. The grades are arbitrary numbers that indicate the viscosity range at a temperature of 100deg Centigrade (212deg Fahrenheit). A

"W" added to the number indicates that the measurement of viscosity was taken at a temperature of 0deg Centigrade (32deg Fahrenheit). Because of the importance of viscosity, the SAE classification system refers to viscosity alone and makes no reference to any other physical or performance characteristics.

Using oil that's more viscous than required creates several problems. In cold temperatures it may not pump as quickly to all parts of the engine. Too-viscous an oil may create cooling problems because it doesn't carry heat away from bearings as quickly. Higher fluid friction will also increase gasoline consumption. Oil that's thinner than required will (surprise!) have its own set of problems. Of most concern is its lower film strength and inability to separate moving parts as well as it should. Related problems are increased oil consumption, potential leakage, and increased engine noise.

Oils are sold in single grades, like SAE 30, or "multi-grades," like SAE 10W-30. Many collector cars were designed during an era when oil came only in single grades. Most oil refiners still supply single-grade oils, usually SAE 30 and 40. *There is nothing old-fashioned or inferior about these oils.* The additive package is usually the same as in the multi-grade oils, testified to by the same API service classification on the bottle or can. Under some circumstances, this is still a satisfactory recommendation.

Multi-viscosity oils are supposed to have the characteristics of each grade at different temperatures. A 5W-30 oil will behave like a 5-grade oil at 32deg Fahrenheit and like a 30-grade oil at 212deg. That does not mean that it gets more viscous as it gets warmer. All oils get less viscous as they get hot. This 5W-30 oil gets thinner more slowly than one would expect of a 5-grade oil, so when 212deg is reached, it's no thinner than 30-grade oil would be at that temperature.

Multi-viscosity oils are created by starting with a very low viscosity base stock. Then a very viscous polymer is added. These have little effect at low temperatures. At high temperatures, they keep the low viscosity base stock from getting even thinner. Refiners call these additives Viscosity Index Improvers, or VI Improvers for short. They're a mixed blessing. At heart, wide range conventional (not synthetic) multi-viscosity oils are 5W or 10W base stocks. Keeping their viscosity up at high temperatures demands the use of a lot of polymers. Fewer polymers are best for all engines because it's the oil that lubricates, not the polymers.

Other Additives in the Oil

The crude base oil stock, no matter how carefully refined, is not capable of meeting the lubrication needs of engines running today, whether modern or vintage. In addition to VI Improvers, refiners add chemical compounds to the base oil

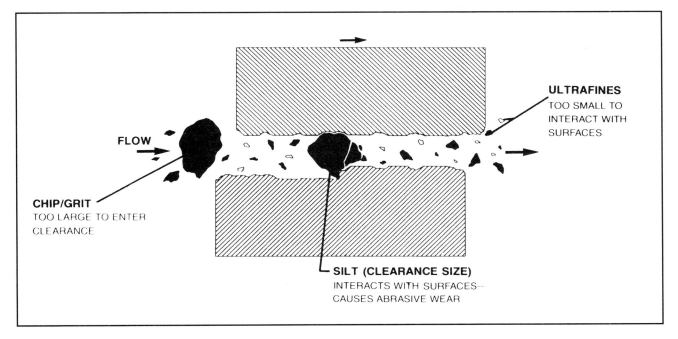

Abrasives bury themselves in bearing surfaces and act as cutting tools. Most damage is caused by particles about equal in size to the bearing's operating clearance.

to deal with specific problems created by the operation of internal combustion engines. These are generally referred to as additives, and they're in every container of oil that you can buy today.

Anti-wear agents provide boundary lubrication. *Dispersants* help control deposits. A pinch of *silicones* controls foam. *Corrosion inhibitors* reduce rust and neutralize acids.

You may have read that the modern oils with detergents should not be used in old engines. You've heard that it will loosen dirt and particles, which will then clog passages and result in burned bearings. That doesn't happen. The detergents in oil are better described as detergent/dispersants. They do keep interior surfaces clean, but the rest of their job is to hold dirt particles in suspension, so they may be carried to the oil filter and there removed from the oil.

Synthetic Oils

Viscosity, we've seen, is the most important characteristic of a motor oil. This is the area in which so-called synthetic oils shine. Synthetic lubricants, like conventional oils, are made from petroleum. It's the treatment that's different. There are different types of synthetics, so any definition must be broad. Generally, synthetic lubricants are the result of reactive chemical processes that create substances of higher molecular weight than the original reacting substances, *with planned and predictable physical properties.* That's the key difference between synthetics and familiar conventional oils.

A petroleum motor oil starts out as a base stock with a grab-bag of ingredients and properties. Some of the harmful molecules are separated out by distillation, extraction, and filtration. What's left are the most useful molecules from the original crude oil stock, but the molecules themselves are largely unchanged. Chemicals are then added to bring the final blend as close as possible to the requirements of an engine lubricant. A synthetic motor oil is produced by chemical reactions, and its molecules are tailored to meet the specific needs of engine lubrication. So synthetic oils require far smaller quantities of additives to meet those needs.

Synthetic oil technology goes back to the 1920s. Synthetics saw some use in WWII but came to the public's attention when they became the only lubricants that could handle the heat and pressure of the new jet airliner engines and the extreme cold of the Alaska pipeline.

Today synthetics are produced by major oil companies like Mobil and Amoco, as well as by some fine chemical companies like Emery.

The several classes of synthetics that are applicable to automobile use each have multi-syllabic names. If you're interested in the chemistry, texts are available at your library to elaborate on this subject. For our purposes, using a synthetic oil produced by a well-known supplier is safe advice.

The major advantage of synthetics is their inherently greater viscosity stability over a wide range of temperatures. A synthetic 5W-30 oil contains a far smaller quantity of VI Improver than does a conventional 10W-30 oil. Most synthetics react far less with water than do conventional oils, so they produce less corrosive acid. Higher film strength means they need smaller quantities of anti-wear additives. Their superior lubricity means less engine friction, which can translate into less wear and better gas mileage.

These properties of synthetics make them outstanding motor oils. They also cost more. For our collector cars, whose oils may be changed once or twice a year, the cost burden will not be onerous.

In years past, synthetics displayed some problems of compatibility with neoprene and other seal compounds used in older engines and transmissions. Synthetic producers have worked toward solving these problems, but caution is still advised. If you decide to try the superior lubrication of synthetics, keep an eye out for leaks for the first few thousand miles of driving. Sometimes, a seal that held oil because it was nicely coated with years of engine gook starts to leak when cleaned up because of the tendency of synthetics to dissolve sludge and lacquer deposits. A new seal may fix the leak.

Marketplace decisions are bound to become even more complicated with time. At least one major refiner now offers a "semi-synthetic" 10W-30. It's a blend of synthetic and conventional motor oil. As might be expected, the ads offer the best of both types at half the price of synthetic. Can others be far behind?

The Numbers on the Bottle

The typical car driver is in no position to evaluate the additive package or real-world capabilities of a quart of engine oil. Beginning in 1958 the American Petroleum Institute (API) created "service classifications" for motor oils. Oils were graded in tests conducted by the American Society for Testing and Materials (ASTM). Three gaso-

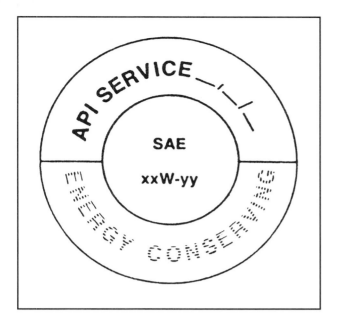

The API symbol describes the oil in the container. The API "Service" designation and the "SAE" grade are described in the text. Any special energy-conserving attributes of this oil appear in the lower half of the circle.

line engine categories were established: ML, MM, and MS, for Light, Medium, and Severe service. The grading method didn't prove entirely satisfactory, and a joint effort by API, ASTM, and SAE resulted in a new system that better communicates between the oil producers and the engine manufacturers. This system is defined as SAE J183 Engine Oil Performance and Engine Service Classification. In 1988 API established the symbol that appears on containers of motor oil to help motorists match the needs of their engines to the quality of the oil.

The first letter of the API service category indicates the kind of engine this oil was intended for. "S" is for gasoline engines, "C" for diesels. The second letter designates oil quality. The higher the letter, the higher the quality. Each new quality level indicates that the motor oil has passed tests designed to meet the increasingly stringent needs of newer engines.

Oil Pressure

The most important thing about oil pressure is to have some. Normal oil pressure varies from engine to engine, and with engine speed. Pressure is higher when oil is cold and viscous and drops as it warms up. Look for oil pressure that doesn't change dramatically from one drive to the next. So long as pressure remains within the range indicated as "normal" on a car with a gauge, or the oil pressure light stays off, there's little need for concern. Remember that some oil pressure sending units won't turn the warning light on until pressure has dropped to 4 lb/sq-in.

A sudden drop in gauge pressure that stays down or a gauge that falls to zero at driving speeds or a light that comes on suddenly is reason to *immediately* pull off the road and stop. If a check reveals that oil level is correct, call the tow truck. If you continue to drive you'll still need the tow truck, a few miles and a seized engine later.

Greases

Greases are oils gelled with compounds like soap. A variety of gelling agents are used commercially to make grease. The grease is often named for the gelling agent. If a sodium soap is used, the grease is called sodium-based. The same for calcium soaps and lithium soaps. Nearly all of the name brand "chassis greases" are lithium-based. Some modern greases are gelled with synthetic chemicals or specially-treated fine clay. The more soap used with the oil, the harder the grease.

NLGI numbers describe the "hardness" of a grease and in that sense relate to the amount of soap in it. The numbers run from one to six, with the lower numbers denoting softer greases. Chassis grease, for comparison, is usually #2.

The purpose of using a grease rather than oil is to avoid the need for an oil pan, pumps and tubing. It's the oil weeping out of the grease that does the lubricating job. The soap simply holds the oil. The bulk of the gelled compound that we call grease is just the soap carrier.

Greases are not as good as oil for lubricating for several reasons. (As you consider these, think about a wheel bearing or a tie rod end, both of which are lubricated by grease.) Greases do not carry away heat, since the grease does not circulate. There's no pressure moving the lubricant in grease to where its needed, as there is with motor oil. So, if the grease was not introduced into all the spots where it might be needed, the possibility of oil starvation exists. Further, wear fragments and contaminants in grease remain in the immediate vicinity of the lubricated parts and can damage them. Lastly, it's difficult to completely flush these contaminants out of a greased bearing without complete disassembly.

CHAPTER TWO

Oil Changes, Grease Jobs, and What Oil to Use

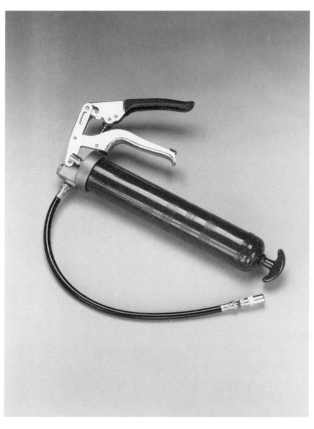

Hand-operated grease gun with flexible extension.

What should you look for in a motor oil? Put simply, buy a major brand. These suppliers spend large sums on research and on the development of a balanced package of additives. While its certainly true that many 'house brands' and unknown labels are produced by major refineries, some aren't. And even those that are may be of a less expensive formulation. It's true that *any* motor oil today is a better lubricant than the best motor oil of forty years ago. Still, even the most expensive oil is much cheaper than steel. Don't skimp here.

Get the highest, most current API designation. The engines of our collector cars originally used motor oils now designated as SB and SC. You can't find these in stores anymore, and you wouldn't want them even if you could. The highest grade available is the one whose additives are the most effectively fight sludge, foaming, rusting, valve train wear, and oil thinning at high temperatures. That's the one to use.

The best viscosity for your engine is the "lightest" SAE grade that will maintain proper HDL yet not result in excessive consumption. If multi-viscosity oil was recommended for your engine by the automaker, follow that recommendation. Single-grade oils were originally specified for cars built in the years before multi-viscosity oils were available. If your collector car dates to this era, you have choices to make.

If you live in a part of the country where winter temperatures are very mild, the single-grade oil recommended by your car's owner's manual will serve you well. The oil will flow sufficiently when starting to lubricate engine parts quickly. At high engine temperatures, the viscosity rating will be appropriate to your engine's needs. You can feel comfortable resisting the siren song of synthetics and other exotic lubricants.

If you live where winter temperatures are cold and if you plan to drive your car on very cool spring and fall days, take advantage of the lower viscosity of multi-grade oil when it's cold. If it's 10deg in your garage in the early morning, 10W-30 oil flows better that straight 30 does. Oil can do its job best with the fewest additives necessary, VI improvers included, so choose the narrowest viscosity span for the temperatures you're likely to encounter. For this kind of use, consider a synthetic. Mobil 1, for example, offers a 5W-30. The cost per mile will be much higher since you'll be draining and replacing your oil well before the typical extended drain interval claimed by the manufacturers of synthetic oil. You'll be getting the best protection when starting in cool weather though, and that's worth a lot.

If you live where temperatures get very hot in the summer, consider a synthetic for its superior performance at very high temperatures too.

Pre-Oiling

The subject of "pre-oilers" comes up regularly in hobby publications. Pre-oilers are devices that pump oil under pressure into the engine's oil galleries *before* the engine is started. The purpose is to prevent "dry starts." Figures have been bandied about in print suggesting that every start takes years off the life of an engine. Some of the prose has been so graphic that the reader could almost hear the engine's bearings and cylinder walls shriek in protest. So the idea of separating the journal from the bearing with pre-start oil pressure certainly seems like a good one.

There are two general types of pre-oilers on the market. One uses a motor-driven, external pump. It draws oil from the crankcase and pumps it into the oil pressure sending port, which usually opens directly on the engine's main oil gallery. As far as I know, this device is available only in a 12V configuration.

The second type of pre-oiler uses a hydraulic accumulator. This is simply a pressure vessel filled half with oil and half with air. More sophisticated versions separate the oil from the air with a diaphragm. This pre-oiler is attached by a hose to the oil pressure sender port. When the engine is running, oil under pressure is pumped into the accumulator until oil and air pressures are equal. The oil is held in the accumulator by a solenoid operated valve. When the ignition key is turned on before starting the engine, the solenoid valve opens. Oil under pressure now flows back from the accumulator into the engine, to provide pressure as the engine starts.

Pre-oilers are an attractive concept. But the purpose of your spending money on such a device would be to add life to your engine by eliminating dry starts. All the tribologists to whom I have spoken say that "dry start damage" is mostly a creation of the advertiser's imagination.

The equipment that makes up a pre-luber driven by a motorized pump.

The basic theory is that the crankshaft journals, cylinder walls, and cam lobes are "dry" when your engine is not running. In fact, most of the oil film that was on them when you stopped the engine is still there when you start it again. It's held by capillary action at the points of HDL, BL, and EHL contacts. What about storage over the winter? Actually, cold oil is even less likely to drain off the walls and journals.

But what about pressure? Don't the journals and bearings touch until the engine oil pump can supply full pressure? Nope. It's the oil *film* that separates journal and bearing. The wedge of oil is created by the turning action of the journal, independent of any outside oil pressure. (Remember the example of hydroplaning?)

So starting your engine is not a terrible thing to do. (Starting it without running it until it's hot enough to burn off acids, is!)

I love gadgets, and a pre-oiler certainly can't hurt your engine. I just don't believe that it's necessary.

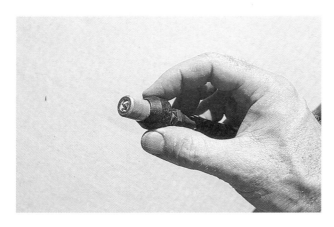

A coupler that hangs on the grease fitting.

Chassis Lubing

The "grease job" is a thing of the past, as far as modern cars go. If you take your new iron to a quickie-lube place, you'll note when they're finished that they've marked "N/A" next to most of the potential lubrication points on their checklist. (That's after you've paid your $35!) Modern cars use sealed grease points, intended to last the life of the car, such as that is.

Not so our precious collectibles. Nearly every point in the steering linkage had a grease fitting. So did kingpins and some ball joints. So did suspension arms. On some cars, the pedal linkage had grease fittings too. In addition, several points on the engine and drive train required grease or light oil periodically.

Grease your car yourself. It's a great way to feel close to your toy and to know that what you're doing has a direct positive effect on its longevity. You'll also get a regular opportunity to inspect undercarriage items for safety or potential failure.

Device for greasing ball and tapered-roller bearings. It's handy, but you can do the same job with your fingers just as effectively and with less waste.

You want to get the car up in the air a bit to do this job comfortably. My preference is to put the rear wheels on ramps and put jack stands under the front. Place them under the frame because you want the tension off the front suspension for this job. (Despite what you may have read, *never* support your car on four jack stands. Even a light sideways push can send it crashing to the ground.)

Your main tool will be a grease gun made for a 14oz grease cartridge. That's the standard size sold in auto supply stores everywhere. (Avoid the mini-guns. They have to be refilled often, and the selection of available lubricant cartridges for them is very limited.) Get a gun with a flexible neck, or add it afterward, to enable you to reach some half-concealed fittings. The coupler at the end of the nozzle is supposed to be pushed over the end of the grease fitting and held there while you pump grease. Throw it away and buy a coupler that locks onto the grease fitting by turning a collar. There'll be times when you'll need one hand to hold the gun and one hand to pump the lever. That's when you'll appreciate that the nozzle hangs on to the grease fitting by itself.

Auto shops used to require an inventory of greases to meet all of a car's requirements. Short-fiber greases were sodium greases for wheel bearings. Other greases were used for steering linkage lubrication, still others for ball bearings. Modern lithium greases replace this inventory with a single cartridge. My favorite is Lubriplate 1200-2. It's available at bearing supply houses. One cartridge will supply sufficient grease for several jobs.

Keep a bunch of shop towels with you as you grease. You'll want to wipe off each fitting before you lock the coupler onto it and after you've greased each fitting. That's because dirt will have been sticking to the grease film on the fitting since your last grease job. If you don't clean it off, you'll push it right into the polished surfaces of the ball joint with your first pump of the grease gun handle. To make this unnecessary, and help lengthen the life of your joints, nylon caps are available that snap onto each grease fitting. The caps have a ring tab that keeps them from falling to the ground and rolling around in the dirt while you grease the fitting.

As you pump grease into the fitting you'll see the dirty grease coming out. Some instructions suggest that you stop pumping when you see grease emerging. I like to pump until I see clean grease follow the dirty grease that comes first. Then I know that clean grease has reached the working parts of the joint I'm greasing. It's messier, and may cost another nickel's worth of grease, but I prefer it. Wiping off the surplus grease will use up those shop towels.

Manual Steering Boxes

This simple-appearing mechanism has several contradictory needs. Pressures are great between the gears and cams and rollers, so an anti-scuff or extreme-pressure lubricant would seem desirable. But most older steering boxes used felt seals, and many incorporated bronze bushings. Neither works well with the common EP additives. Oil, even a viscous oil, tends to leak out of older steering boxes. Chassis grease won't leak, but the gear teeth cut "channels" through it and don't get lubricated. (Generally speaking, you shouldn't use any lubricant in your steering box that you can't pour in there.)

The answer is a lubricant made especially for steering boxes, viscous enough not to leak but soft enough not to channel even in cold weather, and laden with EP additives of a type compatible with steering box components. One such is Penrite Steering Gear Lubricant, imported from Australia. I've used it for years with good results. In cold weather you'll have to warm the plastic bottle to get it to pour into the box's filler hole.

Wheel Bearings

The bearings on which the non-driven wheels turn are lubricated by grease. There's usually a pair of them, the inboard ones slightly larger in diameter than the outboard ones. Most are of the tapered roller design, although ball bearings are used in some cars.

Periodically the old grease should be cleaned out of these bearings and replaced by fresh grease. In a collector car, every two or three years is sufficient. The process is referred to as repacking.

Instructions for removing and replacing the brake drums will be found in your car's service manual. Here are some additional tips:

De-grease bearings carefully in fresh solvent and keep them surgically clean. We've all seen the service station mechanic throw bearings into a hubcap as he removed them. That's a no-no.

Packing a tapered roller bearing with your fingers. It's messy, but it works.

Remember that whatever you put into a greased bearing stays there. A bit of abrasive can do a remarkable job of destroying a freshly greased bearing. Lay parts out on a clean paper towel.

You can repack bearings as well with your fingers as with any tool. Use your palm and fingers to work grease through until it comes out the other side of the bearing. Pack the bearing about 2/3 full.

Tapered roller bearings must have a bit of end play. When you re-install the drum assembly, use large channel pliers (the so-called "water pump pliers") to tighten the nut firmly. That will seat all the parts. Then loosen the nut and tighten it back up snugly by hand. In the unlikely event that a slot in the nut lines up with the cotter pin hole in the spindle, put the pin in; you're done. If it doesn't line up, you'll need a package of arbor shims, which you can purchase in a tool supply shop. Get them with an ID the same as the diameter of the spindle at the nut end. Remove the nut and its washer and

A box of paper "rags." For the limited use made by most car owners, disposable biodegradable paper works better than cloth shop towels.

New plastic ramps won't rust. These are made to accommodate low-riding cars.

add a single arbor shim underneath. Pick a thickness at random. Tighten the nut by hand again. Keep trying different washers until one of the nut slots lines up with the hole. It's tedious, but it'll give you just the right end play and contribute to the longevity of the bearings. (The importance of this adjustment was well known to many car owners in the 1950s. A two-piece nut marketed as "The Educated Nut" made it simple to get this adjustment right. I guess not enough owners of what are today's collector cars thought it was worth the three bucks.)

Other Lubrication

Your collector car's service manual will show other points that need to be lubricated as well. (In the old days, lubricant makers published charts showing all lubrication points and which of their products should be used. You'll find the charts at swap meets occasionally.)

There may be oil cups on the generator and starter bushings and on the distributor. A wick under the distributor rotor may need some oil. So may the clutch throwout bearing. Don't be lavish with oil on these parts. The excess runs into the mechanism, and neither generator commutators nor clutch plates benefit from a dose of oil. Check the lube chart to be sure you're not missing anyplace.

Lubricating body points will help prevent squeaks. Door strikers, trunk latches, hood latches, and trunk props all have metal parts that slide over other metal parts. You'll use a small amount of stick lubricant for some, oil for others.

Keeping grease and oil on everything that needs it, in the right amounts, is one of the most important paths to longevity for your collector car. Doing it on a sunny weekend morning can almost make you feel that George Burns and Gracie Allen should be coming out of the car radio.

CHAPTER THREE

Additives and Other
Kinds of Snake Oil

Here's a typical auto supply store inventory of products that will "improve" or "revive" your engine's oil.

Want to start a heated discussion among collector car (or modern car) owners? Voice an opinion one way or the other on the benefits of some of the currently more popular motor oil additives. Your local auto parts store probably stocks between five and twenty different brands. Few list their ingredients, except for the one that they tout the loudest. All offer "Increased-Engine-Life-And-Better-Gas-Mileage-In-A-Bottle." Most include effusive testimonials, some from respected racing professionals. Who can you believe?

Fred Rau did an intensive investigation of four basic "groups" into which motor additives can be placed. Here is a condensation of the results of his research, and his conclusions. It's reprinted with the permission of *Motorcycle Consumer News*, of which Rau is editor.

1. Products With PTFE Added

Among the most popular oil additives on the consumer market are those whose primary ingredient is PTFE powder suspended in petroleum or synthetic motor oil. PTFE is the common abbreviation for polytetrafluorethylene, commonly known as "Teflon," a registered trademark of the DuPont Chemical Corpora-

tion. Some of the most heavily-advertised brands fall into this category; few list any other ingredients. Though they have gained rather wide acceptance among the motoring public, oil additives containing PTFE have also garnered their share of critics among experts in the field of lubrication.

The most damning statements originally came from DuPont, inventor of PTFE and holder of the patents and trademarks for Teflon. Said they, "Teflon is not useful as an ingredient in oil additives or oils used for internal combustion engines."

DuPont threatened legal action against anyone who used the name "Teflon" on any oil product destined for use in an internal combustion engine, and it refused to sell its PTFE powders to any one who intended to use them for such purpose. Some additive makers simply went to Europe to buy their PTFE powders. Others filed suit. The courts ordered DuPont to resume selling their PTFE to the additive producers. The additive makers claim this is "proof" that their products work. In fact, it is only proof that the American legal system works. The decision against DuPont involved "restraint of trade"; you can't refuse to sell a product to someone just because there is a possibility they might use it for a purpose other than that for which it was intended. The court's decision made no mention of PTFE's effectiveness as a motor oil additive.

Some PTFE powders (from manufacturers other than DuPont) appear to be made with larger sized flakes that are more likely to "settle out" in your oil or clog up your filters. One fairly good indication that a product contains this kind of PTFE is if the instructions for use advise you to "shake well before using." If the manufacturer knows that the solids in his product will settle to the bottom of a container while sitting on a shelf, its likely that the same thing is going to happen inside your engine when it is left idle for any period of time.

The additive makers claim that PFTE, in the form of suspended solid particles, "coats" the moving parts in an engine. Hard to believe. In manufacturing PFTE-coated cookware, the base material must be rendered scrupulously clean and free of oil during manufacturing in order to get the PFTE to stick to it. Those are hardly the conditions inside your engine.

Indeed, PFTE solids seem more inclined to coat non-moving parts, like oil passages and filters. And if your engine's oil filter is doing its job, it will collect as much of the PTFE as possible, as quickly as possible. This can result in a rapidly clogged filter element. To assure oil pressure, the filter's bypass valve will open, and your engine will lose the benefits of oil filtration until the filter is next changed.

The PTFE sellers state that their particulates are of sub-micron size, capable of passing through an ordinary oil filter unrestricted. This may be true when the additive is first poured into your car's crankcase. But PTFE expands when exposed to heat, and particles may stick together forming fewer, much larger ones. So even if those particles are small enough to pass through your filter in their original state, they very well may not be when your engine reaches normal operating temperature. Researchers at the University of Utah Engineering Experiment Station tested an additive with PTFE. Their test report states, "There was a pressure drop across the oil filter resulting from possible clogging of small passageways." In addition, oil analysis showed that iron contamination doubled after using the treatment, indicating that engine wear didn't go down; actually, it appeared to increase. This particular

report was paid for by the additive's maker; still, it was not all bad news for its product. The tests, conducted on a Chevrolet six-cylinder automobile engine, showed that after treatment with the PTFE additive, the test engine's friction was reduced by 13.1 percent. Also, output horsepower increased between 5.3 percent and 8.1 percent, and fuel economy improved from 3.8 percent to 11.8 percent, depending on engine load. These are the kind of results an aggressive marketing company can really sink its teeth into. Based only on these power and economy results, you'd be inclined to think that this PTFE-laced product was indeed a magic engine elixir.

The benefits, however, appear to be temporary. Some of the testimonials in favor of oil additives come from professional racers or racing teams. In the world of professional racing, the split-second advantage that might be gained from using such a product could be the difference between victory and defeat. Virtually all of the detrimental effects attached to these products are related to extended, long-term usage. For a short-life, high-revving, ultra-high performance racing engine designed to last no longer than one race or one racing season, the long-term effects of oil additives need not even be considered. Readers of this book, on the other hand, are primarily concerned with engine longevity, and no laboratory tests have indicated any reduction in long-term wear in engines using PFTE as a motor oil additive. Instead, such tests have raised concerns regarding increased wear, clogging of oil filters, and potential starvation of bearings as a result of oil passages clogged by accumulations of the particulate in the additive.

Manufacturers and publicists persevere regardless. New products shout about "technological breakthroughs." These often involve smaller particles, so as to lessen concerns regarding oil filter clogging. Future tests will determine the accuracy of these claims. At this writing, however, there is no credible evidence that adding PTFE to your motor oil in any form will result in increased longevity for your precious collector car engine.

2. Products with Zinc Added

The latest "miracle ingredient" in oil additives is zinc dialkyldithiophosphate. Purveyors of the new zinc-related products claim they can prove superiority over the PTFE-related products.

Zinc is included in the standard additive package in virtually every major brand of engine oil sold today. Organic zinc compounds, as we've seen, come into play only when there is danger of actual metal-to-metal contact within your engine and boundary lubrication is required. This may very well occur during racing conditions. In your collector car engine, BL is only likely to be needed when starting or shutting down your engine. (We assume that you never intentionally engage in jackrabbit starts, sudden acceleration, or lugging up hills.)

However—and this is the important part to remember—available research shows that more zinc does not give you more protection. It may prolong the period of protection if the rate of metal-to-metal contact is abnormally high or extended, but, for collector car engines, adding extra zinc compounds to your oil is usually a waste. Also, keep in mind that high zinc content can lead to deposit formation on valves and spark plug fouling.

Additives with zinc compounds are easy to identify. The zinc phosphate they contain is a known eye irritant, so they carry a Federally mandated warning label indicating that they contain a hazardous substance. Zinc phosphate is capable of doing serious harm if it comes in contact with your eyes. If you insist on using one of these products, please wear protective goggles and exercise extreme caution.

3. Products with the Additives Already Found in Motor Oil

Though some additives may not contain anything harmful to your engine, and even some things that could be beneficial, most experts still recommend that you avoid their use. The reason for this is that oil, as purchased from one of the major oil companies, already contains a very extensive additive package. This combination of additive components is blended to a specific formula that will meet the requirements of your engine. Usually several of these additives are synergistic. That is, they mutually interact to create an effect that none of them could produce individually. Changing this formula can upset the balance and negate the protective effect the formula was meant to achieve, even if you are only adding more of something that was already included in the initial package.

Think of your oil like a cake recipe. If the original recipe calls for two eggs, is adding four more eggs going to make the cake better? Not likely. You're going to upset the carefully calculated balance of ingredients and magnify the effect the eggs have on the recipe to the point that it ruins the entire cake. Adding more of a specific additive already contained in your oil is likely to produce similar results.

4. Products with Detergents and Solvents

Many of the older, better-known oil treatments do not make claims nearly so lavish as the new upstarts. Standbys like Bardahl, Rislone, and Marvel Mystery Oil instead offer the benefits of "quieter lifters," "reduced oil burning," and a "cleaner engine."

Most of these products are made up of solvents and detergents designed to dissolve sludge and carbon deposits inside your engine, so they can be flushed or burned out. Wynn's Friction Proofing Oil, for example, is 83 percent kerosene. Other brands use naphthalene, xylene, acetone, and isopropanol. Usually, these ingredients will be found in a base of standard mineral oil.

In general, these products are designed to do just the opposite of what the PTFE and zinc phosphate additives claim to do. Instead of leaving behind a "coating" or a "plating" on your engine surfaces, they are designed to strip away such things. All of these products will strip sludge and deposits out and clean up your engine, particularly if it is an older, abused one. The problem is, unless you have some way of determining just how much is needed to remove your deposits without going any further, such solvents also can strip away the boundary lubrication layer provided by your oil. Overuse of solvents is an easy trap to fall into, and one which can promote harmful metal-to-metal contact within your engine.

The Infamous "No Oil" Demo

We've all witnessed or read about live shows put on to demonstrate the effectiveness of certain oil additives. The demonstrators usually have a bench-mounted engine which they fill with oil and a prescribed dose of their "miracle additive." After running the engine for a while they stop it, drain out the oil, and start it up again. Instant magic! The engine runs perfectly well for hours on end, seemingly proving the effectiveness of the additive which had supposedly "coated" the inside of the engine so well that it didn't even need the oil to run. A pretty convincing demonstration—until you know the facts.

Since some of these demonstrations were conducted using its engines, the Briggs and Stratton Company itself decided to run a similar, but somewhat more scientific experiment. Taking two brand-new, identical engines straight off its assembly line, they set them up for bench-testing. The only difference was that one had the special additive included with its oil and the other did not. Both were operated for twenty hours before being shut down and having the oil drained from them. Then both were started up again and allowed to run for another twenty hours. Neither engine seemed to have any problem performing this "minor miracle."

After the second twenty-hour run, both engines were completely torn down and inspected by the company's engineers. What they found was that both engines suffered from scored crankpin bearings and other internal damage. That's the part you never see in the "miracle additive" demonstrations.

Testimonials Versus Scientific Analysis

Most producers of oil additives rely on personal testimonials to advertise and promote their products. A typical print advertisement may include letters from satisfied customers stating something like, "I have used Product X in my engine for two years and 50,000 miles, and it runs smoother and gets better gas mileage than ever before. I love this product and would recommend it to anyone." Researchers refer to such evidence as "anecdotal." While it has its place in the examination of any product or process, it is used responsibly only as an adjunct to scientific testing. Instead, we find it most commonly used to promote such things as miracle weight loss diets. Compiling personal testimonials for a product is one of the easiest things an advertising company can do—and one of the safest, too. As long as they are only expressing someone else's opinion, they don't legally have to prove a thing.

Why Do We Buy This Stuff?

With the volume of evidence accumulating against oil additives, why do so many of us still buy them? Part of the answer may lie in what might be called "the chicken soup effect." Maybe they won't help, but maybe they will.

And they can't hurt. Unfortunately, some people are allergic to chicken soup, and, as you have already seen, some oil additives can hurt.

Then again, perhaps it comes from an ancient, deep-seated need we all have to believe in magic. There has never been any shortage of unscrupulous types ready to cash in on our willingness to believe that somewhere there's a mystery potion that will help us lose weight, grow hair, attract the opposite sex, or make our engines run longer and better. I doubt that there's one of us who hasn't fallen for one of these at least once in our lifetimes. We want it to be true so badly that we just can't help ourselves.

Accredited institutions and researchers have done documented, careful scientific analysis on numerous oil additives. In addition to the studies already cited, engine manufacturers have performed their own. No-one would be happier than an engine manufacturer to discover a product that would protect his engine from wear and improve its reputation with consumers. Still, Avco Lycoming, a major manufacturer of aircraft engines, states, "We have tried every additive we could find on the market, and they are all worthless." Briggs and Stratton, builders of some of the most durable engines in the world, say in its report on engine oil additives, "They do not appear to offer any benefits."

Not all engine oil additives are potentially harmful. But the best that can be said of those that have not proved to be harmful is that they haven't been proved to offer any real benefits, either. In some cases, introducing an additive with a compatible package of components to your oil in the right proportion and at the right time can conceivably extend the life of your oil. Consider, though, that in every case it would actually have been cheaper to simply change the engine oil.

In my opinion, you should not add anything to your motor oil. First of all, the major refiners work constantly to improve the quality of their product, for good reason. The better it is, the more they'll sell, and the more money they'll make. So the additive package they put in their motor oil is already the best they are capable of. Second, the additives incorporated in motor oil are chemically balanced. If you add other chemicals to the oil you may upset this balance and prevent the oil from performing to specification.

CHAPTER FOUR

When Should You Change Your Oil?

A suction gun used to remove an oil sample through the dipstick tube.

We live on a dirty, wet planet, and dirt and water manage to get into the nice clean oil we put in our engines. Water is also a product of your engine's combustion process and contaminates the clean oil with water. Soot, sulfuric acid, wear particles, and other materials get in, too. These contaminants increase wear and encourage corrosion. Filtration doesn't remove all of them, so the oil must be changed periodically.

Auto manufacturers conduct tests to determine a drain interval that will keep their engines safe while not unduly frightening their customers, or financially burdening them. Drain intervals found in owners manuals stress that this interval is for "normal" service, whatever that is.

The problem is compounded for our collector cars. What's found in a forty-year-old owner's manual is based on tests conducted by the car manufacturer way back then. The automaker had no way of knowing the characteristics of the motor oils used today, so its recommendations are a poor guide. Changing the oil more often to be safe is good practice but how often is often enough? A quart of oil isn't very expensive, but the dollars add up quickly if you empty some of our big old crankcases more often than necessary.

Your collector car may be limited, by insurance agreements or by you, to relatively few miles per year; 2,500 miles is a typical figure. So when do you change your oil? The simple answer for the typical collector car: At least twice a year, in the spring and in the fall. If you store your car for the winter, change its oil just before you put it away and again as soon as you take it out. The more complex answer: sometimes the oil needs changing between those times, too.

Later in this chapter we'll discuss lab analysis as a tool. But there are ways to judge the condition of your oil without full lab analysis. Performing these checks periodically will help you determine a "normal" oil change interval for your specific car. Several times a year you can send an oil sample in for a lab test, both to check your own findings and to look for things your simple home test can't determine.

First, the bouquet. Smell the oil in a fresh container. The odor of fresh oil is usually somewhat "soapy." That's the desirable smell. Now smell a service station. That's the sour, acidic smell of used-up oil. (To avoid people looking strangely at you, you'll want to conduct your smell tests unobtrusively.) Now remove the dipstick and smell the oil. A sour smell means that

Settling out an oil sample.

the anti-acid additive has been depleted, and the acids in the oil are not being neutralized. Change it. Now protect the floor and let the oil drip from the dipstick. Good oil will flow off like thin honey. Pay little attention to the color. Many modern oils darken quickly, although the oil is still quite suitable for engine lubrication. What you're looking for is a homogeneous flow—a smooth film. If the oil has bubbles, specks or discolorations, change it.

There's another test you can perform in your own garage. It's a bit more elaborate, but worthwhile. You'll need a hand-operated pump, often referred to as a "suction gun." You'll also need a tall glass jar, like the ones olives come in (carefully washed and dried), and a strong magnet.

You need a sample from the bottom of the oil pan, where all the junk falls. Be sure that the plastic inlet tube on your pump gun is of a length that the gun can pump out a cup or so through the dipstick tube. Expel what you've pumped into your olive jar. Let it sit for a couple of days.

Now examine the bottle. If there's any water in the oil, it will have settled to the bottom. Sludge and sand will also be visible. Hold your magnet against the side of the jar for a few minutes. If particles move to the side of the jar, where

Looking for iron in the oil.

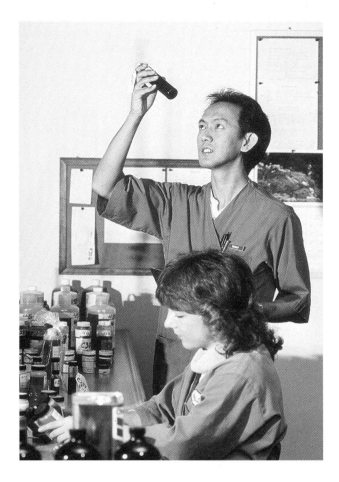

Standardized American Society for Testing Materials (ASTM) standards are applied to all samples recirved at Herguth Labortories. Every sample is first inspected visually for gross abnormalities in color, clarity, and separation of different liquids or solids and liquids.

you can move them around with the magnet, you have found iron and steel wear fragments.

If there's no water or sand, and little sludge or metal in your oil, and if it's homogeneous and smells soapy, no need to change it yet.

Caveats

There are circumstances when you should change your oil more often even if it smells, looks, and feels fresh.

My collector car has no oil filter at all. I change the motor oil about every 500 miles. There's no other way to get the accumulated abrasives out of the engine. And changed oil every two months or so is hardly an onerous or financially challenging routine.

If your car has only by-pass filtration, 1,000 miles is a good interval.

If your car is blessed with full-flow filtration, you can comfortably change twice a year, checking with the look/smell/feel tests.

Oil Analysis

In diagnosing the ills of the human body, doctors have found that minimally invasive techniques can give valuable information without the dangers that attend the major surgery necessary to actually look inside. The fluids that run through us, for example, can be analyzed to help determine the condition of the rest of our organs.

Cars have body fluids too. There are now techniques that can help us diagnose existing or potential problems, without requiring the dismantling of the engine or transmission.

Oil, as we've discussed, performs multiple functions in a car engine. While circulating through the oil galleries, separating metal from metal and washing the walls of the cylinders, the oil picks up and carries with it a variety of contaminants produced by the engine's operation or introduced from outside. Analysis of used oil can identify these contaminants. The type of contaminant points to its source and suggests corrective measures.

Transmission lubricant is subject to fewer potential contaminants than engine oil, although here, too, a sour odor should be a red flag. Analysis can also be a great tool for checking the condition of gears, synchronizers, and ball or roller bearings.

Oil analysis has been used by the U.S. military for more than forty years, and by railroads and fleet operators for almost as long. Today, few operators of heavy equipment or commercial trucks would consider running for long without oil analysis. An oil analysis costs about as much as two pizzas. If you change your oil just before and after the car's winter snooze, you'll want to submit the fall sample. It'll take several years for you to see a trend. If you change your oil more often, consider analysis at six-month intervals. You'll get the trend picture more quickly.

The procedure is performed by several laboratories throughout the country. In the 1980s, some labs began to offer their services to the individual car owner. Some make it more convenient than others. A list of labs you can contact appears in the appendix.

In each case, the lab supplies you with a clean container in which to capture the oil and

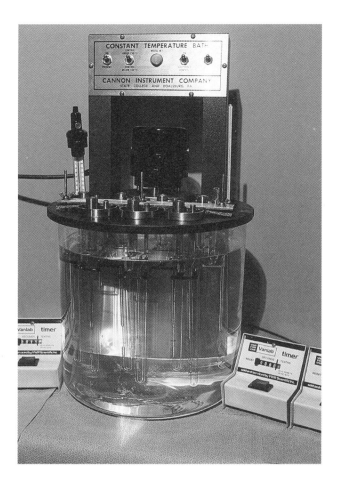

Testing for metals is done using emission spectrography. The oil sample is burned in a chamber in the spectrograph. The light from the burning process is separated by a diffraction grating into the characteristic wavelengths of light, which are different for each element. Photomultiplier tubes measure the light output for each wavelength. A computer compares the intensity of the outputs and converts the result to metal content in parts per million. The spectrographs used are fully automated, which is primarily what has made the cost of such testing affordable.

While spectrography is extremely valuable, it is not perfect. The physical size of the wear particles, for example, affect the results. The spectrograph test usually misses particles greater than ten microns in size. But for a non-invasive report on what's going on inside your engine, you can't beat it.

When you receive your first oil analysis results, you may find that one or more wear

Oil is maintained at 100deg Celsius (212deg Fahrenheit) in this constant temperature bath. Visible in the glass container are kinematic viscometer tubes that measure the oil's viscosity at the high end of its working range.

a mailer in which to return it to the lab. In about a week, you receive in the mail a form that tells you what the lab found in your oil. As labs have begun to go after the patronage of the individual car owner, they've modified and simplified the form to make it more easily understandable.

When your sample arrives at the lab, it's handled very much as a blood or urine specimen would be in a medical lab. It's labeled with a control number and stacked in a rack with other samples. To make the analysis process affordable, many of the testing procedures have been automated.

The lab's analysis can be divided into two categories. Testing for metals normally detects wear rates. Testing for physical properties normally detects contamination from antifreeze, water, gasoline, combustion by-products, and dirt particles. Physical properties testing also indicates the acidity of the oil and its viscosity.

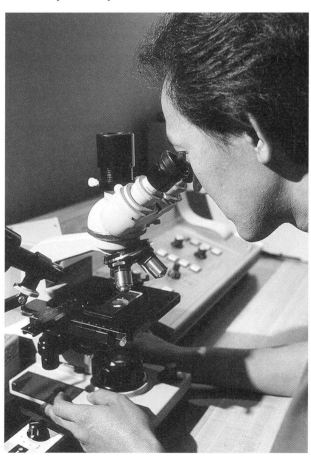

Herguth's technicians examine samples microscopically, looking for dirt, debris, and wear materials. Magnification ranges from 50X to 800X. Colored or polarized light may be used to bring out suspicious abnormalities.

metal concentrations show higher figures than the lab's "normal" rating. This should not be cause for immediate panic, unless the figure is grossly beyond the normal limits. What you'll look for, over several analyses, are trends. If an important metal, like iron, shows a high reading, your oil should be sampled and analyzed again a few hundred miles or a month later. If there's a problem, you'll see it happening and can take action. Sometimes it will turn out that one high figure was an anomaly. Better to know that quickly, too.

The sample you send to the lab must be representative of the oil in your engine or transmission. You want what the medical labs call a "clean catch." That is to say, the sample should be uncontaminated by outside environments. You don't want to submit for testing the first oil that comes out of the crankcase, or the last dregs. You also don't want to dip a sample out of the pan you use to catch the waste oil. You don't know what else has been in there, and even dirt from the air can contaminate the sample. (I heard about a man who repeatedly got oil analysis reports indicating excess silicon in his inboard boat engine. Turns out he was siphoning the oil out of the pan with a silicon rubber tube!)

Follow these procedures: Wear latex gloves. Drain the oil when the engine is warm. Wipe off the area around the drain plug to avoid getting outside dirt into your sample. Remove the plug, let the oil flow for a second, then put your lab-provided container under the stream until the vial is nearly full. If you're working in your own garage without a lift, this can be a messy procedure. The container may overflow, and you'll get oil on your hands. (That's what the gloves are for.) Your technique will get neater with practice. What you'll have, though, is an accurate sample of your engine's oil.

Different labs offer different lab report formats. Some report on more metals than others. Some provide more interpretation of the results than others. The better labs will use all the information you can give them to particularize your report to your needs. Make of oil is an example. On the information form that you submit with your sample, note the brand and weight of oil you use. The lab knows the exact chemical makeup of each brand and will adjust the report to accommodate. Boron, for example, is used in tiny amounts by some motor oil refiners as an

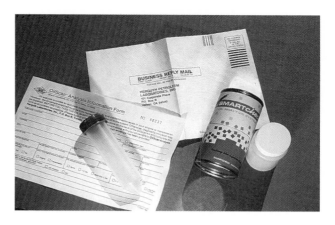

Analysis kits offered by AAA and a private company.

additive. Boron is also an ingredient in many anti-freezes. When the lab finds a boron content in your oil sample, they may note on the report that you should check for a possible anti-freeze leak. Given the make of the oil that you're submitting, the lab's computers will indicate that a trace of boron is normal. (For even more accuracy, ask your lab if you can submit a fresh sample of the oil you use, which they can use as a reference for comparison.)

Be aware that strange readings may occur immediately following an engine rebuild. A newly-rebuilt engine will show relatively high iron readings until the engine is fully broken in and the inevitable debris of machining is flushed out of the engine. Tin is sometimes used to coat new piston rings to provide supplemental lubrication during break-in. Make the lab aware that this is a recent rebuild.

Here are some of the metallic elements in the lab's report that are most important to the collector car owner.

Iron. Wherever iron or steel parts wear, iron will appear in the oil analysis. As we've seen, a small amount of wear is unavoidable. The lab report will give the amount of iron present in parts per million, or ppm. When the engine is new, iron concentration will be higher than normal. After break-in, and for most of the engine's active life, iron concentration should remain relatively stable. When the concentration readings begin to rise again, it indicates that failure is taking place. Look at the reports on other metals to help identify where the failure is occurring:

Copper, tin, and lead. The working surfaces of crankshaft, rod, and camshaft bearings are made of these. A rapid increase in a combination of these metals in the oil is a

A report on an oil sample from the author's car showing all's well.

warning of bearing deterioration and imminent failure.

Nickel. Nickel is often part of the alloy steel of which crankshafts, camshafts, and exhaust valves are made. A nickel reading by itself is inconclusive. Look for high combinations of nickel in conjunction with other metals. As always, trends are more informative than a single high reading. High nickel readings, along with high iron, copper, tin, and lead readings, indicate possible shaft failure. High nickel and iron may show valve stem or guide wear, or cam lobe wear.

Chromium. This is another alloying metal. Chromium plating is used on some piston rings, and in the steel of which roller and tapered roller bearings are made. Abnormal chromium readings, especially when accompanied by high iron readings, can mean piston problems. In a transmission, high chromium may indicate failure of one or more bearings.

Some labs report on aluminum, silver, and manganese as well. Others don't. The lab's report will indicate what an abnormal presence of any of these metals might mean.

Silicon. Sand is silicon dioxide. High silicon readings are an indication that abrasive dirt is entering the engine from outside. The entry point is most likely the carburetor air cleaner. A secondary suspect is the crankcase breather. Silicone is sometimes used, in small quantities, as an anti-foaming additive in motor oil. Again, this is where a good lab, knowing the brand of your oil, can narrow the possibilities.

The lab will also examine the physical properties of your oil or transmission lubricant. Here's what they'll report on:

Viscosity. As vital a property as this is, some labs do not provide this information in the report format they use for their least expensive tests. These kind of bargain tests are often provided through auto clubs. The reason the infor-

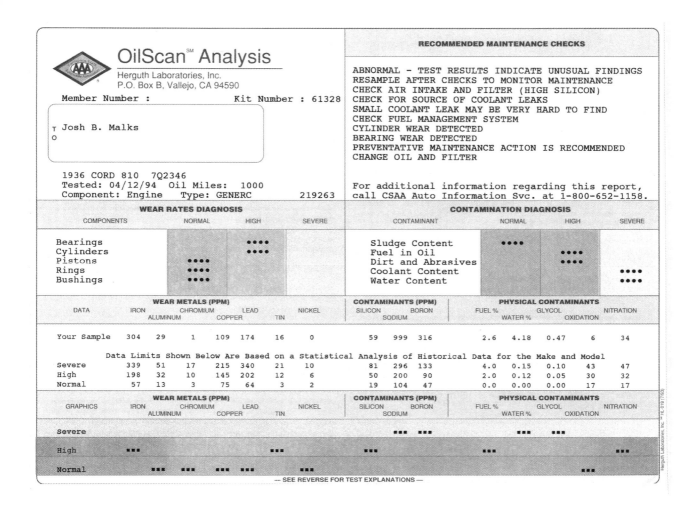

A report six months later indicating a leaking head gasket. No other symptoms were evident yet.

mation is omitted is not an attempt by the lab to save a few pennies at your expense. It's omitted because this particular type of test is usually provided to the owner of an everyday passenger vehicle who doesn't keep the kinds of logs and records that fleet owners do. Different brands of oil may have been used to top off the crankcase, for example. Sometimes these added quarts were of a different viscosity from the original filling. As a result, a viscosity reading on the used oil is meaningless and could create needless concern by the owner and problems for the lab.

Collector car owners are much more scrupulous about maintenance. So, if nothing but straight-30 Quaker State has gone into your crankcase, information on how the oil held its viscosity will be useful and of interest to you. Tell the lab that this is what you want, and you'll get a more comprehensive test and report. This is the test that fleet operators and truckers

request. The cost is a bit higher but not inordinately so.

The lab should give you viscosity results in the standard SAE grades. Given reasonable drain intervals, your oil sample should test at the viscosity of the fresh oil. If it's viscosity has changed with use, and if the same result appears in two consecutive tests, it may be time to try another brand.

Water. Most motor oils contain a few parts per million of water. The test report will indicate this as normal. A higher concentration of water in the oil is abnormal. Water can get into the oil by condensation in the fuel tank or crankcase. This usually means that the engine is being attacked by acid corrosion and rust. Water can also enter the crankcase from an internal coolant leak or a leaky head gasket. All these conditions warrant immediate attention.

Antifreeze. Some tests used to attempt to detect the presence of antifreeze in the oil, a sure

Using a large oil pan with spout in conjunction with the oil pan drain valve may make it possible for you to change your car's oil without getting under the car.

sign of an internal leak, by testing for boron and sodium, both ingredients of anti-freeze. Trouble was, both of these could get in the oil by other routes as well. Most labs now run a test for glycol, which is much more positive. If the analysis shows antifreeze in the oil, don't wait to see a trend. Ethylene glycol in oil forms a sludge that can quickly damage your engine. (If you've switched to propylene glycol antifreeze, rather than ethylene glycol, be sure to let the lab know.)

When choosing a laboratory, ask about some of the tests and procedures described here. You'll be using the lab you pick for a while because only reports from the same lab are useful in examining trends. The same sample, sent to two different labs, may result in widely different reports. Think trends.

You'll be fascinated by the results of your first oil analysis. I know I was. If there's trouble a-brewing, you'll benefit by knowing about it early. If the analysis is all normal, the feeling is just wonderful.

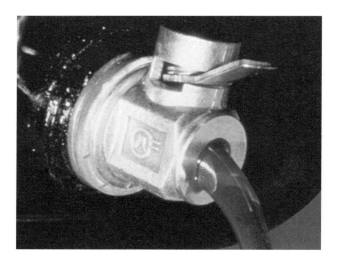

Changing oil is easier on you and on the oil pan threads if you replace the plug with a finger-tip valve. The lever locks when in the closed position. Painting the valve body black will render it less obvious.

CHAPTER FIVE

Filters

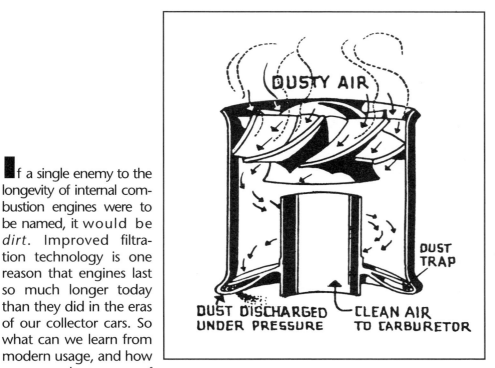

A centrifugal air cleaner of the 1920s.

If a single enemy to the longevity of internal combustion engines were to be named, it would be *dirt*. Improved filtration technology is one reason that engines last so much longer today than they did in the eras of our collector cars. So what can we learn from modern usage, and how can we adapt some of these new techniques to make our beloved cars last longer?

Filter manufacturers have been active for decades in testing the effects on engine wear of contaminated air, oil, fuel and coolants. Ditto for piston ring and valve manufacturers. Much of the data presented here is excerpted from their technical bulletins and test reports.

Air Filters

If you could have only one filter on your precious engine, what should it be? Oil? No cigar. The component that your engine uses more of than *anything* else is air. And, unfortunately, air is the dirtiest component of the liquids and gases that enter your engine.

A typical six- or eight-cylinder inhales about 1 million gallons of dirty air for every 100 gallons of gasoline it burns! The particles in that air include sand, clay and carbon, vegetable matter,

insects, soot, and tire dust. Hard particles gouge and scrape at metal surfaces. They tear away oil films and cause frictional heat and wear.

Analysis by a piston ring manufacturer in the 1950s indicated that 40 percent of worn piston rings removed from engines had worn due to excessive abrasive wear. An air cleaner manufacturer determined that the wear rate for cylinder bores not protected by "an effective air cleaner" was forty to fifty times greater than when a efficient air filter was in use.

The first carburetor air cleaners were introduced about 1925. They were designed to extract, by centrifugal force, the larger particles being carried by the air stream. In that era, 20,000 miles was a normal interval between ring jobs. The next step was the copper mesh filter. In this design the air passed through a copper mesh, like a pot scrubber. The mesh was wetted in oil. Every 1,000 miles or so the mesh was to be cleaned in kerosene and re-dipped in oil. This design denied entry only to insects and to the largest particles of dirt. Also, because mesh filters clog quickly, they soon begin to restrict the air flow into the carb. That created a richer mixture, with two adverse effects:

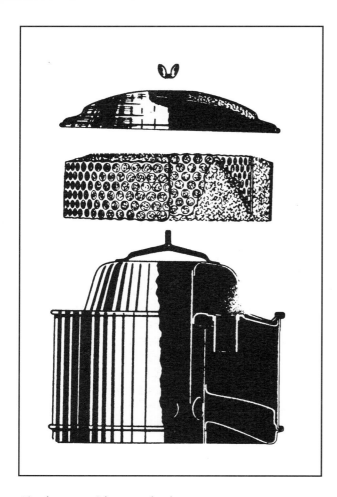

Air cleaner with a mesh element.

Replaceable paper air cleaner elements were introduced on American cars in the 1950s. Since then, they've been joined by reusable polyurethane filters. Properly used, either can provide 98 percent to 99.9 percent clean air to your engine's induction system. If you care for your car, these are the *only* types of air filter that you should use when in Touring Trim.

The limitation in air filter design is providing adequate filtration while not restricting the engine's enormous appetite for air. Manufacturers generally refer to their paper air filter elements as "light duty" and "heavy duty." Light duty filters are designed for cars. Since space is restricted, so is the size of the element. Paper filter media that block the smallest particles would clog up quickly. So the porosity of the filter element is a compromise, balancing free breathing and filter media efficiency. Heavy duty paper filters are used in trucks and large equipment, where space is of less concern. Larger elements can be used, with "tighter" porosity to trap smaller particles.

Several manufacturers make air filters that use one or more densities of oil-wetted polyurethane foam. These filters are cleaned and re-oiled at intervals, not discarded as paper elements are. Tests have shown these filters to be even more effective than paper air filters. They're more expensive to buy, but their reusability makes up for that.

If your collector car provided a replaceable air filter element as stock equipment, consider yourself lucky. For added protection, consider

decreasing gas mileage and increased wear as the excess fuel washed the oil film off cylinder walls. Mesh filters remained in use until the 1950s. While oil bath filters were available for most cars by this time, they were standard equipment only on higher priced lines.

The oil bath filter, introduced on expensive cars in the early 1930s, still used a mesh filter as its primary element. Incoming air was caused to make a 180-degree turn across the surface of a pool of oil. As the dirt-laden air made the turn, some of the heavier particles of dirt stuck to the surface of the oil, eventually settling to the bottom. The air, carrying droplets of oil with it, then passed through a mesh element where more dirt was caught. This device was to be cleaned and the oil replaced every 2,000 miles. Oil bath air cleaners are about five times as effective as copper mesh filters, which in turn can only be considered as better than nothing. But even the best oil bath air cleaners are only effective if the mesh and the oil bath are scrupulously maintained.

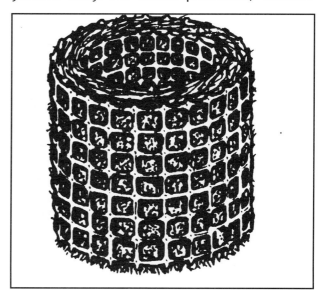

The mesh element still found in some older cars.

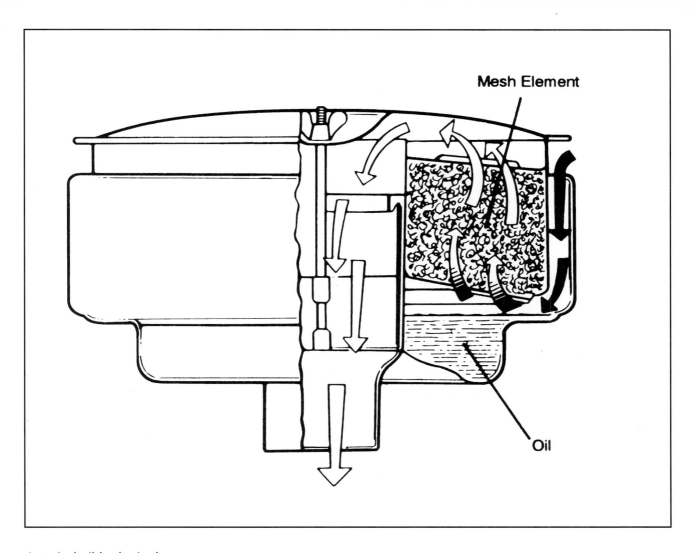

Mesh Element

Oil

A typical oil-bath air cleaner.

using a polyurethane element; a direct replacement should be available. If your car pre-dates the era of the replaceable element, you'll need to fit one. This may require some ingenuity, but its a rare car for which this can't be accomplished.

Fortunately for us collectors, manufacturers have never been able to standardize on lengths or diameters or shapes of air cleaner elements. There are literally dozens of shapes and hundreds of sizes. To retrofit an air cleaner, you'll need to do some calculations first.

Because of the variety of air cleaner designs, it isn't possible to present specific plans. Here are some points to consider. If you can find a stock air cleaner that uses a modern element and will fit your car properly, use that for Touring Trim. Candidates are a later year of your car, or a more expensive make and model by the same manufacturer. Physically, a paper or polyurethane element will have to be larger

than the copper mesh fitted to an older air cleaner enclosure, so you can't just replace one with the other. Conversion to a modern element may require destructive modifications to an original air cleaner. This is a last resort, but balance this vandalism against the protection of an original engine. To choose an element, check the interchange charts for the size of engine this element was originally fitted to. Look for the same displacement as your engine, or *larger*. Just because they aren't as messy or obvious as water or oil leaks, don't ignore air leaks. Filter elements have soft plastic sealing surfaces that must fit tightly against the air cleaner. Also watch for and correct leaks permitting dust-laden air to enter around the carburetor throat or around any tubes into the air cleaner.

Once fitted, maintain your air cleaner element religiously. Replace paper elements once a year. While polyurethane elements can go

An oil-bath air cleaner on a well-used Ford.

longer before cleaning and re-oiling are needed, it's best to do this on the same yearly schedule. For simplicity, do your element maintenance every spring before the touring season starts.

Crankcase Ventilation and Breather Filters

There are only four ways for dirt to get into your engine. We've discussed the major one above. Next in order is the breather for the crankcase ventilation system.

Ventilation of the crankcase is necessary to remove acid fumes which encourage the creation of sludge and to prevent the pressure in the crankcase from pushing oil out through the seals. Well into the 1950s, most American car engines ventilated the crankcase by means of a road draft tube. Opening into the crankcase and pointed down toward the road, the tube had its bottom end cut at a 45deg angle. The resulting mild vacuum when the car was moving was supposed to draw air through the oil filler cap and out the tube, carrying with it noxious crankcase vapor. The fumes were released into the air; environmental concerns were still decades in the future. (Tests with older cars and

trucks have shown that the emissions from road draft tubes often equal those from the tailpipe as a source of polluting hydrocarbons!)

Those collector cars equipped with rudimentary positive crankcase ventilation (PCV) systems have a hose or tube connecting the engine interior with the air cleaner or intake manifold. Fumes are sucked from the engine to be burned in the cylinders, and fresh air is drawn in to replace the evacuated fumes. The breathers through which makeup air enters are usually part of the oil filler cap and are most often equipped with the simple mesh filter used on early carburetor air cleaners. To eliminate this source of entry for engine-destroying dirt, you'll again need to adapt modern filter technology.

Unlike the situation with the large carburetor air cleaner-silencer, you probably will not be able install a replaceable element in your crankcase breather cap without modifying its appearance. So, use a Touring Trim cap equipped with an effective filter and replace the original cap only for shows.

Replaceable air filter elements are made for the small gasoline engines used on lawnmowers. They're essentially a polyurethane foam

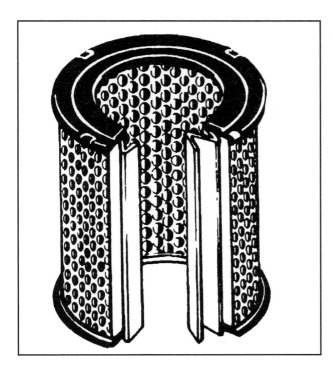

Above and below: Two styles of replaceable paper elements.

"sock" and may be just the right size to use on a modified Tour Trim cap for your crankcase breather. They come in a variety of proportions, too, to suit the location of your cap and the clearances available. If the style of your breather cap lends itself, there's a simple conversion possible. Remove the mesh from the inside of the cap. Then install the polyurethane filter over the existing cap, holding it in place with a radiator hose clamp.

Oil Filters

As with air cleaners, the vital engine-saving nature of oil filtration was increasingly recognized with the passing decades. Few stock cars of the 1920s had any type of oil filter. By the 1930s, many cars offered by-pass filters as standard or optional equipment, although some still had no filters at all. For these, aftermarket by-pass filters were available. In that era full-flow oil filtration was already in use in some luxury car engines. Beginning in 1949, all of the newly-designed V-8s in American cars were designed with integral full-flow filtering systems.

The concept of by-pass filtration is simple. Oil leaves the engine through a port that's fed from the main oil gallery supplied by the engine's oil pump. It passes through the filter, then is returned to a point on the engine from which it drains into the crankcase. The by-pass filter is not in the main line of oil circulation. It taps off about 10 percent of the oil on each pass and filters it. The line to the filter is usually a 1/4- or 5/16in pipe or tube. Opening a "hole" of that size in the engine's pressure lubrication system could cause a serious pressure drop. So a calibrated orifice in the line out of the by-pass filter restricts the volume of oil to an amount that will not cause a drop in oil pressure. Over a period of driving, all of the oil in circulation will probably pass through the filter.

Full-flow filters install directly into the main line of oil circulation. All engine oil passes through the filter, so all the oil is filtered all of the time. That's certainly a more positive arrangement than the by-pass filter system, but its effectiveness depends on proper maintenance.

By the nature of their work, filters clog. The particles removed by the filter gradually block the filter's pores. Delay long enough between filter changes, and the filter element may plug solid. When this happens in a by-pass filter, no more oil can flow through it. This doesn't cause a catastrophe. Oil pressure continues to be provided directly to the main oil gallery, and the engine simply runs on unfiltered oil until you get around to replacing the filter element. The full-flow filter element, by contrast, is in the main line of all circulation. If it clogged up, the results would be catastrophic. So the base of each full-flow filter, the part to which you screw the spin-on element, is provided with a by-pass valve. This spring-loaded device opens if the filter begins to clog and permits oil under full pressure to flow around the filter element. (The valve may also open when the oil is cold and

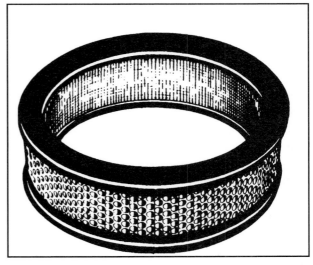

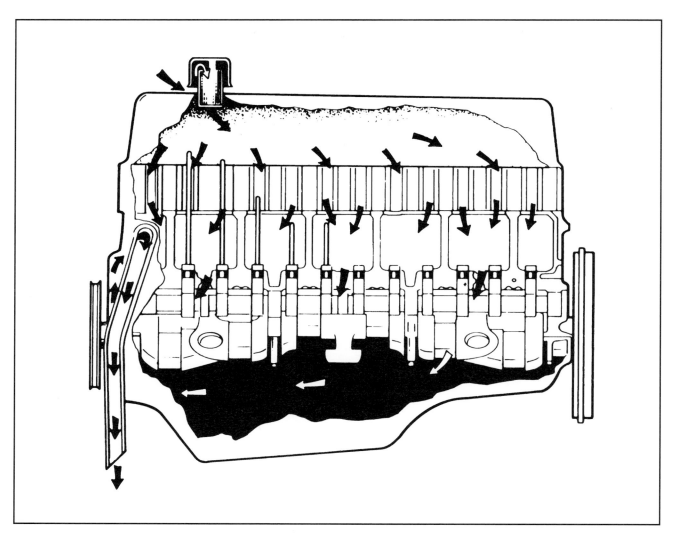

How the road-draft-tube system works. Air enters the crankcase at the top and exits through the tube.

Right: An early, closed crankcase ventilation system. The idea was to bring in filtered air from the air cleaner and pull vapors from the crankcase into the intake manifold. A side advantage was that the air entering the crankcase was filtered.

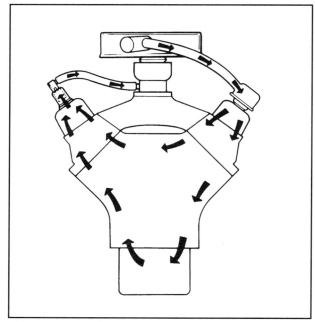

very viscous, and would have difficulty flowing through the filter.) In both by-pass and full-flow systems, the result of a dirty filter element is the same; full volume of oil flowing through the engine, but with no filtration.

Collector cars made since the mid-1950s usually incorporate full-flow filters. From then to the mid-1960s they usually used a canister type-filter, with a replaceable element. These were superseded by spin-on elements, which are easy to obtain and easy to install. When you install a new filter, ignore any flats or wrenching surfaces on the can. Lubricate the gasket, use a strap or

About Oil Filter Elements . . .

An oil filter element has a tough job. In addition to its work as a lubricant, *Skinned Knuckles* contributor Matt Joseph calls engine oil "a sewer for an engine's wastes." Sludge, varnish, wear particles, soot, water, unburned fuel, carbon, and miscellaneous debris all circulate in the oil. The filter must attempt to remove these as they pass through. And it must remove the smallest particles it can, without plugging up too quickly. This is where the compromises begin.

A filter that can remove particles small enough to properly protect an engine will clog quickly. To avoid this problem, large truck diesels, stationary engines, and engines powering construction equipment have huge filter canisters for their full-flow filters, containing large filter elements. The small full-flow elements that will fit in the space available in a car's engine compartment must permit the passage of larger particles in order to make it through the oil change interval without clogging. Cummins Diesel's study indicated that most engine damage is done by particles of 5 to 20 microns in size. Few automobile full-flow filters will remove 5 micron particles; many will permit 20 micron particles to pass.

The photos on page 40 and 41 are micrographs, or photographs taken through a microscope. They are enlargements of the filter media of two well-known brands of full-flow oil filter cartridges, fifty times actual size. The dots on each depict particles 5 and 20 microns in size, respectively. Note the difference in porosity. While photographs alone can't accurately gauge filtering ability, they do indicate the differences between products on the consumer market.

The filtering medium of full-flow oil filters is generally treated paper. It is the practice of the service departments of dealers in heavy machinery to regularly cut open new and used filter elements. Used elements come from customers' equipment. They're looking for metal particles that might indicate problems about to occur. Cutting open new elements permits examination of the quality of filter construction. Standards are extremely high because an engine failure in some of their massive earth-moving equipment could result in replacement costs resembling the total price of some of our finer collector cars. Their work has lessons for us, as revealed in the photos on these pages.

If you and a local group of car enthusiasts want to invest in a simple "can opener" tool, you can autopsy some of your cars' oil filter elements periodically. Here's what to look for.

Check the outside of a filter first. Are the threads clean and deburred? Peer into the spin-on hole with a fiber-optic light. Is there manufacturing debris in there? The sealing gasket should turn freely in its slot, so it won't bunch up when the cartridge is tightened against the engine adapter.

Inside a new filter, expect cleanliness. There shouldn't be any loose glue, dust, grit, or metal fragments from machining. Examine the quality of the glue job where the pleated paper element is attached to the ends. Since the paper comes around in a full circle, there'll be a seam somewhere around the circumference. See how well this is made. Cracks let unfiltered oil pass right through.

Light construction in itself is not necessarily cause for condemnation. An oil filter element is, after all, a temporary part. I'd prefer a well-assembled cartridge with cardboard ends to one with steel ends and missing glue.

When you cut open a used filter, you'll be looking for particles that the filter removed from the oil. Brass or copper-colored flakes may come from bearings. Aluminum specks may come from pistons. A magnet will help you find iron and steel particles.

coil-type wrench, and tighten only to the manufacturer's prescribed torque.

Before the 1950s, most cars used by-pass type oil filters. Early by-pass filters were of several types. There were cartridges which were to be thrown away when replaced; Handy and Purolater made these. Edge type filters did not require the replacement of an element. (These were often called Cuneo filters, after a leading manufacturer.) Their filtering media were steel discs; a handle on the outside was turned periodically to scrape off accumulated sludge. These and the throwaway cartridges were eventually superseded entirely by replaceable-element filter housings. The housings and the elements for them were supplied by Fram, AC, Purolator, and others.

On cars not equipped with oil filters, filters were often added later by the owner or dealer. These were always of the by-pass type. Generally, two types of elements were used. Surface-type filters were made of pleated paper, treated with resins. This is not unlike the construction used in spin-on full-flow filters today. Depth-type filters used a thick section of a wool-like material. Everything from wood and cotton fibers to old rags has gone into such filters. Given equally limited dimensions, depth filters can trap much smaller particles than can surface filters. They can also remove water from the oil. On the other hand, they plug up more quickly. Depth-type elements were also prone to 'channel', as oil under pressure cut passages through the medium permitting unfiltered oil to flow through without filtration.

If your car used no filter at all and you want to add one, you can respect authenticity by installing a by-pass filter housing dating to the era in which the car was built. The depth-type cartridge elements that these filters used are still available in the replacement market. Wash up the old element when you remove it, and you should find the manufacturer's name and a part number. Most dealers can locate an exact

replacement of the same brand or an interchangeable one from another. If you can't identify your element, contact a filter manufacturer's technical service. They can help specify an element based on the dimensions of the element. I've found these folks to be very knowledgeable and equally friendly.

Avoid NOS by-pass filter elements that can be purchased at flea markets. They may be many years old. Two of the major components of oil filters are glue and paper. Both dry out with time, and the cartridge may be absolutely useless as a filter element.

In tests by respected laboratories, using the standard J806 SAE protocol for filter testing, by-pass depth filters have removed 99.9 percent of particles 3 microns and larger. But remember that a by-pass filter works on only some of the

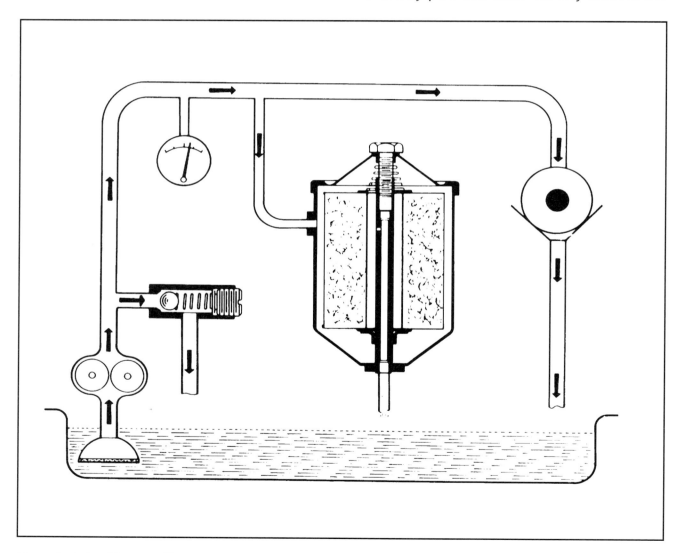

The principle of by-pass filtration. Only some of the oil is filtered on each pass.

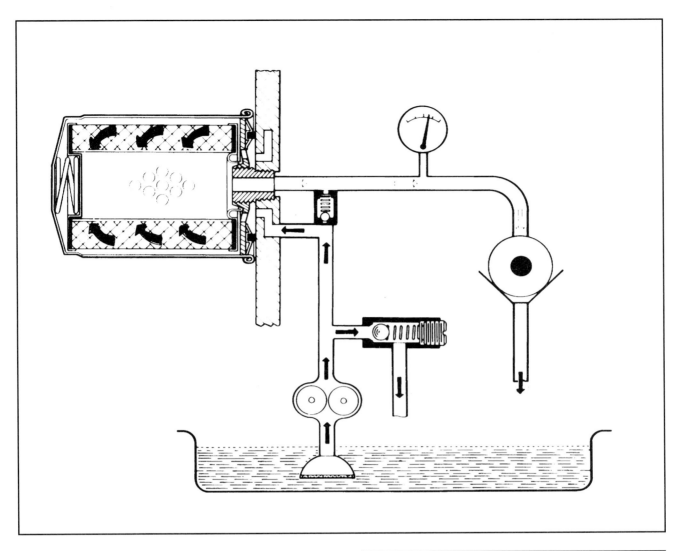

How full-flow filtration works. All the oil passes through the filter, until it clogs. Then the oil passes through the spring-loaded by-pass valve.

oil. Before it theoretically filters all of the oil, abrasive particles have made many passes through engine bearings. Still, it's a better solution than no filtration at all.

If you agree and if your car is one for which no filter was ever available, you can leap across generations of technology. Several filter manufacturers offer remote bypass filtration systems. Wix and Amsoil are two of these. The filters used are spin-on density types. This can be an admirable modification for some of our older cars. Since we collector car drivers change our oil more often than most manufacturers recommend, we minimize the depth-type filter's drawback of early clogging.

To protect your car's authentic appearance as much as possible, you can install the remote filter in a hard-to-notice location. Oil is picked up

Exotic Elements Of The Past

The car-loving market of the post-WWII years was host to an explosion of products intended to make your car more glamourous, more comfortable, more economical, or more long-lived. Into this latter category fell exotic filter media. Since most oil filter systems were still of the by-pass design, various replacements for the stock filter cartridges were offered by mail and in stores. Sintered bronze elements came in cone and cylinder shapes and never needed replacing, just cleaning. An adapter that permitted the use of a standard toilet tissue roll as the filter element was heavily advertised and has its adherents to this day.

from a tee at the oil pressure sender port. Amsoil provides a self-tapping, self-sealing fitting to return oil to your crankcase through a hole you drill in the oil pan. You can buy this separately. Your engine may have a more convenient loca-

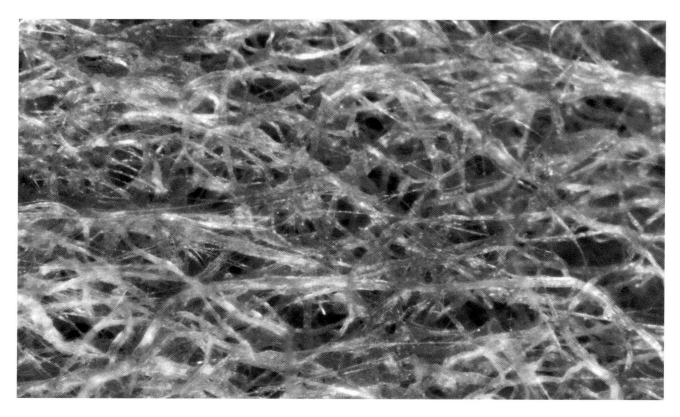

A micrograph (photograph taken through a microscope) of the element of a used consumer oil filter after washing with solvents. This is fifty times actual size.

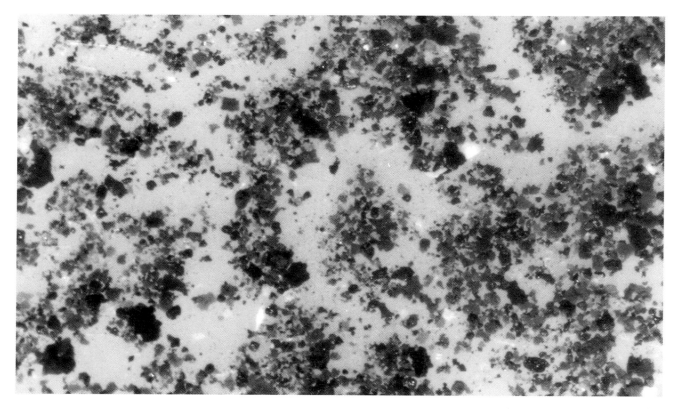

This is what was captured by 3sq-in of this filter.

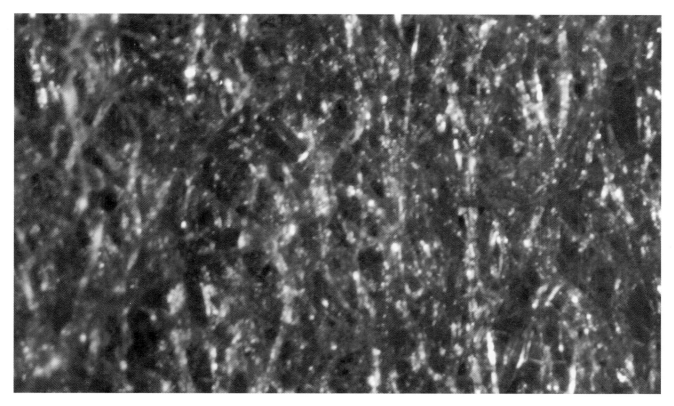

A micrograph of a different brand of filter. Notice
how much denser the weave of the paper element is.

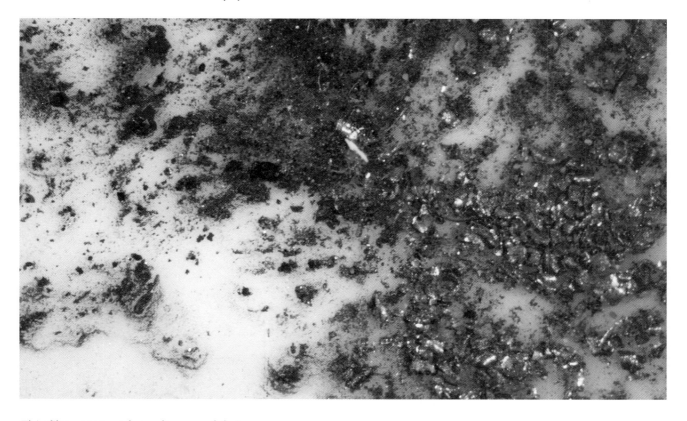

This filter captured much more debris.

This company even takes care to grind square the end of the spring in the oil filter element. This prevents any possible damage to the paper filter.

engine; the larger volume helps keep oil temperature down. In addition, the filter can itself radiates heat to the air and acts as a simple oil cooler.

Providing clean oil is a good way to extend your engine's life. And yes, in some cases adding a by-pass filter involves modifications to an authentic car. Only you can decide whether it's worth it.

Magnetic Drain Plugs

The lubricants in your transmission and differential are not subjected to all of the abuses to which motor oil is exposed. Transmissions and differentials do generate abrasive particles continuously though, as gear teeth slide against

The internal parts of a quality oil filter element. The paper filter medium is carefully glued to steel end caps. Heavy-duty parts make up the bypass

valve; some cheaper elements use just a sheetmetal "flapper."

tion where you won't have to drill a new hole. If you don't mind the appearance, Amsoil also offers a swivel fitting that returns the oil through the oil filler cap and so requires no holes in the oil pan.

There are other advantages to the added remote bypass filter besides cleaner oil. The filter adds between 1qt and 2qt of oil capacity to the

each other. These particles are steel, and what better way to capture them than with a magnet?

A practical way to put a large magnet right into the flow of lubricant is to attach it to the transmission or differential drain plug. Heavy equipment and aircraft have followed this practice for decades. Magnetic drain plugs used to

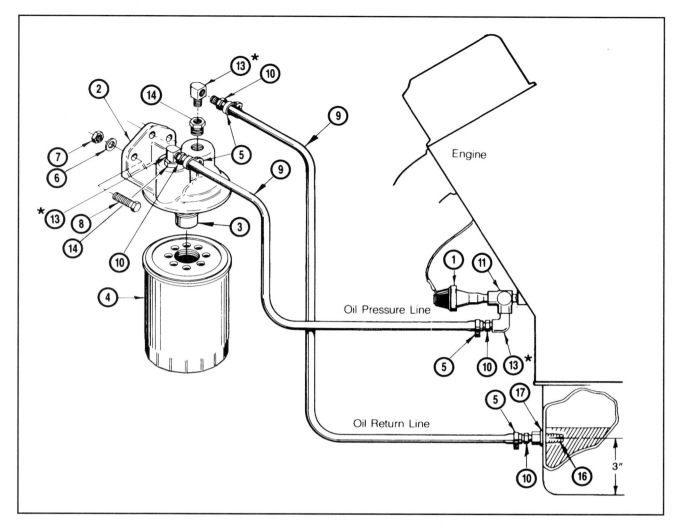

How an add-on remote by-pass oil filter is installed. A tee (11) is installed at the existing port for the oil pressure gauge sending device (1). A special self-sealing plug (16) can be installed in a hole drilled in the oil pan. Alternatively, a fitting is available which will return oil through the oil filler cap. It requires no holes, but it has visible hoses.

be a popular aftermarket item for cars too, but I have not seen them in auto advertising for some years.

The Lisle Manufacturing Company offers a complete range of sizes of magnetic drain plugs. They're available in straight threads, from 3/8 to 1-1/4in, and in pipe threads, from 1/8 to 2in.

Before you install a magnetic drain plug, be sure that the magnet projecting into the housing will not interfere with any rotating parts. *With the engine off,* stick a finger into the plug hole and feel around for clearance with the nearest internal parts. You want to be sure that there's clearance during the entire rotation cycle. Remove finger, turn the engine a bit, feel around again. Please do it in that order. And *don't* let someone else turn the machinery while your finger is inside.

Fuel Filters

As with air and oil, the key word in the operation of a fuel system is cleanliness. A speck of dirt in the carburetor needle valve can cause engine flooding. Internally, carburetors have a multitude of small passages. Dirt in any of them can cause serious problems with engine operation.

Dirt gets into fuel system in one of several ways. Poorly sealing gasoline caps can admit airborne dirt. Rust, a mild abrasive, can flake off from the inside of the gas tank and fuel lines of old cars. Attempts to seal the inside of the gas tank, if faulty techniques or improper materials are used, can result in particles of sealant floating in the gas. And, once in a while, improperly filtered gas enters the tank from your local gas pump.

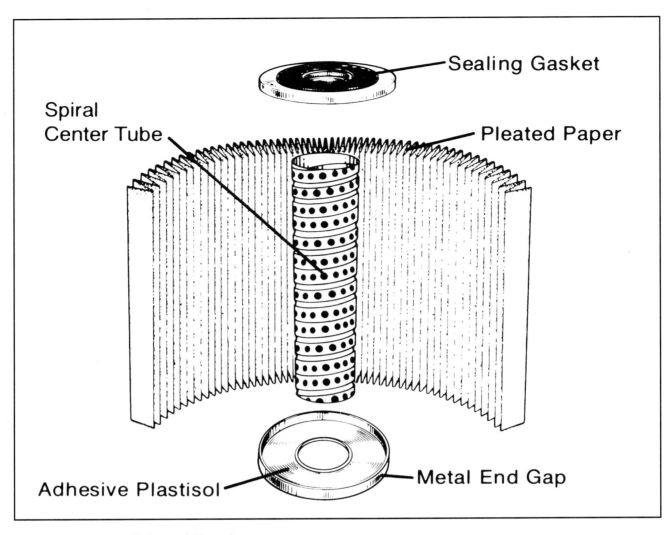

Sealing Gasket

Spiral Center Tube

Pleated Paper

Adhesive Plastisol

Metal End Gap

Construction of a full-flow oil filter element.

Many mechanical fuel pumps have a brass strainer in the bowl. So do many electric fuel pumps. A pleated paper disposable in-line filter is an excellent supplement to these. It's easy to install and replace and is quite inexpensive. Install it on the output side of the fuel pump. When installing or replacing an in-line filter, use clamps to close down the rubber hoses before removing the filter.

Gasoline is a familiar fluid, but a very dangerous one. Be sure all parts of the car are cool before you begin opening gas lines. Be sure there's no one smoking and no open flames anywhere near where you're opening a gas line.

Bringing your filters up to modern standards can be a chore. The outlay in time and money, while not enormous, may still be substantial. You won't see immediate changes in performance, comfort, or appearance. But no other improvements can have as profound an effect on your car's longevity.

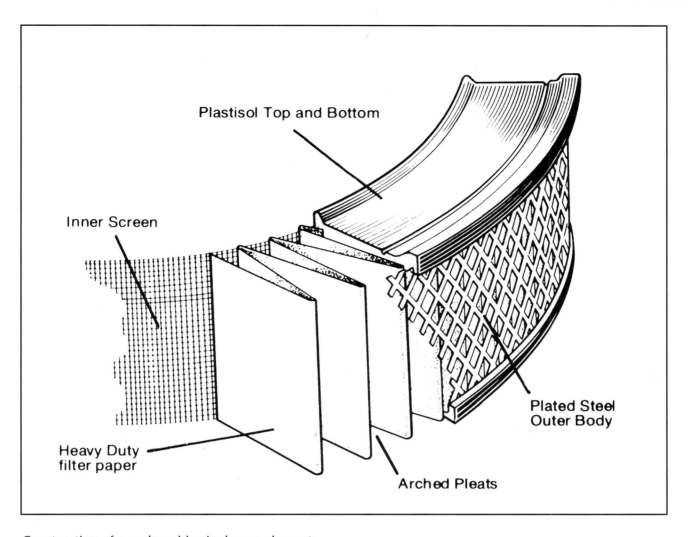

Construction of a replaceable air cleaner element.

By-pass oil filter elements are available in sizes to suit the size of the engine.

A home-made magnetic drain plug. Magnets like these are available at home supply and hardware stores. A generous quantity of epoxy adhesive holds the magnet in place.

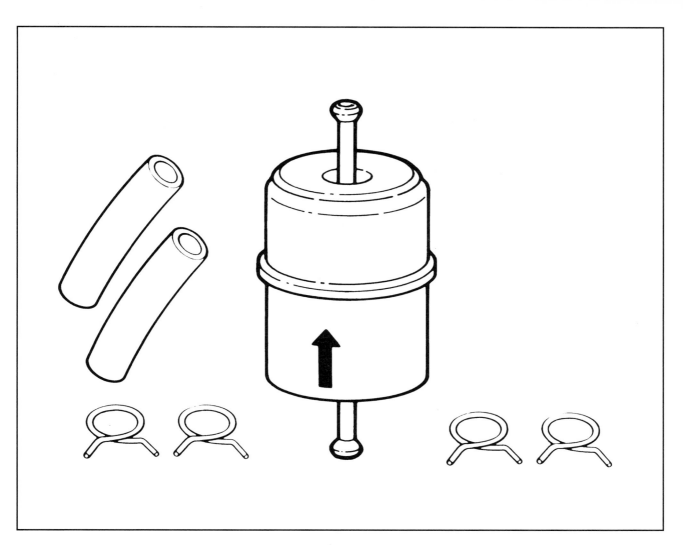

A common style of gas line filter.

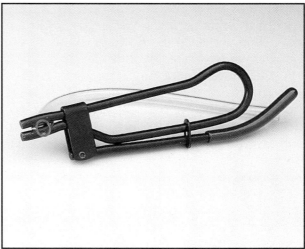

A handy tool for closing down fuel lines while you're changing the filter. This clamp can be operated with one hand.

CHAPTER SIX

The Environment and Us

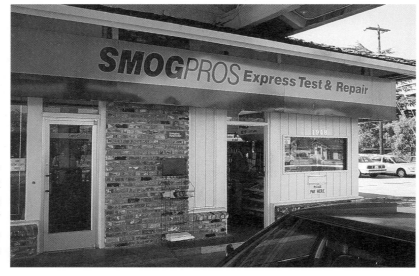

Above and opposite: Emissions or "smog" testing has become a major industry. Much of the pressure to continue with current testing methods comes from the makers of the test equipment.

Most people will agree that we have done damage to our natural environment. If you are not a believer, step outdoors on many days in Los Angeles or Denver or a host of other cities and breathe deeply. Most of us can also agree that some steps need to be taken. First, we have to reduce the rate at which we are causing damage. Then, we need to find ways to undo some of what we have already done.

Our government has responded to these genuine needs with all the delicacy for which governments everywhere are justly infamous— acting before all the facts are in, doing delicate surgery with a sledgehammer, and mandating and banning without fully thinking through the consequences of its bans or mandates.

Collector car owners are a diverse population united by the common interest we share. That diversity has driven a variety of responses to our government's heavy-handedness. Some of us, convinced of the righteousness of our cause, rely on Americans' love of liberty—and of the automobile—to protect our hobby. Others impute dark and devious motives to the bureaucrats and vow civil disobedience. Still others throw up their hands and predict an end to car collecting as we know it. And the vital few to whom we are all beholden examine the issues and recommend actions that can influence the future of car collecting.

Reams of paper and miles of film have chronicled America's love affair with the automobile. Most of our collector cars are still exempt from the plague of regulations, inspections, and licensing procedures that increasingly engulf modern cars. That's so because most citizens still view old cars on the highway as a friendly phenomenon. But there are strong forces who feel otherwise and who write and lobby with a vehemence that a car-lover will find shocking. Many want our cars regulated and taxed off the highways, and they want it now.

Stanley I. Hart and Alvin L. Spivak are typical of those who prefer to rely on government coercion to implement their agenda. In *The Elephant in the Bedroom* they call cars and trucks "the most wasteful element of our consumer society." Their remedy? Taxation of gasoline at "between five and nine dollars per gallon", with the revenue to be diverted, of course, to the construction of public transportation. The authors acknowledge that such extortion-like taxation might decrease the usage of gasoline, so "the tax may have to adjusted to even higher levels in the future."

While we bask in the smiles and admiration of fellow drivers on the road or at shows, we must not mislead ourselves about the fickleness of the public. With each repetition of even the most outrageous statement, more people believe it. When that statement has a germ of truth and where ignoring it may carry risks to our health and that of our loved ones, a tipping point in public opinion is not far off. The Harts and Spivaks of the nation are not in the majority yet, but only our organized opposition will keep them from making the rules for our game.

Car-lovers *can* respond constructively and effectively to the anti-car atmosphere being fostered by today's Luddites in high places. Those responses can effect long-term solutions. For right now, until our influence can be fully felt, there are changes we need to live with. To influence the future, indeed just to live with the changes of today, requires a basic level of understanding of matters chemical and governmental that was unnecessary in the earlier years of our hobby. Still, one of the hallmarks of the successful car hobbyist has been the ability to integrate new knowledge and adapt it to our needs. If we can learn to weld and to spray-paint, we can learn what we need to know about fuels and pollution and emissions testing.

Concerns about the pollution of the air we breathe are responsible for several governmental fiats that affect car collectors. Two that are of immediate concern are changes in the fuel our cars run on and pressures to make it increasingly difficult to drive our favorite cars on the public way. Further in the future, but looming large, are intrusive and expensive testing procedures which may no longer exempt collector cars, as most of the current regulations do.

Why is all this being done? If you begin with the notion that pollution is a creation of big government and that everything would be fine if we were only left to our own devices, then you can't help solve the problem. We *do* have a pollution problem to deal with. The issue is how to get elected officials to make laws that respond to the hard facts that we can present favoring our cause.

When this book was written, the legislation that governed federal and state actions with

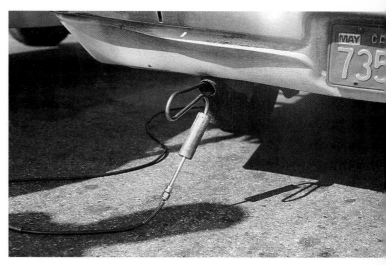

regard to pollution control was the Clean Air Act Amendment of 1990. This legislation identifies 100 areas of the country where there is a problem with air cleanliness. It calls these "airsheds." It establishes acceptable levels of pollution and sets dates by which those levels must be attained. It mandates inspection programs for vehicles. These are called I/M programs, for Inspection and Maintenance. And it gives the Environmental Protection Agency (EPA) the authority to work with states on the development of solutions. Among these is providing incentives to those who contribute to air pollution to do things that will eliminate it.

This last provision is the rationale for car-crushing programs. Instead of spending millions to clean up its own smokestacks, an oil refinery can crush cars and gain "pollution credits" to offset the damage that it does to the environment. So long as legislators and regulators believe old cars to be a major source of environmental damage, these programs will flourish.

Burning gasoline in cars creates three major air pollutants. You ought to know what these are because you'll find them mentioned wherever pollution control is spoken. They are: Volatile Organic Compounds, Carbon Monoxide, and Nitrogen Oxides. (The Environmental Protection Agency also tracks lead, particulate matter, and sulfur oxides, but these are of marginal importance when discussing pollution caused by automobiles.)

Volatile Organic Compounds (VOC) are sometimes referred to as "hydrocarbons." They basically comprise unburned vapors of fossil fuels like gasoline and vapors of solvents and other chemical products derived from fossil fuels. VOC's contribute to the formation of ozone, the primary component of smog. Ozone contributes to the damage of biological tissue and to respiratory problems.

Carbon Monoxide (CO) occurs when a hydrocarbon fuel is burned in circumstances where there either is not enough oxygen or not enough time for carbon dioxide (CO_2) to be formed. CO reduces the ability of the body to deliver oxygen to organs and tissues. It creates a special problem for those with heart conditions.

Nitrogen Oxides (NOX). When hydrocarbon fuels are burned in air, the heat that makes power is created by their reaction with the oxygen that makes up about 20 percent of the atmosphere; the nitrogen that comprises most of the remaining 80 percent is usually thought of as inert, or passive. Under certain circumstances, however, some of the nitrogen will combine with some of the oxygen to make various nitrogen oxides. These irritate the lungs and are another ingredient of smog.

EPA statistics are often broken down into "mobile" and "stationary" sources of pollution. Mobile sources include cars, trains, planes, lawnmowers, tractors, boats, etc. If it moves, it's mobile. Stationary sources are everything else: homes, factories, refineries, steel mills, etc.

Considering all the rhetoric, you may be surprised to discover that 1990 figures indicated that, on a national level, cars were NOT the major source of two of the above three pollutants. Stationary sources produced 48 percent of the VOCs while cars produced less than 18 percent. Stationary sources produced 60 percent of the NOX, cars only 11 percent. Only carbon monoxide is produced more by cars than by stationary sources, 31 percent to 20 percent. In all three categories the pollutants produced by cars have gone down since 1970 by 5–9 percentage points while those produced by stationary sources have gone up 3–8 points.

EPA continues to mandate ever more stringent tests for motor vehicle emissions. Current proposals call for equipment that is so expensive that it would have to be located in central testing stations, to which motorists would have to drive and line up for testing. Little thought appears to have been given to the value of the motorists' time wasted in this exercise. More important, this may not even be the best way to identify which vehicles, regardless of age, are actually creating the pollution problem.

Dr. Donald Stedman of the University of Colorado is one of the developers of remote emissions testing apparatus. His emissions testing equipment is designed to be set up by the side of a busy highway, identifying the worst polluting cars as they go by. Cameras record the license plate, and the state can deal directly with the owner regarding needed repairs. Tests of hundreds of thousands of vehicles have proven to Dr. Stedman that, regardless of the age of the vehicle, only 10 percent of all cars are polluters, due to defective computer chips, lack of periodic tuning and maintenance, and tampering with emission control equipment. The real need is to identify these specific cars, not to spread a net that will catch the 90 percent of motorists whose cars contribute little to the problem.

So why pick on old cars? It's hard to pinpoint all the exact motives, but generally there are three. First, to the EPA, destroying old cars has a "green" feeling and sells well to the congress that appropriates funds to government agencies. Second, the more cars that are destroyed, the more that will have to be manufactured and sold to replace them. The term "harvesting" of cars has even been used. Finally, and perhaps most important, nearly everyone who attends the committee meetings where regulatory decisions are made represents an industry that is regulated by these laws. It

Dr. Donald Stedman and the University of Denver's remote emission sensing setup.

stands to reason that they'll be pushing for the best deal for themselves. We unorganized hobbyists and our cars become the chess pieces in the game.

So what do we do? Dr. Mark Warden (a leader among those making a favorable case for car collectors) and others point the way to protecting our automobile hobbies for the future. First, we must clearly understand the issues. We must not act before we think because that will simply destroy our credibility with the public and with legislators. In the world of politics the good guys are not protected because they are good or because they have reason and logic on their side; they are protected because they are organized. So organize we must. That will make it possible for us to make our case reasonably, accurately, and persistently to those who make the laws. As voters and taxpayers, we *can* get our message across. But we must do it together.

Join the groups which lobby on our behalf. Membership dues are a tiny fraction of your investment in your car. COVA—The Council of

Vehicle Associations—whose address is listed below, is one of the most active national organizations. You'll find others, as well as local groups, listed regularly in magazines for the car hobbyist. COVA is an association of car clubs, state car-club councils, companies, and individuals that serves as an information resource to people and organizations nationwide. COVA contributes regularly to several automotive publications, and publishes a quarterly newsletter.

Public opinion will be a vital factor in determining the future of our hobby. There are ways that we car lovers can show our best face to our communities. Matt Joseph has passed on a couple of ideas from a friend of his.

As tinkerers with old machinery, we have expertise that can be useful to our local governments. Every city and town has old equipment in its inventory. Such equipment is often disabled for want of an obsolete part or by the inability of today's mechanics to fix it. So, otherwise usable machinery is discarded and replaced, at great cost to the taxpayer. Car

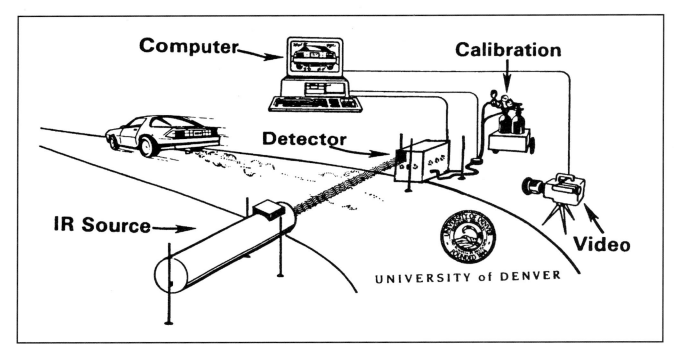

A schematic of how remote sensing works. "IR" means infrared. This system has shown itself capable of monitoring the emissions of hydrocarbons (VOC) and carbon monoxide (CO) by vehicles traveling between 2.5 and 150 mph. The computer generates its results in less than one second per vehicle.

clubs, or individual restorers, can offer their services to their local government. Make them aware that you're ready to help them with the rebuilding or repair of aging equipment. You'll save money for yourself and fellow citizens. You'll get a kick out of making something work that might otherwise have been junked, *and* you'll help change our image with local officials from anti-environmental cranks to "good guys."

Local governments regularly sponsor clean-up campaigns of various kinds. Local car clubs should participate in projects like collecting and disposing/recycling of old batteries, crankcase oil, tires, and antifreeze. Activities like this will help officials and the public recognize the concern for the environment that we share with them, too often obscured by loud voices and finger-pointing.

Offer you, club's services to local civic organizations for parades and festivals. Suggest exhibits of old cars to local museums. Historical and service organizations are always looking for speakers for meetings. Get your most articulate members to offer their talents. Include in your message the fact that old cars are not the enemy and that we're all in the good fight together.

It's important to remember that what we are organizing against is not the issue of the danger to our environment but rather our government's misguided approach to dealing with a genuine problem. Only you and you and I can make certain that our hobby has a future. Give it some thought, and take some action.

Getting our points across will make it possible for us to leave to our grandchildren not only our precious collector cars but a safe and beautiful country through which they can drive them.

Wall Street Journal "Dirty Driving" Response

On August 17, the well respected Wall Street Journal took a mis-informaed approach to so called "clunker" laws. It prompted a response from Dr. Mark Warden. So far, WSJ has not published his reply. We're hoping they will, however, and maybe even provide their readership with a better researched follow up article.

The Editors
The Wall Street Journal
200 Liberty Street
New York, NY 10281

Dear Sirs:

Your front page report of August 17, 1994 entitled "Dirty Driving" concerning the so-called "clunker" laws and EPA regulations requires a response.

It seems the success of any public policy depends upon the poiny of view it incorporates being repeated enopugh in many different places for it to be taken as gospel. A case in point is the one about older cars being dirty and new ones clean.

The U. S. EPA and its state counterparts have targeted cars as major sources of pollution, specifically those of theh 1970's and prior. Thus we have the various purchase programs of older cars and the trading of pollution credits between mobile and stationary sources.

The identification of pre-1980 cars for special treatment makes about as much sense as writing a crime bill that targets brunettes for special surveillance and stop-and-frisk since more brunettes commit crimes than blondes and redheads. (Just look inside your local jail and you will see this is the case.)

The absurdity of such a proposal should draw attention to the unreasonableness of targeting cars on the basis of age rather than their actual contribution to dirty air. Dirty air is ostensibly what the EPA wishes to fight, whether that dirty air is produced by new or old cars.

Using actual tests on literally hundreds of thousands of cars (not computer models employed by the EPA) Dr. Donald Stedman of the University of Denver has found that about 10% of the cars on the raod contribute 50% of the pollution, regardless of age. Most of this pollution production is due to tampering with pollution control devices, computer chips out of whack, and very poorly maintained cars.

It is admitted that the technology of earlier years did not allow a car to be so easily kept clean burning as is true of more recently manufactured ones, but older cars can nevertheless be tuned to run very clean. For example, in a study conducted by Automotive Testing Laboratories, Inc. of cars in the Chicago area found that the degree of pollution emissions went from very clean to very dirty. Three cars of the 1975-77 vintage tested, as they were taken off the street without any special tuning, were anywhere from 0.01 to 2.2 grams dirtier in pollutants than the standard mandated for 1993 cars. While dirtier, the degree is minimal. We are not talking about radioactive plutonium here.

From the hyperbole used, one would think that it is the car that is the evil machine that is choking us to death. Yet if we look at the figures of the U.S. EPA as reported in the Regional Interim Emission Inventories (1987-1991), Volume II: Emission Summaries, the pollution attributable to highway sources is 30% for VOC's, 38% for NOx, and 61% for CO in the Chicago-Gary-Lake County airshed. While this is not a pretty picture, what is usuall;y not pointed out by EPA spokespersons is that highway sources are not the same as the passenger car source which they

> *The identification of pre-1980 cars for special treatment makes about as much sense as writing a crime bill that targets brunettes... since more brunettes commit crimes than blondes and redheads.*

A page from COVA's publication, which keeps members up-to-date on government actions and proposals.

CHAPTER SEVEN

New Fuels and Old Cars

The Ethyl sign on early gas pumps was more than an ad—it was a warning label.

Life After Lead

In 1970 General Motors announced that it intended to meet federal emissions standards by the use of catalytic converters. The platinum alloy used in these devices is incompatible with lead compounds, so the eventual elimination of tetraethyl lead (TEL) from gasoline became inevitable. The Clean Air Act of 1970 led to the introduction of the necessary unleaded fuels in 1974 and to the beginning of the phase-out of TEL as a gasoline additive. It should be noted that there was little concern when these decisions were made about toxic emissions of lead fumes from automobile exhaust pipes. Lead had to go simply because it clogged up the catalytic converters.

When the federal government first announced its intention to eventually ban the use of tetraethyl lead in automobile gasoline, loud were the cries of the gloom-and-doomers in the car hobbies. Magazines carried editorials and articles condemning the move. Many pre-

dicted the demise of older internal combustion engines, suggesting that remedies would be expensive or impractical. At meets and shows, knots of enthusiasts (this author among them) discussed in somber tones a non-driving future.

As always, the free market sprang to life. Companies manufacturing fuel and oil additives included a "lead substitute" in their lines. Some drivers of collector cars use one, some don't. But nearly everyone worries.

My advice is . . . relax. Having to use unleaded gas should not stop you from fully enjoying your collector car. Nor is it likely to cause the prompt demise of the typical collector car engine. To understand why, it's helpful to know something about the history of TEL in motor fuels.

In 1922, Dr. Thomas Midgley, Jr., was working with Charles Kettering at the General Motors Research Corporation. (This company was a descendant of Kettering's own Dayton Engineering Laboratories Company, later abbreviated "Delco.") Midgely and Kettering knew that the performance potential of passenger cars could be greatly advanced by the use of higher compression ratios, but work in that direction was stymied by "knocking" caused by the existing commercial gasolines. An uncontrolled knock caused by the fuel can quickly destroy an engine. It was believed at the time that the knocking was caused by pre-ignition—a tendency of the fuel to begin burning spontaneously, before the spark occurred.

Midgley and Kettering fitted a quartz window to the combustion chamber of a running engine, so they could actually watch pre-ignition occur. They found that the knock was caused by a rapid rise in combustion chamber pressure after ignition and not by pre-ignition, as had been assumed. Thus began the long search for anti-knock agents. They experimented with various chemical compounds mixed into gasoline; the most practical was tetraethyl lead.

TEL added to gasoline reduced the tendency of high compression, heavily loaded engines to knock. That was its function, period. Although gasoline refining methods continued to improve, it was far less expensive for refiners to further increase the knock resistance, or "octane rating" of the gasoline by adding this compound than by more costly improved refining techniques.

The first public sale of what Kettering himself named "Ethyl gasoline" took place at a gas station in Dayton, Ohio, in 1923. The TEL in it was produced by the General Motors Chemical Company. A year later Standard Oil of New Jersey developed an improved method of manufacturing tetraethyl lead. The two giants promptly formed the Ethyl Gasoline Corporation (the middle name was dropped in 1942). TEL had begun its long march into the gas tanks of the world.

Gee, It Seemed Like a Good Idea . . .

Dr. Thomas Midgeley, Jr., is generally acknowledged as one of the great geniuses of the science of chemistry. He certainly could not have known that his brainchildren would be so vilified in decades to come. In addition to tetraethyl lead, Dr. Midgeley also discovered dichlorodifluoromethane, later trade named Freon!

Most gasoline marketers used Ethyl's TEL only in what became known as "premium" gasolines. On these pumps, Ethyl Corporation's logo was prominently displayed. The "regular" gasolines supplied to service stations by most oil companies used no TEL at all for a decade. Not until 1933 was lead first used in a "regular" grade gasoline and even then not in all brands.

The notion of a role for lead as a cushion or lubricant for exhaust valves was not even considered by engineers during the first thirty years of TEL's use as a gasoline additive. Quite the contrary. Most of the engineering time related to the use of TEL in motor fuels was devoted to getting rid of the lead deposits that TEL left behind! Dozens of papers at SAE conferences in the 1940s and 1950s dealt with methods of eliminating lead deposits from automobile engines. Lead was such a known nuisance that some brands advertised that they obtained their higher octane without resulting to harmful additives like TEL. Blue Sunoco and Shell No-Nox were two of these. As late as the 1960s, at least one major gasoline distributor advertised its premium product as containing no lead. Remember Amoco White?

The pesky lead deposits built up on piston crowns, valve guides, and valve seats. Spark plugs could be "fouled" (shorted out) by lead accumulation. Midgeley and his colleagues discovered and developed the chlorine and bromine scavengers that, added to the TEL mix, helped eliminate the build-up.

As another part of the assault on the deposits TEL left behind, Ethyl Corporation engineers teamed up with auto manufacturers to change engine designs. Valve guides were counterbored. Valves and valve seats were ground to slightly different angles to produce a narrow line of contact between valve and seat that cut through the lead build-up. Valve rotators were developed by Thompson and Eaton, and saw increasing use in original engines and in the aftermarket. These devices caused the valve to rotate 10–15deg each time it opened and closed, eliminating local hot spots on the exhaust valve and seat. In the process, they also wiped away the unwanted lead deposits.

The worry today about the dangers of lead-free gasolines to older engines is based on concern about excessive wear of the exhaust valve seat, referred to as "valve seat recession" or "exhaust valve recession." This refers to wear of the valve seat, which causes the valve clearance to steadily diminish. Hydraulic valve lifters will compensate, until their operating range is exceeded. If clearance reaches zero, the valve will not seat fully and will burn.

In the 1930s, the typical interval between valve jobs was 25,000 miles; a ring job wasn't needed until much later. The goal of the engineers was to extend the interval between valve jobs to approach ring longevity. The changes in valve design described above, along with improved metallurgy, accomplished this. Valve recession, as such, was not an issue. As a matter of fact, those who own cars built between the 1930s and the 1950s are driving vehicles that spent their early years running on gasoline with little or no lead in it. It's unlikely, therefore, that the engine in a collector car of those eras will be damaged by the lack of a substance that it wasn't designed to use in the first place.

Serious research on the effects of unleaded gasoline was not even begun until the late 1960s. Remember that American cars of this era were reaching new levels of horsepower and performance. Recreational vehicles were growing in popularity. Highway speeds of 70 and 80mph were legal in many parts of the country. Engines had to be designed for reliability under such conditions, so testing was done to severe standards of speed and load. And valve recession *under these conditions* was found to be much greater with unleaded fuels.

The research found that valve recession starts with the transfer of material from the valve seat to the exhaust valve. The hard particles become embedded in the valve, where they act as an abrasive, grinding away at the seat as the valve opens and closes. As the seat is ground away, the valve recesses into the cylinder head or engine block, upsetting the clearances.

The tetraethyl lead deposits that engineers had so diligently worked to wipe away in earlier decades had the completely unintended effect of acting as a solid lubricant, preventing metal to metal contact between the valve and its seat.

Many papers dealing with the effects of unleaded fuel were presented at SAE conferences. All that I have seen date to 1970 or later. In nearly every case, test engines were run at high speeds and heavy loads. Road testing was done at 70mph for long periods of time, with very high engine temperatures. Bench testing was done at engine speeds as high as 4400rpm, with coolant temperatures of 230deg Fahrenheit. Under these conditions, exhaust valve

recession in pre-1971 engines running on unleaded gasoline was measurable and seriously affected engine performance.

The same tests found that engines run at moderate speeds, and moderate loads did not suffer serious valve recession as a result of using unleaded gasoline. A 1971 paper presented by TRW engineers suggested that ". . . the average driver, who seldom exceeds 70mph, should not experience significant engine deterioration." Ethyl Corporation engineers found that "Operation at 60mph instead of 70mph reduced valve seat wear . . . by about two-thirds." Union Oil people stated that ". . . exhaust valve seat wear with zero-lead gasoline is responsive to engine speed . . . at 2300rpm and 16.0-in vacuum, exhaust valve seat wear was very low."

Don't these conditions describe how most of our collector cars are driven? (Drivers of muscle cars of the 1960s should obviously be prudent about using all the power of which their engines are capable.) The findings suggest some guidelines for driving with unleaded fuel, all of them easy to take: 1) Stay within the highway speed limits. 2) Keep your cooling system in shape. 3) Don't pull trailers or haul heavy loads.

Recent studies also indicate that there *may* be some benefit from using some of the additives sold as lead substitutes. If you want extra insurance, use them until the day that you need a valve job.

If your collector car is running well, there's no need to overhaul your engine just to protect it from unleaded gas. Eventually, the regular driving that I hope you'll do will create the need for valve work. That's the time to invest in modern technology and metallurgy. Good machine shops now have considerable experience in fitting hardened valve seats. This will resolve the unleaded gas issue permanently. (All American car engines have boasted hardened valve seats since 1974.)

Two more points for when you have that valve job done. Back in 1971, TRW engineers found that, in engines without hardened valve seats, changing the valve face angle from 45deg to 30deg reduced recession by 75 percent. And recent studies seem to indicate that the valve rotators that helped remove lead deposits in the TEL years can actually increase wear on valve seats with today's fuels. When you have other valve work done, have the rotators removed.

Finally, celebrate the good things that lead-free gasolines have brought us. Studies have shown that combustion chamber deposits have

You'll always find driving more enjoyable when your car has plenty of pep and power. And the best way to get full power is to use high-octane gasoline. You see, the amount of power gasoline can deliver depends on its octane rating. So, no matter what other qualities you want in your fuel ... be sure you get a *high-octane* gasoline. Look for the yellow-and-black "Ethyl" emblem when you buy gasoline. Enjoy the powerful difference!

ETHYL CORPORATION
New York 17, N. Y.
Ethyl Antiknock Ltd., in Canada

An Ethyl ad from a 1950s magazine, urging drivers to choose gas with Ethyl in it. Not all fuels contained TEL. If they did, why would Ethyl Corporation spend money on advertising?

been reduced, used oils contain fewer acids, internal engine rusting has been reduced, and spark plugs and exhaust systems last much longer. See, there *is* a silver lining after all.

The New Fuels

Gasoline has been modified to reduce air pollution. In addition to the removal of all tetraethyl lead compounds from regular gasoline, changes have included the use of alcohol (an oxygen bearing compound) to "oxygenate" fuels and the introduction of "reformulated" gasolines. What effect will these new fuels have on our older cars?

Oxygenated gasolines, now in use in most states during winter months, will have little noticeable effect on your driving, though you will note a small decrease in gas mileage. A greater concern is that oxygenated gas appears to attack some of the material used in the fuel systems of old cars. Buna rubber is especially vulnerable. This was often used for the accelerator pump on carburetors. Some of the compounds of which old fuel lines were made may be attacked, too. Jeff Dreibus, who has extensive experience rebuilding old carburetors, warns that the worst problems occur with old rubber compounds that have been in contact with old gas. Fuel pump diaphragms and valves can also be a source of concern. "NOS" is no longer a plus when applied to rubber parts in the fuel system. When you buy repair kits or

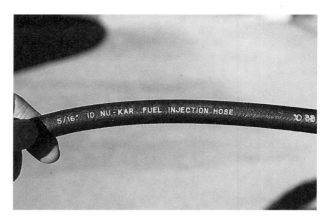

Be sure your new fuel line is marked with something like this or "30R9."

rebuilt fuel pumps or carburetors, find out what materials the "rubber" parts are made of. Choose neoprene, fluorocarbon rubbers, synthetics, and yes, leather.

Hoses are vulnerable, too. It's a good idea to gradually replace all the fuel hoses in your car with the hoses made for fuel injection systems. You probably won't be able to find these hoses in the correct lengths for your old car and with the right fittings. You'll have to make them up yourself. Just be sure that the new hose is stenciled "309R." (The old SAE standard was 30R7.) These lines are expensive by the foot, but they are a good investment.

Attempts to introduce "reformulated" gasolines (RFG) in 1995 were met by a ground swell of opposition from motorists. Concerns were raised regarding toxicity of the fumes, among other issues. Still, there's no doubt that some reformulations are inevitable. Used correctly, reformulated gasolines may even have some advantages for our older cars.

RFGs have a higher initial boiling point, which may actually reduce the problem of vapor lock. Be careful, though. All gasolines now have different formulas for winter and for summer. So if you put your car to bed for the winter, having followed advice to fill the gas tank beforehand, you'll be driving off on a nice warm spring day with winter gas in the tank. That winter gas was formulated with increased gasoline volatiles, for easier starting in cold weather. Be aware that this tankful is *more* prone to cause vapor lock.

The down side of RFG's higher boiling point is that some cars may be harder to start. All the more reason to be sure that your starting system is as good as you can make it.

Installing an Electric Fuel Pump

An electric fuel pump may be installed by cutting into the fuel line at a convenient location near the gas tank. That will put electric and original mechanical pumps in series. This is the easiest way to do it, but not the safest. That's because if the diaphragm in the mechanical pump should leak, the electric pump can pump gasoline directly into the crankcase. That's a potentially explosive situation.

The best way to install an electric fuel pump while retaining the mechanical pump is as a *parallel* system. Provide a toggle switch to turn the pump on and off. Be sure to run the supply wire from the ignition switch, so the electric fuel pump cannot run with the ignition off. Now the electric pump can be used to fill the carburetor bowl before starting or as a supplementary pump on hot days or long hills, or shut off completely.

CHAPTER EIGHT

Hot and Cold

The baffles on this Plymouth direct all the air through the radiator core. They're essential to proper cooling.

The warm months of the year are the most popular ones for touring in collector cars. The higher ambient temperatures, though, lead to some of the most irritating of collector car problems: the dual specters of overheating and vapor lock.

First, some definitions. For purposes of this discussion I define overheating as a condition in which engine temperatures rise steadily until a point is reached where the coolant boils, or is lost. If coolant is not being lost, just running at a high temperature is not in itself an overheating condition. Vapor lock is a condition in which heat causes the fuel to change from liquid to vapor so that it can no longer be delivered to the carburetor in a form that is usable by the engine. (This is a kin of percolation, when the pressure of the boiling fuel forces some of it to bubble out of the carburetor.)

Though some systems were marginal even when new, production cars of the collector car era had cooling systems that were capable of handling ordinary driving conditions while maintaining engine temperatures in an acceptable range.

As years and miles go by, scale and chemical residues build up inside the cast-iron block, insulating the coolant from the cylinder walls. Deposits in the radiator passages reduce the core's ability to transfer heat to the air. So do several layers of paint on the core. Add in a long grade on a hot day, and the fun drive becomes a steaming nightmare.

Many hot-weather problems are avoidable through maintenance. Some may require judicious modifications.

Before you begin to dismantle your car's cooling system to repair cooling problems, consider some of the other factors that cause an engine to run hot. For checking some of these I recommend the use of the services of a good local radiator shop, as some tests are best done with specialized equipment. Using their test gear and their technicians is much cheaper than buying your own, and some of the professional tests are more reliable. Ask fellow car owners for recommendations for good shops, and be sure to take your common sense with you when you visit.

Originality

Since your car did not overheat when it was brand new, the first step is to be sure that its parts and specifications are as they were when it was new. Unless you're the car's original owner, you can't be sure that some critical part was not

The asbestos insulation on this exhaust pipe is a feeble attempt to keep its heat from affecting the radiator.

changed during the car's earlier life. Experience with old cars will soon convince you that it is impossible to imagine all the things that people will do to machinery, let alone comprehend why they did it. So you'll find water pumps with the wrong impellers, fan drive pulleys of incorrect diameters, belts that slip because they don't fit, incorrect carburetors or carburetor jets, distributors with incorrect spark advance parts, fans that are smaller or that have fewer blades than the original, and other abominations.

If your engine originally had insulation around the exhaust pipes, it was put there to lower under-hood temperatures. See that it's in place.

To begin to solve cooling problems, first restore the car to its original design. Many problems solve themselves just like that.

Ignition Timing

Determine that the basic timing setting is correct. Check the distributor's centrifugal and vacuum advance mechanisms to be sure both are working. To be certain that they are main-taining the advance curve to original specifications, seek out a shop with a distributor machine. For a collector car, you'll probably have to supply the shop with the specs for spark advance and dwell. You'll find these in your car's service manual.

Fuel Mixture

An old car may run quite well on a mixture that's leaner than specifications called for, but lean gas mixtures increase the heat that the cooling system has to carry away from the combustion chambers. The result can be overheating and even burned exhaust valves.

Besides checking carburetor specifications, look for vacuum leaks. The entry of additional air through a point other than the carburetor will lean out the mixture. The old method of finding leaks involved squirting gasoline at suspected leak points and listening for the engine to speed up as the gasoline was drawn in by vacuum. This method is messy and dangerous. A safer method using the same principle involves a propane torch. Install a nozzle with a flexible hose on it. (The long nose is so you can keep your face and the rest of you far back from the test area.) Run the engine at idle. Crack the torch's valve, but *do not light it.* Play the end of the nozzle around suspected leak areas, including the base of the carburetor, the end of the throttle valve shaft, and the intake manifold gaskets. The engine will speed up when the propane enters a leak.

Thermostats

Thermostats permit your engine to warm up quickly and to maintain temperature in the optimum range. If your engine takes a very long time to warm up, suspect a thermostat stuck open. If the temperature just rises steadily, the thermostat may be stuck partially or completely closed.

One way to *not* solve an overheating problem is to run the car without a thermostat. Some cars will run too cool as a result, creating problems with sludge and acid corrosion. Oth-

ers may actually overheat, without the thermostat doing its part in the hydraulic design of the coolant flow.

The thermostat designed for your engine is the one you should be using. The engineers balanced cooling needs, sludge and acid control, and other factors when they specified the thermostat. Unless you fancy yourself a better automotive engineer than they were, don't tamper with thermostat temperature specifications. Do make certain that the thermostat is opening fully and at the specified temperature. This is easily checked by placing the thermostat in a pan of water and gradually heating the water while monitoring the temperature with a thermometer. Look for the temperature at which the thermostat is fully open.

Radiator Cap

Water boils at a higher temperature when it is pressurized, so modern cooling systems are kept under pressure by a specially designed radiator cap that fits a matching neck on the radia-

Testing for vacuum leaks with a propane torch. This nozzle attaches to the tank with a long flexible hose for ease of moving the nozzle around the intake manifold area. The hose is available at most industrial suppliers.

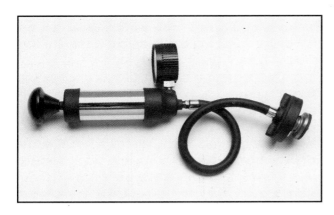

A pressure cap tester.

tor. Many collector cars had pressurized systems too. Be sure that the cap is holding pressure and that coolant is not being lost through the overflow pipe. A properly maintained pressurized system should rarely, if ever, need water added. A radiator shop has the testing device to check the cap. If your cooling system was not designed to be pressurized, you should still check the gasket on the radiator cap. Much water can be lost through a leaky gasket here.

Shrouds and Baffles

Most cars use baffles to direct all of the incoming air through the radiator core. Shrouds around the fan assure that the fan draws air only through the core and not from the engine compartment. All of these sheetmetal devices are carefully engineered to make the cooling system function efficiently. Be sure they're all in place, fastened tightly, and that they retain their correct original shape.

Head Gaskets

Exhaust gas entering the cooling system will increase its temperature rapidly. Exhaust gas (or oil) can get in through a blown head gasket, or through a crack in the block or head(s). While there are several home tests to determine whether this is happening, the best is an inexpensive leak test conducted by your radiator shop.

The Radiator

Despite all the sophisticated analyses, the most common cause of an overheating car is still a dirty radiator. If you suspect this, have a flow check performed at the radiator shop. If plugging is extensive, it may be possible to mechanically "rod" the obstructions out. ("Boiling,"

using a caustic chemical, will not remove the dried accumulation of gunk in narrow radiator tubes.) The shop can tell you whether they can rod out your radiator. Some core designs don't lend themselves to rodding; in other cases, the tubes may be deteriorated too far to save. If a new core is recommended, find out first from

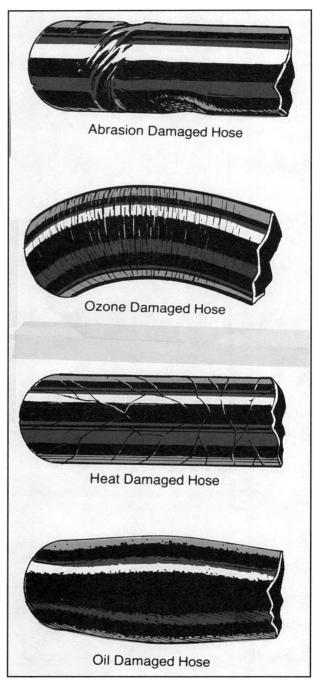

Abrasion Damaged Hose

Ozone Damaged Hose

Heat Damaged Hose

Oil Damaged Hose

This is what different types of hose damage look like. Hoses are relatively easy and inexpensive to replace in your garage, but much more difficult and costly on the road. Inspect and replace them regularly.

your car club's technicians what other owners have done to restore the radiator's cooling capacity while maintaining original appearance.

Leaks

While most of us are concerned about coolant leaks that leave drips on the floor of the garage, the more dangerous leaks are often less noticeable—when the engine is running, they aren't letting coolant out; they're letting air in.

Air in the cooling system reduces the heat transfer capability of the coolant. This leads to overheating which, in turn, can force water out of the overflow. Worst of all, it provides the final component needed for rust: water, iron, and air.

How to keep air out? Keep your cooling system filled to the maximum. (This is more important for early non-pressurized systems. A pressurized cooling system with an overflow tank is always full of water, keeping air out.) Fill the radiator when the engine is hot. When the engine is cold, the thermostat is closed and will not permit complete filling.

Your radiator shop can check for air leaks into the system. They can also tell you whether they're caused by loose hose connections or by exhaust gases from a leaking head gasket.

Hoses

The rubber hose in a cooling system has always been the system's weakest point, structurally. It had long been assumed that hose failure was due to cracking of the rubber caused by

---

Refinishing Your Radiator

If the radiator is removed from your car for repair, you will likely want to refinish it before it's reinstalled. Before you pick up that spray gun, consider the virtues of a new coating system that has effects well beyond the cosmetic. It's used in racing and hot rod applications, where a radiator of adequate size won't fit in the space available. One such coating process is a specialty of Swain Tech Coatings, in New York. Swain caters primarily to the racing and street rod fraternity. Their heat dissipating coating is called a "black body emitter." Its ingredients include copper oxides, vanadium, and some ceramics. The coating is applied approximately 0.0005in thick and dramatically increases the heat exchanging ability of the fins on your radiator's core. This modification is invisible and could be an answer if everything else has been tried.

---

heat or to failures of the yarn with which the hose was reinforced. Research done by the Gates Rubber Company eventually discovered that the real culprit was in the same family as the cause of rusting chrome, corroded brake lines, rusty fenders, and damaged engine bearings. Its our old enemy, the electro-chemical reaction caused by dissimilar materials in the presence of a weak electrolyte. When it affects rubber hoses, Gates calls it ECD, for "Electro-Chemical Degradation." The rubber is assaulted by the electrical charge and develops tiny cracks, or striations. Coolant seeps through and weakens the reinforcing fiber. It wicks along the fiber until it finds a weak spot, which is where the hose eventually bursts.

The damage continues whether the car is in use or not. Since it's done from the inside out, a hose that looks just fine may be about to go. Damage usually occurs 1 or 2in from where the hose is connected to a pipe or nipple, not in the middle. Check hoses by squeezing near the ends with your thumb and forefinger. Squeeze the middle, too. If the ends feel significantly softer than the middle, replace the hoses. You may also detect a cracking sort of feeling near the ends, as the weakened hose splits on the inside under the pressure of your fingers. If hoses appear hardened or are cracked on the outside or bulging, replace them immediately. If they're oil-soaked, find out how the oil is getting into the cooling system; a leaking head gasket is a good bet.

Smaller hoses on your engine carry coolant to the heater or to the carburetor or other heated components. It's hard to tell the condition of these hoses by squeezing, so replace them regularly.

All the hoses on your collector car should be replaced every four years, no matter how nice they look. ECD is attacking from the inside. Murphy will make certain that the rupture occurs while you're on a tour.

When replacing a hose, drain the cooling system down below the level at which you're working; you can capture the coolant for reuse. Use a funnel to guide the flow. Open the petcock only partially, or the rush of coolant will overwhelm the funnel. Put a paper coffee filter into the funnel to catch the inevitable junk that'll come out when you drain coolant—no point putting that stuff back in the engine. (Sometimes when you open a petcock in the engine jacket, only a trickle comes out. That's

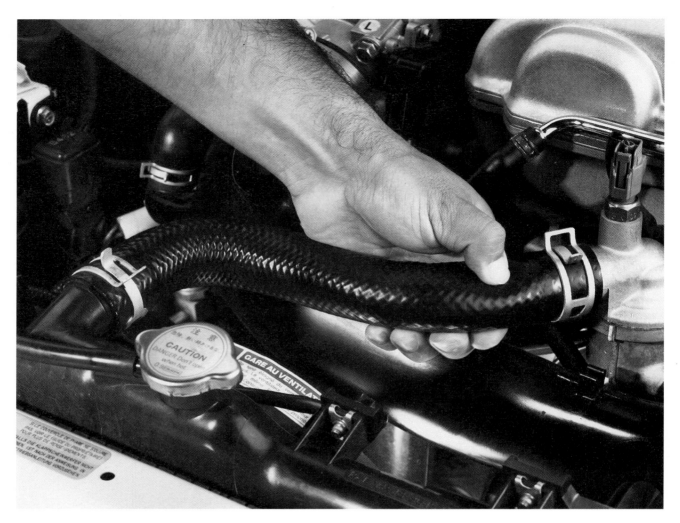

Above and opposite: When checking for hose weakness, squeeze with your fingers not your whole hand. Squeeze within 2in of the end not in the middle of the hose. Left hand photo: Correct way. Right hand photo: Wrong way.

usually because the petcock is clogged with scale and old core sand. Remove the petcock completely. You may still have to poke a piece of mechanic's wire into the hole, but you'll be rewarded by a rush of water and crud. Replace the petcock before you refill the engine.)

Next, loosen the hose clamp and slide the old hose off the fitting. If it's stuck, as it often will be, do not pry it off with a screwdriver; you risk damage to the radiator nipple or the other component to which the hose is attached. Use a new blade in a utility knife to cut the hose off. Be sure the blade is new; a dull blade is much more difficult to control. Make light cuts in the direction shown in the illustration in this chapter until you've cut through the hose. Avoid deep cuts in the nipple, which can provide a leakage path later.

Make certain that the nipple is clean and smooth. Use a wire brush to remove old stuck

rubber. File smooth any sharp or ragged edges that could cut the new hose.

Dip the end of the new hose in coolant, to lubricate it for easy installation. Most radiator nipples have a raised bead at the end. When you install the new hose and replace the clamp, be sure that its positioned between the bead and the end of the hose; a clamp tightened on top of the bead will eventually cut through the hose. Tighten the clamp snugly, but not with all the force you can muster on the screwdriver. The inside surface of most radiator hoses is of a softer rubber than the outside. It conforms well to the nipple and seals against leaks.

Refill with coolant to the correct level, then start the engine and check all hoses for leaks. If you find any, tighten down on the clamp a bit. Leave some turns for a final tightening after you've had the car out on the road and given all

the components the opportunity to warm up and cool down.

Hose Clamps

Hose clamps had different designs during different eras. You'll want to use the correct clamps for your make and year of car. Although modern worm-drive clamps can exert the most force, that isn't really necessary. Authentic hose clamps, correctly installed, can keep your hoses leak-free.

Filters

In our older cars, the installation of a coolant filter will help keep scale, rust, and other particles from reaching and clogging the radiator. One tested device is the Gano filter, available in several sizes. It is made of a clear plastic, so you can watch your coolant flow. That's pretty and useful, but not authentic. With only a bit of head-scratching you should be able to invisibly install the two parts of the filter/strainer in an existing hose or tube. Instead, you could

make up a cone-shaped strainer from bronze window screen wire. The Gano filter has the advantages of a mesh smaller than window screen and a neat trap to keep captured particles from re-entering the coolant stream.

If you install a filter, be sure to remove and clean it at least once a year. A filter plugged with crud restricts coolant flow.

Water Pump

It seems reasonable and logical that the longer the water stays in the radiator while it's passing through, the more time there will be for heat exchanging and the cooler the engine will run. This has led to suggestions for modifying the water pump to decrease its output by reducing the size of its impeller. Bad mistake. Thermodynamic analyses make it clear that the *more* water you can push through the radiator and block and the *faster* it moves, the more heat exchanging will take place. And heat exchanging, after all, is what a cooling system does.

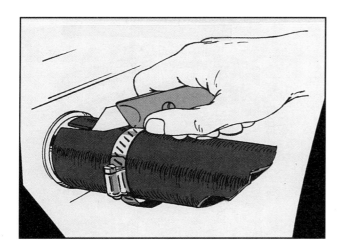

Don't try to pry off a used hose. Use a sharp knife, and avoid cutting into the fitting.

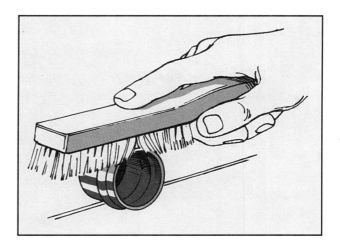

Clean the fitting with a wire brush before installing the new hose.

A rebuilt water pump provided by a reputable vendor of parts for your make of car should move all the water flow you need.

Head Bolts
Even torquing of cylinder head bolts is vital to leak-free, long-lived head gaskets. Follow the sequence given in your service manual, and use an accurate torque wrench.

The design of some engines is such that the cylinder head bolts actually enter the cooling system passages of the engine block. This creates the opportunity for leakage around the bolt threads. Also, rusting of the threads of the bolts or the block make it difficult to apply uniform torque.

For engine designs of this type, you need to apply a compound designed to seal and to permit adequate torquing. Fel-Pro's "Pli-a-Seal" is available at auto supply stores. It appears to be unique in both maintaining a seal and providing lubrication that permits uniform torquing.

Coolant
Here are coolant choices for collector cars:

Straight water
Don't even consider it.

Water with anti-corrosion compound added
This choice has the advantage of the best possible heat-transfer ability. Consider this if you live where the temperature of your car storage space will never drop as low as 32deg. Or use this coolant in the warmer months of the year, but be scrupulous about changing to an anti-freeze mixture in the fall. Actually, this was standard proce-

dure when some of our older collector cars were new. In those days, the corrosion inhibitor would have been some variety of soluble oil; there are better products available today. Particularly popular in northern California is "Red Line Cooling System Rust and Corrosion Inhibitor." A useful additive in this product is what Red Line calls "WaterWetter," essentially a surface-tension reducer. It decreases cavitation and permits the coolant to maintain closer contact with the walls of the passages of the engine cooling system, which contributes to more effective heat transfer. The result is a measurable drop in engine temperature. Anti-corrosion additives do not affect the 212deg boiling point of water.

Water and antifreeze in a 50-50 mixture
Back in the 1930s and 1940s, ethylene glycol was referred to as "permanent" antifreeze. Prestone was the best-known brand name. Its permanence was by comparison with methanol antifreezes, which boiled away if the engine's temperature rose too high. Now, the last thing that Union Carbide (Prestone's manufacturer) wanted was for people to believe that once they'd installed Prestone it was good for the life of the car. That dramatically reduced potential antifreeze sales. They outsmarted themselves, though, because people did believe it. Prestone solutions often stayed in cooling systems for years. After the corrosion inhibitors were used up, untold damage was done to engines and radiators.

If you live in an area where temperatures drop below freezing in some months of the year, a 50/50 water-antifreeze mixture is what you'll use. Plan to drain the cooling system and replace the coolant once a year. You'll start with fresh inhibitors and do your engine a real favor.

Until recently, glycol-based antifreeze available to collector car owners would have been based on ethylene glycol, or EG. This tried-and-true solution has protected cars from freezing for more than sixty years. It does have a serious flaw, unrelated to its use in the car—it's highly poisonous. Even a small puddle of spilled anti-freeze, lapped up by a thirsty pet, can be deadly. Worse yet, it has a sweet smell and taste that encourage such a tragedy. Colorado State University Veterinary Hospital reports that 50 percent of all poisonings of dogs and cats involve ethylene glycol antifreeze.

There is a safer alternative. Antifreeze formulations are now available based on propylene glycol. PG, for short, has been used for years as an ingredient in foods, cosmetics, and medicinal products. Because of its lack of toxicity, the regulations regarding disposal of PG are less stringent in some states than those for the disposal of toxic EG. Check on this locally; these rules have a habit of changing suddenly.

In corrosion protection and stability, you'll find little difference between the two types of antifreeze. There are areas where the differences are more substantial, and they explain why ethylene glycol so dominates the antifreeze market.

PG's freeze protection is 5–6deg less effective than EG's. PG boils at a 3–4deg lower temperature, too. Of more concern is that PG is more viscous than EG, especially at very low temperatures. At -20deg, PG's consistency is about that of SAE 20 oil at room temperature. This reduces its heat transfer ability, especially at very low temperatures. If you switch to PG, your old hydrometer won't work anymore, though that's a small loss. Simple dip strips can now tell you the freeze point and other useful information.

The bottom line: Ethylene glycol is a marginally better anti-freeze than is propylene glycol. This can be an issue if you live in a very cold climate or if your cooling system needs every break it can get. If the toxicity issue is an important one to you, then PG is the way to go. Just be aware of the down side.

In the normal operating range, your car will run a bit warmer with any antifreeze in it than with water. Ethylene and propylene glycol have only about 60 percent the heat transfer ability of water. Mixing the two results in heat transfer characteristics proportional to the mix. So, a 50-50 mixture of antifreeze and water has about 80 percent of the heat transfer ability of water.

The up-side of the trade-off is that at sea level in an unpressurized cooling system, 50/50 EG antifreeze boils at 227deg, PG at 223—11 to 15deg higher than plain water. That can be

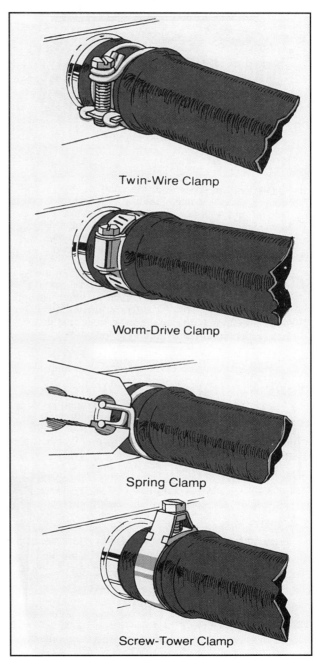

Twin-Wire Clamp

Worm-Drive Clamp

Spring Clamp

Screw-Tower Clamp

Many types of hose clamps have been used over the years including some not shown here. While some are capable of greater tension than others, all will do the job. Try to keep it authentic; use the type originally specified for your car.

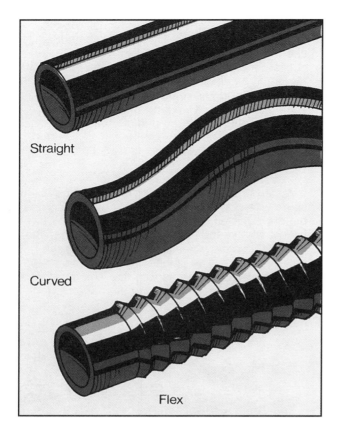

Straight

Curved

Flex

Straight hose was used on early cars. Curved hoses fit specific later installations. Avoid using the flex-hose shown at the bottom. Despite a spring molded into the walls, flex-hose can crimp if used for sharp bends, reducing water flow.

an important margin on a very hot day. The engineers tell us that this margin makes a 50/50 antifreeze coolant the best one to use. Some experienced collector car drivers swear by a water-inhibitor mix, like Red Line. You may want to experiment.

Another situation in which you'll want to consider the use of an antifreeze mixture is if you live or will be touring at high altitudes. At 5,000ft in an unpressurized system, water boils at 202deg Fahrenheit. A 50/50 EG mixture boils at 217deg, PG at 212deg.

Electrolytic corrosion occurs inside your cooling system, too. All the ingredients are there: dissimilar metals (like an aluminum head and iron block) and immersion in a conducting electrolyte (the coolant). The battery action causes the transfer of material from one surface to the other. Interfere with this process by keeping the corrosion inhibitors fresh. That means changing the coolant no less often than once a year.

When it comes to your cooling system, there's water and then there's water. Mercedes-Benz and a few others have gone to the extent of specifying the characteristics of the ideal water to use in coolant. They make the strong point that distilled water *not* be used in your radiator. Distilled water is "mineral hungry," and will look to your engine block and other cooling system components to try and absorb those minerals. Also, avoid very hard water. In the area that I live, tap water is so hard that any spillage on the outside of the radiator dries to a crusty white film. I don't even want to think about what that might leave on the inside surfaces of the engine block and radiator. So I use bottled water for my coolant mix. It costs little. Not all bottled water falls within the ideal specs. Purveyors of water will, upon request, provide you with the specifications of their products. In my area, Black Mountain brand falls within Mercedes' specifications.

Vapor Lock

If your car vapor locks regularly, you'll have to deal with the twin causes: hot fuel and low fuel pressure. First check for originality. If your engine originally had insulation on the fuel lines and exhaust pipes, be sure that its there. (Original insulation was often asbestos; today you'll have to use a replacement material, which usually abandons authentic appearance.) See that any original heat shields are in place around fuel pump, fuel lines and carburetor.

Examine the routing of the fuel lines. You want them far away from exhaust pipes and exhaust manifolds. If a line must cross an exhaust manifold, keep the crossing as close to right angles as possible, for the least heat transfer. If you can't reroute the fuel lines, consider insulating them.

Next, be certain that your fuel is under pressure for as much of the run of the fuel line as possible, especially in warm underhood areas. Since the mechanical fuel pump is often

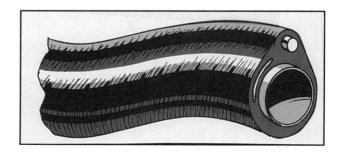

This heater hose has a spring molded into the walls and a wire molded into the side so that it can maintain the curved shape you give it. Just don't try small-radius bends.

The results of electro-chemical degradation (ECD).
This hose looked fine on the outside.

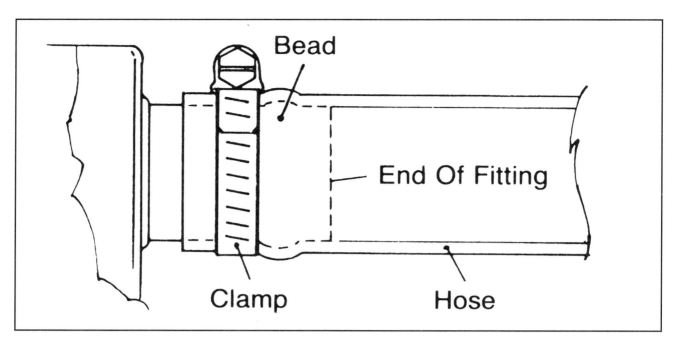

If the fitting on which you're installing the hose has a "bead," place the clamp on the inside of the bead. A clamp directly on top of the bead can cut through the hose.

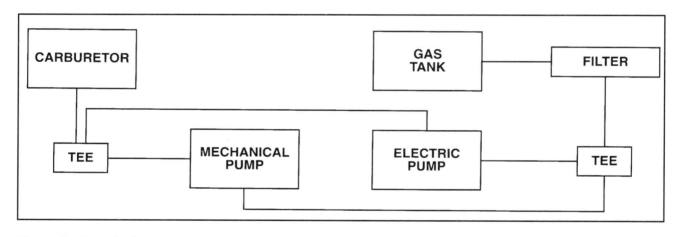

How to hook up the lines to a combination of electric and mechanical fuel pumps. Consider installing a one-way flow check valve. In the event of a rupture of the diaphragm on the mechanical pump, this will prevent any gas from being pumped into the crankcase by the electric pump.

located close to the carburetor, its action creates a mild vacuum in the fuel line all the way back to the gas tank. That's the least desirable condition because the boiling point of gasoline drops as its pressure is reduced. To put your fuel lines under pressure, you'll have to install an electric fuel pump. A way to do this while retaining the use of the mechanical pump is described in an accompanying sidebar.

Percolation feels like vapor lock but has a different cause. It's a result of gasoline actually boiling in the carburetor float bowl. When the gasoline boils, it creates pressure and expands. Since the pressure can't return down the line to the fuel pump, it forces gasoline out through the jets. The resultant flooding stalls the engine, and makes it impossible to restart immediately. Some carburetors have an anti-percolation valve that automatically vents the float chamber to the intake manifold when the throttle is closed. If your car isn't blessed with this design, you can relieve the situation by decreasing the temperature of the bowl. One method is to increase the insulation between the carburetor and the intake manifold by adding more gaskets. If there's sufficient clearance between the top of the air cleaner and the

These handy test strips replace your hydrometer. They give you an instant reading of the freezing and boiling point of your anti-freeze mixture.

They also verify the state of the corrosion-inhibitor in the coolant. The strips are available for either EG or PG.

underside of the hood, you can add two or three gaskets to improve this condition.

The mechanical fuel pump in many cars is located at the top of the engine, where it provides another opportunity for heat to be exchanged between the engine block and the fuel, making percolation problems even worse. In some cars with chronic problems, relief has been obtained by running the fuel line directly from a rear-mounted electric fuel pump to the carburetor. The original fuel pump may be left in place to preserve the illusion of authenticity, and to supply vacuum for windshield wipers. (If your car is equipped with vacuum-powered windshield wipers, a separate section of the original fuel pump may function as a vacuum pump. This is necessary because engine vacuum drops when you accelerate or when you're pulling hard as on a steep hill. This causes the wipers to slow down just when you need them most. The "vacuum booster" in the fuel pump keeps vacuum high all the time. This is another reason to keep the original pump in place.)

The carburetor's needle valve shuts off the flow of fuel to the bowl when the float signals that the

Compare the colors on the strip pad with the color chart that comes with each strip.

bowl is full. It's exactly the same action that takes place in the toilet tanks in your home. If you install an electric fuel pump, you may need a pressure regulator to reduce the output of the pump to a pressure that the needle valve can handle. Many electric pumps put out enough pressure to push the valve open even though the float bowl is full. Consider

The Gano cooling system filter.

replacing your stock needle valve with a tested device called Grose-Jet. It uses two ball bearings to replace the needle valve and is far less sensitive to fuel pump pressures. It's available for most old cars.

If your car chronically vapor locks no matter what you do, the installation of a modern vapor-recovery system will probably solve the problem. You'll have to install a three-outlet fuel filter near the carburetor. Like an ordinary filter, one line carries fuel in from the fuel pump, one other delivers fuel out to the carburetor. The third outlet carries vapor back to the gas tank; you'll need a second line for this purpose. Such a system is best installed by a knowledgeable mechanic—preferably one who's done it before—for a couple of reasons. The outlet size on the three-out-

let filter is engineered to work with the engine on which it was originally installed. Getting to work correctly on your engine may take some experimentation. Even more important, the return vapor line must enter the gas tank through a hole that must be added for this purpose. Gasoline and its vapors are not to be trifled with. Drilling holes in any part of a gas tank that's in place in the car is not suggested practice for the neophyte. If you need this modification, ask your club members for referrals to a competent mechanic.

Your car ran within its normal temperature range once, and it can again. Once the system is in good shape, reasonable, regular maintenance will keep it so. Stay cool!

CHAPTER NINE

Brakes

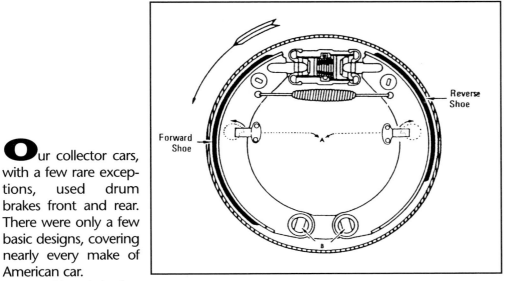

A Lockheed brake as used on the front and rear of Chrysler cars in the 1930s and 1940s and the rear of these cars in the 1950s.

Our collector cars, with a few rare exceptions, used drum brakes front and rear. There were only a few basic designs, covering nearly every make of American car.

Lockheed brakes were manufactured by the Wagner Electric Company under Lockheed patents. Their basic design called for brake shoes pivoted at their bottom end on one or two anchors. The primary shoe provided most of the braking power and was "leading." This means that its brake cylinder end pushed it into the direction of drum travel; the secondary or "trailing" shoe provided much less braking power. Shoes were adjusted using cams. Some later versions used a special design with two single-ended wheel cylinders. Each operated a single brake shoe, both of which were leading. That resulted in very powerful brakes. With the car in reverse, however, brake power would be inadequate since, with the drum turning in the opposite direction, both shoes would become trailing. For that reason, the "two-leading-shoe" design was used only on the front; conventional Lockheed brakes were used at the rear. Two-leading-shoe brakes were particularly popular in England. A modified version was used on Chrysler cars from 1956 to 1962. Chrysler called them "Center-Plane" brakes. Ford hydraulic brakes, before they switched to the Bendix design, were similar in design to Lockheed.

Bendix brakes are based on designs patented by the Bendix Aviation Corporation between 1929 and 1950. They had come into widespread use by the late 1930s. By 1955 all American cars used the Bendix "duo-servo" design front and rear. The Bendix design permits the two shoes to float on the backing plate, connected at the bottom by an adjustable link. When the primary shoe contacts the drum it moves with the drum, and transfers this movement to the secondary shoe through the link. In effect, the shoes "wrap into" the inside of the drum. The result is significant increase in braking power.

This Bendix brake was one of the most successful and long-lasting designs in American automobile history. Its safe to say that, because of the Bendix brake, there have been fewer revolutionary changes in drum brake design than any other automobile part. While there have been minor improvements in details over the first sixty years of the use of this brake in production cars, the only significant change was the addition of self-adjusting linkage in 1960. Parts for Bendix brakes of the 1930s can be purchased off the shelf at your local auto supply store.

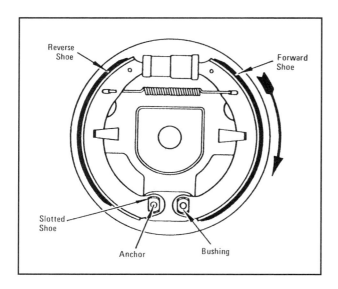

The typical Ford brake used until Ford switched to Bendix.

Among American production cars of our collector car era, there have been only a few other deviations in brake design. Chevrolet used the Huck brake for some years, then switched to Bendix. The other exceptional designs were the caliper brakes made by Goodyear for the Crosley Hotshot in 1949, the first use of disc brakes on a production car, and the Chrysler Imperial of 1949–1951, which featured a Kelsey-Hayes disc brake. Chrysler cars for many years used a small supplementary drum brake on the driveshaft as a parking brake.

Brake Maintenance

For the typical collector car owner, the most important brake maintenance chores will be inspecting the lining for wear, adjusting the brakes, and keeping brake fluid clean and up to the correct level.

You can learn to do much of your own brake service work, too. Consult one of the texts on the subject and your car's service manual. Brake adjusting procedures are covered there, too.

Brake linings wear thinner every time you apply the brakes. That's why mileage driven is a poor gauge of lining wear. A car that commutes fifty highway miles per day will still have plenty of lining left at the end of a year. A car that spends fifty miles a day delivering pizza could need new linings long before the year is up. The method by which lining is attached to the brake shoe makes a difference, too. Since World War II most makers have attached the lining to the shoe by a bonding process involving adhesives

and heat. This makes nearly the full thickness of the lining usable. Older cars used rivets to attach lining to shoes, which limits the usable thickness to the depth of the counterbored hole in the lining through which the rivets pass.

If you let the lining wear too far down, you run the risk of scratching the brake drum with the lining rivets or the shoe. The only way to determine the amount of brake lining wear is by inspection. A minimum 3/16in of usable brake lining thickness is considered safe. Most cars provide an inspection slot at the edge of the brake drum that permits you to see the edge of the lining and shoe; so check the remaining thickness of the lining. In order for this to be a useful exercise, you must first know whether your linings are bonded or riveted and, if the latter, the lining thickness from shoe to rivet head. The usable lining thickness is the difference between that dimension and the total thickness of the lining, as viewed from the edge.

If you've never seen your car's brake linings, you'll have to remove each drum to verify the lining installation method. Removing one drum won't do; different shops may have used different methods during your car's lifetime. Drums on some makes of cars are easily removed. Others require a wheel puller. Consult your service manual.

Until the 1990s, brake linings contained large amounts of asbestos. The dust that you'll find covering the brake components and the inside of the drum is largely asbestos. *Don't blow it away, either with your breath or with an air gun*—there is strong evidence that asbestos dust is toxic. Lay pads of newspaper on the floor under each brake. Using a rag soaked in a bucket of plain water, wash the brake backing plate, cylinder, and springs. Use a fresh clean cloth on the shoes. The asbestos dust will become muddy dirt. Wash the inside of the brake drums the same way. Discard the rags and rinse out the buckets. Now you can use a can of brake cleaner to clean off the brake parts and the inside of the drum. Wipe with clean shop cloths.

Your life depends on those brakes. No grease can be permitted to contaminate the lining; even a greasy fingerprint can make a brake grab. If you're working on brakes with the drum off, wrap the clean shoes in plastic food wrap. That'll keep errant fingers and tools from transferring grease to the linings.

Brake Fluids

Electrolytic corrosion occurs inside hydraulic brake systems, too. Our dissimilar metals in this case include aluminum pistons and cast-iron cylinders. The conducting electrolyte is created by the water that most brake fluids absorb from the air.

That's why it's so important to keep the fluid in your brake lines free of water. Chemically, traditional brake fluid, now labeled Department of Transportation (DOT) 3, is a glycol compound. It's been a quite satisfactory fluid for hydraulic brakes since the 1920s. It's incompressible, as a fluid must be for transmitting force through hydraulic lines. It doesn't freeze at any temperature likely to be encountered by the motorist, and it boils at a relatively high temperature. Boiling point is an important issue because a tremendous amount of heat is generated inside drum brakes. Remember that in most cases your braking system actually produces more horsepower than your engine does. The arithmetic is simple. Horsepower is a measure of work done in a certain time span. The 135bhp V-8 in your 1949 Olds 88 will get your car from 0 to 60mph in about 12sec. The brakes will get you from 60 to 0 in about 3sec. That's a lot of power, and your brake shoes and drums turn it into a lot of heat. (DOT 4 brake fluid is the same formulation as DOT 3, but with a slightly higher boiling point for hard use.)

Glycol-based fluid does have two serious flaws. It's an effective paint remover, therefore a hazard to us shade-tree mechanics. Worse yet, it is hygroscopic. That means that it absorbs water from everywhere, including the humidity in the air. Water in the brake fluid reduces the boiling point, and that's dangerous. Water in the fluid also causes steel brake lines to rust and corrode from the inside out, and that's even more dangerous. Changing the brake fluid regularly, a chore few perform, is the only way to maintain a glycol-based system in a safe and efficient condition.

On older brake systems the fluid reservoir was usually vented to the air. That provided plenty of opportunity for the brake fluid to find water. Later reservoirs had a diaphragm between the fluid and the air. That permitted the fluid to contract and expand without coming into contact with air.

Silicone-based brake fluid came on the market in the 1960s; it too came with advantages and

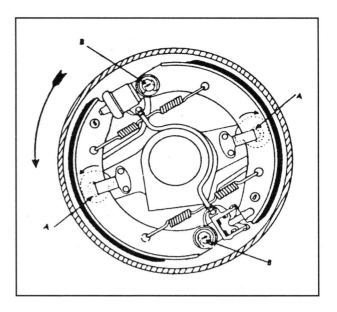

The British call this a two-leading-shoe brake. Chrysler used it on the front wheels in the 1950s.

disadvantages. The most important point in its favor, and it's a big one, is that it does not absorb water. That means that you can leave it in your brake system for much longer periods before changing it. Also, happily, when dripped on your newly-painted fender, all it does is make it sticky. And, its boiling point is even higher than DOT 4.

At first silicone brake fluid was sold for off-road use only. That did not deter many of us from purchasing and using it in our collector cars. In 1972 silicone brake fluid was approved for road use by DOT and labeled DOT 5. Most of the early use was in motorcycles.

During the decades that silicone brake fluid has been available for legal road use, a surprising amount of controversy has surrounded what seems like a simple product. Early silicone brake fluid leaked a bit at the master and wheel cylinders. That's when we discovered that glycol fluid swells rubber a fraction and that the manufacturers of the rubber cups and seals used in brake systems had been taking this into account in the manufacture of their components. The silicone fluid caused no swell and therefore a poorer seal. Silicone fluid manufacturers added chemicals to produce a controlled swell, but it took some years of experimentation to get fluid and rubber parts to cooperate smoothly. On some cars the problem may not have been fully solved yet. As a result some folks were made unhappy and probably won't try silicone brake fluid again.

For the advantages of silicone brake fluid there are several prices to pay. The fluid itself is

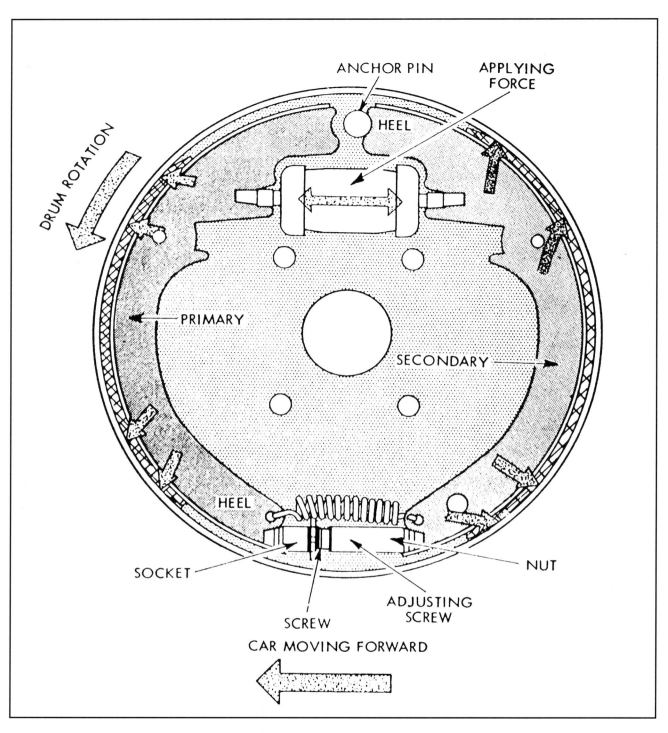

The nearly immortal Bendix duo-servo brake design.

more viscous, or thicker, than DOT 3. Entrapped air is more difficult to remove. To ease this problem, pour silicone brake fluid into the master cylinder reservoir as slowly as you can. Pour the reservoir half full and let it stand for an hour. Because the fluid is thicker, air bubbles rise more slowly. Top off the reservoir and let it stand again. (You'll want to avoid shaking the container of sil-

icone brake fluid before you use it; you'll just be creating more hard-to-bleed bubbles.)

The other price is the eventual destruction of most hydraulic brake switches. Restorers and collector car owners have reported a disproportionate number of switch failures. In a typical switch, the contacts are separated from the brake fluid by a rubber diaphragm. It seemed that silicone brake fluid was weeping through the diaphragm and contaminating the switch contacts. Restorer Paul Chemler explored this possibility with the technical experts at Echlin, one of the makers of these switches. Their response: "Our brake light switches are manufactured in accordance with SAE J1703. These units are designed for use with DOT 3 brake fluids. I am not familiar with DOT 5 brake fluids and therefore will not comment on the use of DOT 5 silicone. Some silicone oils do have great penetrating properties and if these oils penetrate the seal into the contact area, contamination of the contacts would result."

If you want to use silicone brake fluid and if your car uses hydraulic brake switches, you ought to rig a mechanical switch in its place. Depending on the configuration of your brake pedal linkage, such a switch will be more or less visible and a departure from authenticity. (The alternative may be regular replacement of the brake switch. In your particular car, this may not be a problem. But if you're using silicone brake fluid, be sure to check the operation of your brake lights regularly.)

The last problem, a small one, is that silicone brake fluid is marginally more compressible than glycol fluid. The difference is greater at high temperatures. You'll feel this as a very slight sponginess of the pedal. The difference is minimal, and you get used to it quickly.

Years and miles of experience have now made it clear that the use of silicone brake fluid will effectively eliminate corrosion in brake systems. For our collector cars especially, which may stand still for longer periods of time than do ordinary cars, that's of special benefit. (I once drove a collector car home that had been standing in a museum for ten years. My only defense is that I was much younger and still feeling immortal. The 600-mile trip required four stops to rebuild wheel cylinders. When I got it home I flushed the brake lines. Ten years of absorbed water had turned the glycol fluid into a most unpleasant-looking jelly.) Still, you may choose to use DOT 3 brake fluid in your collector car. You'll gain a harder pedal, and your brake switch will last a long time. You *will* have to replace your brake fluid regularly. Doing this every two years should be quite satisfactory. Few of us ever change the brake fluid in our daily drivers, unless hydraulic brake work is being done, but we do want to treat our collector car better than the old beater, don't we? If

you consider this recommendation unnecessary, look at your brake fluid sometime. Use a clean turkey baster to suck some out of the reservoir. (Get it from the supermarket, *not* from the kitchen drawer—glycol is poisonous.) Squirt it into your old standby olive jar and check its color and consistency against fresh fluid.

Remember that glycol absorbs water out of the air. Unless you have lots of cars and are changing the DOT 3 fluid in all of them, buy brake fluid in small containers. If you top off the system and have only a small amount left in the container, dispose of it. A container full of air and a small amount of glycol fluid equals a small amount of contaminated glycol fluid. If you're saving a nearly-full container, be sure the cap is on tight.

Converting to DOT 5

If you choose to use silicone brake fluid, learn from the millions of miles of experience that military, racing, and collector car drivers have had with this product.

There are several situations where silicone brake fluid should *not* be used, unless specifi-

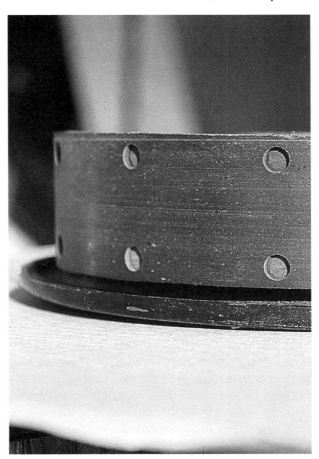

A brake shoe with riveted lining.

cally recommended by the manufacturer. Don't use it with power brake units like the Bendix Hydrovac. Don't use it in slave clutch cylinders. Don't use it in hydro-electric systems, like the convertible top mechanisms in many collector cars. (On modern cars, don't use it in systems that have a master cylinder fluid level gauge—the silicone fluid isn't sufficiently conductive to operate the gauge. And don't use it in Anti-lock

There is much brake work that an owner can learn to do. Brake work must be done carefully, but requires only simple tools.

Brake Systems.) Certain foreign cars have had specific problems with silicone brake fluid; check with your dealer. Volkswagen and Porsche, in particular, have opposed the use of silicone brake fluid from the beginning.

From the time that silicone brake fluid first became available, it was recognized that the best way to convert a system that had previously used glycol fluid was to rebuild all the brake hydraulics, including new or sleeved master and wheel cylinders, all new rubber parts, and new hoses. An alternative that took less time and effort was also suggested. Nicknamed "flush-fill," it involved removing all the glycol fluid by opening the wheel cylinder bleeders and pumping the brake pedal. Fresh silicone

brake fluid was to be introduced into the master cylinder reservoir, with several reservoirs-full pumped through. Cylinder bleeders were then to be closed, and the system refilled with silicone brake fluid. Years of experience have now made it clear that flush-fill is *not* an acceptable alternate method. Glycol residues and water remain in the system, and used rubber parts swell incorrectly when the silicone fluid is introduced. Flush-fill may sound like a time-saver, but it will cost you. Don't do it.

Not even silicone brake fluid should be left in your car forever. Older cars have reservoir caps vented to the atmosphere, so water and dirt can enter through there, as they can when you have the cap off to check the fluid level. Although silicone fluid does not absorb water, any water that enters remains free, and the boiling point of water is much lower even than contaminated fluid. Plan to replace the silicone brake fluid every five years; a complete teardown isn't necessary.

Bleeding Brakes

No, that's not a British expletive. Whenever air is permitted to enter a hydraulic brake system, the system must be bled to encourage the air to leave. Unlike brake fluid, air is compressible. The effect of air in a hydraulic system is a brake pedal that feels spongy when the brakes are applied.

Air enters the system when you replace a wheel or master cylinder. It can also enter if you permit the level of brake fluid in the master cylinder reservoir to fall.

You're best off bleeding your own brakes. Aside from the dollar saving, it gives you some control over this vital safety component. Most brake shops use a pressure bleeder tank, kept full of brake fluid. If you're using silicone fluid, it is unlikely that the shop will have a pressure bleeder full of DOT 5 fluid. If you're using glycol, remember that this quantity of brake fluid may have been standing around for a while busily absorbing moisture. Yes, most brake bleeders do have a diaphragm arrangement that's supposed to keep the fluid isolated from water-laden air. Nevertheless, that's not what I want in my brake system.

The traditional method of bleeding brakes involves two people. One lies under the car and cracks open the bleeder screw at each wheel cylinder in order. The helper sits behind the

DOT 3 and DOT 4 brake fluids. These are glycol-based.

wheel, foot on the brake pedal. In response to commands by the under-car member of the team, the helper alternately depresses and slowly releases the brake pedal. Success of this method depends on clear communication between the parties and good coordination on the part of both. Each time a brake is bled, the master cylinder reservoir must be checked and refilled, to be sure that the fluid level doesn't drop so low that air is drawn right back into the system. The helper is usually a spouse or significant other, often a non-car person, pressed into service. The opportunities for misunderstandings, sulking, and poor brake bleeding are many.

Alternative methods of one-person brake bleeding appear regularly both on the market and in print. They usually involve vacuum pumps, check valves, and other paraphernalia. Reported results have been spotty.

There is one method that requires no outside assistance and that does work. I referred to it earlier. It's used in nearly every brake shop and is called pressure bleeding. You can use this method too. It involves a tank filled with brake fluid, placed under air pressure. An adapter is fitted to the master cylinder in place of the regular cap. When a wheel-cylinder bleeder is opened, pressure forces fluid and air out. No pumping, no trips out from under the car, no refilling of the reservoir. The downside of pressure bleeding is that the equipment is expensive and usually needs filling with a gallon or two of brake fluid.

Sometimes a used pressure bleeder appears at a swap meet. Failing that, though, there is a device you can make easily that does the job just as well, requires only a quart or two of fluid, and doesn't even need an air compres-

sor. Collector John Moody first thought this up several years ago.

Buy a plastic 1 or 1-1/2gal garden sprayer, the kind with a handle you use to pump up the pressure. Remove the spray nozzle at the end of the hose and replace it with a standard female air hose connector; you can get these with a barb fitting at the end to fit into your hose. (Some nozzles have a brass threaded connection, to which you can screw an air hose connector.) The polyethylene sprayer I bought holds 1-1/2gal but works fine with only two quarts of fluid in it. It has a simple built-in pressure gauge and permits you to easily release the pressure when you're finished using it. That makes for neater operation.

Now you need an adapter for your master cylinder's lid. KD makes them and sells them through auto supply stores and tool shops. The adapter is essentially a replacement for the master cylinder reservoir cover, with a standard male air hose fitting at the top. Your older car may no longer be included in KD's list, so you'll

DOT 5 silicone brake fluid.

A hydraulic brake switch.

have to do some research and hunting. If you can't find an adapter for your master cylinder, you can make one out of an old cover that fits your master cylinder. Drill and tap the top for a male air hose adapter. Old caps are usually vented; you must seal up the vents or the device won't work. Braze or solder them shut or use a modern adhesive product like JB Weld.

Put a couple of quarts of brake fluid in the pump container, snap the coupler onto your master cylinder adapter, and pressurize the sprayer container to the maximum recommended by the instructions.

Here are step-by-step instructions for bleeding your brakes, using the Moody pressure bleeder.

Slide under the car. Take with you a supply of shop towels and a wrench to open the bleeder screws. Use a *six*-point box wrench to protect the small hex on the screw. If you need one, special bleeder wrenches come with a very large offset, to help reach bleeders that may be obstructed by suspension or steering parts.

If your car's master cylinder has a bleeder on it, do that one first. Then bleed, working

The garden-sprayer pressure bleeder.

in order from the wheel furthest from the master cylinder to the closest. For most cars the sequence will be right rear, left rear, right front, left front. Cover the bleeder lightly with a rag to avoid squirting brake fluid all over the place. Bleeding is done by opening each bleeder screw no more than a quarter turn. As you crack each bleeder open, the pressure will force out fluid and air. You'll hear the air come out. Close the bleeder when no more

Add this air-line coupler to your garden hose brake bleeder to apply pressure to the brake reservoir adapter.

air is heard. (When you're bleeding with pressure you don't need a tube in a jar to watch for bubbles because you're only just cracking the bleeder screw open.)

When you're done, release the pressure in the garden sprayer and unsnap the coupler from the master cylinder adapter.

This pressure bleeder can be used for the periodic replacement of your brake fluid, too. Since you'll be using a larger quantity of fluid, be sure that the garden sprayer tank is full, so you don't pump air into the system.

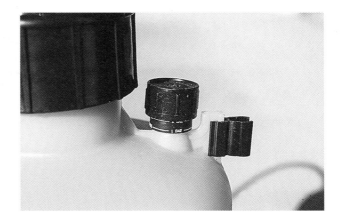

This neat garden sprayer has a pressure gauge calibrated in atmospheres (1 atmosphere is about 15lb/sq-in). The gauge doubles as a pressure release.

CHAPTER TEN

Wheel and Tires

Here's how an expert trues rims. This work was done at Stockton Wheel Service. A dial indicator is used before, during, and after the straightening to insure accurate results.

Even the handsomest collector car will encourage its owner to leave it in the garage if it doesn't perform acceptably on the road. A large measure of responsibility for the quality of that performance rests with the wheels and tires. So does your safety.

Check your wheels visually at least once a year. With disc wheels, you'll be looking for cracks in the wheel and rim; with wire wheels, you'll be looking for loose spokes as well. Cracks can start as a result of metal fatigue caused by thousands of blows from bumps, curbs and potholes, and millions of cycles of rotation. Cracks can also be caused by over-torquing of lug bolts or nuts.

The openings in the wheel include the bolt holes and the holes between wheel and rim, sometimes called "handholes." Look for hairline cracks from any hole to any other and from any hole to the rim. Also look for any rust or corrosion in corners and crevices. If you find cracks or serious corrosion, you should probably discard the wheel. The only possible exceptions are for a very rare or irreplaceable wheel. In these cases, consult a wheel expert. While examining the bolt holes, look for elongation, or holes worn large. Either condition will make it difficult to properly

torque the bolts or nuts and can result in loosening while driving.

Don't tighten the wheels on your collector car with an impact wrench. We're sometimes advised to run the wheels up with an impact wrench, then do the final tightening with a torque wrench. If you do this, you'll need a light touch on the impact wrench's trigger. Besides, you'll lose the feel for stripped or cross-threaded nuts or studs that you get when you install the nuts by hand. It's not that much harder to run the nuts up with a lug wrench. (Snap-On makes extensions especially designed to limit the torque that an impact wrench can apply to lug nuts. I haven't seen many shops using these.)

I prefer not to use an impact wrench to remove wheels from my collector car either. Any rust can lock the nut briefly to the stud, and the impact wrench is fully powerful enough to break the stud loose from the hub. Again, it just ain't worth it. Besides, the interface of human and machine via lug wrench is one of those lost artifacts of the good old days. You may not want to do it too often, but it isn't such a horrible chore once in a while.

On wheels with an odd number of lugs, tighten every other lug around the wheel. On wheels with an even number, tighten opposite pairs all around. Do the final tightening, in the same pattern, with a torque wrench.

Here's a guide to recommended torque. Note that the size given is for the bolt or stud, *not* the head size marked on the lug wrench. The bolt size is usually 3/16in or more smaller than the head size.

Bolt Size in	Torque Range lb/ft
7/16	55–65
1/2	75–85
9/16	95–115
5/8	125–150

Just plain honest mileage will have an effect on the wheels' dimensions; your wheel rims have probably hit many a curb in their lifetime. They may look fine to the eye, but only a dial indicator will tell you the truth. To give acceptable performance on the road, wheels and tires must be round and within acceptable tolerances for radial and axial runout. (If you try bringing such highfalutin' terms to your local tire shop, you risk blank stares. Many use the equally valid and more descriptive terms "hop" and "wobble".) Good standards to adhere for your collector car wheels are a maximum of 0.020in hop, 0.050in wobble.

An impressive selection of tires is available for collector cars, both American and foreign, going back to the classic and antique eras. Few of these tires are made in the original molds; in most cases, new molds have been made, to closely reproduce original sidewall and tread patterns. Since the steel molds are expensive, there are some sizes and patterns that it's not financially practical to reproduce. Collectors of most American collector cars, though, will be able to choose from several brands and several tread designs.

Experience with the driving quality of collector car tires, even those that carry famous old brand names, has been inconsistent. Members of your marque club can often tell you which brands have the happiest history. There's no way to tell how a tire will run just by looking at it, so when you buy tires for your collector car, be fussy. Chances are that the four tires you buy will look and run just as you hoped they would. On the other hand, you may have to invest a good deal of time in mounting, remounting, and returning an occasional tire. Persevere, because your future pleasure may depend on it.

Be prepared to try several tires to get a good one. Like your old wheels, your new tires can be out of round laterally or radially. Most tire manufacturers consider tires adjustable or replaceable if they are 1/16in (0.060) or more out of round.

Choose a tire brand based on how you use your car. If you show your car and have it judged regularly, you'll demand exact authenticity including original correct major brand names. Major brand tires are those that were original equipment on the automobile as it rolled off the production line. This selection may not be as simple as it seems. Many of the automobile companies had relationships with several different tire companies—Goodyear, Firestone, BF Goodrich, U.S. Royal, and General—all during one production year. If you don't have your car judged, you'll still want appropriate appearance and proper sizes, but brand is not quite as important. In that case, consider one of the minor or private-brand tires.

Collector car tires are often purchased by mail or phone order, and delivered by one of the common carriers. They're usually shipped, wrapped in clear plastic. It's important to examine your tires while the delivery person is present. Look for damage done by conveyor belts or rubbing against another parcel. It is normally the responsibility of the consignee or customer to determine if the parcel is damaged and to so advise the delivery person. If the damage occurred in transit, claims are made to the carrier, not the vendor.

Tires are highly complex products. They're manufactured from an array of chemicals including chloro-butyl rubber, natural rubber, carbon black, and calendared fabric made of polyester, rayon or nylon. With time all of these chemicals will break down or oxidize from exposure to the atmosphere.

It is best to put off purchasing tires until the final weeks of a restoration project, so you're sure of purchasing fresh ones. Most tires will begin to deteriorate after five years. If you must buy your tires long before they are to be mounted on your car, here are a few things you can do to limit the damage they suffer in storage. Store your tires in a cool, dry and dark environment. Stack them on top of each other, sidewall to sidewall. Make sure that no whitewall touches black rubber. Black rubber contains carbon black, which will permanently stain any

Above, below and opposite top and below: A hydraulic press and a variety of specially made fittings are used to tweak the rim into shape. Operators in shops like this one have straightened thousands of wheels. If you're having wheel problems, check for roundness and runout.

whitewall. Leave the clear plastic on during storage. It is best to cover tires completely during long term storage, to protect them from sunlight. As for tubes, buy those just before you need them.

Ozone speeds the deterioration of rubber products. While ozone exists in the atmosphere, there's no need to expose your tires to more. Don't store tires near electric motors, since these emit ozone while in use.

Most cars, from Dodge to Duesenberg, were originally purchased with black sidewalls. Today, most collector car owners prefer the look of wide white sidewalls. Whitewalls vary in width from brand to brand. Look for original factory

photos and owner's manuals to help determine correct sizing and whitewall width for your car. National marque clubs like the Early V-8 Ford Club and the National Corvette Restorers Society have printed judging standards listing correct sizes and sidewall configurations.

Wide whitewalls should be cleaned on a regular basis to keep them white. You may have to try several brands of whitewall cleaner to settle on one you like best. Some whitewall tires discolor as they age. Because whitewalls on most collector car tires are somewhat porous, dust and dirt can become imbedded. To completely clean whitewalls, you're going to need some abrasive. One way to handle very dirty whitewalls is to use a quality whitewall cleaner and very fine grit sandpaper. Don't worry about sanding through the whitewall; the white rubber on most collector car tires is over 3/8in thick. (This method for cleaning whitewalls also applies to redlines, pinstripe whitewalls, or raised letters.)

Rubber and vinyl treatments are popular at auto supply stores. The makers claim that they will prolong the life and enhance the beauty of the rubber on your automobile. Frankly, most result in black rubber that's too shiny for my taste. You can also buy tire "dressings" that make your dark gray tires look black. If you use these, be sure not to put them on areas of a collector tire that are not black. Whitewalls, redlines, and raised white letters will be stained by the chemicals in these treatments. It's best to pour or spray the chemical onto a rag and wipe it on the black rubber only, keeping it completely clear of the white rubber.

Although you can mount your own tires by hand, I recommend that you turn this job over to a qualified expert. Not all tire shops are willing to take the care needed to mount your tires with minimal damage to the rim finish. Ask fellow collector car owners for a good shop in your area. Most good shops will also have the proper equipment for balancing and truing.

Rims should be properly prepared prior to the mounting of tires. They must be checked for trueness, sharp edges, or cracks.

Tire balance is more critical on some cars, less on others, but all newly-installed tires should be balanced. Today's computerized machines spin tires for just a few seconds; lights and numbers indicate size of the needed weights, and where to place them. Sure, we all

balanced tires with a bubble balancer when our cars were new, and in most cases it worked just fine. That was partly because the tires were made to pretty good standards, and partly because our own standards of a smooth ride may have been a bit more forgiving. Modern cars spoil one.

It's true that the computerized wheel balancers are intended to make it possible for a minimally trained person to balance a tire well but, frankly, that's who will be working on your tires in many shops. Be thankful that he has clever equipment to help him. I recently watched a balancer called Accu-Balance, made by Assix, Inc., do its work. After balancing is complete, the machine places a load on the tire to simulate the road, then uses abrasive wheels to buff the tire into round wherever it deviates beyond normal standards! Some shops use strobe light balancers, which balance wheel and tire on the car. This method balances brake drums, in addition to the tire and wheel assembly.

If your car vibrates on the road after the tires have been balanced, it's likely one or two tires that are causing the problem. Very seldom does one find all four tires causing a vibration problem. Check the run-out of each tire/wheel assembly. If the tire appears to be out of round, try matching the tire to the rim. This process often corrects the problem without truing or replacing the tire. The tire is broken away from the rim and turned 180deg on the rim. Sometimes an older rim is out of round a few thousands. If the out-of-round positions of the rim and tire match, the problem is amplified. If the 180deg turn does not relieve the problem and make the tire assembly more round, try the same process again, this time turning the tire 90deg on the rim. If the assembly is still out of round and the rim is determined not to be the problem, the tire should either be trued or replaced. (It is important to note that most tire manufacturers will not adjust an out-of-round tire after it has been trued or shaved.)

If you decide to keep the tire, a minor amount of truing may correct the problem. Some collectors shudder at the thought of cutting rubber off a new tire, but tire-rim matching and truing or shaving can make the tire more nearly round, which will extend the life of the tire by insuring that it rolls down the road surface instead of hopping or bouncing, wearing irregularly in spots. The best experiences

I've had with tire truing used older Hunter equipment, which trued the tire on the car. If the tire is trued on a separate machine, you're at the mercy of the machine's accuracy. That's why it's important to seek out a clean shop; odds are that the equipment will be well-maintained as well.

Many times other mechanical problems of an automobile are blamed on the tires. If you're still experiencing vibration with round and balanced tires, check for proper front end alignment. Shocks

Above: Hunter and others now use a stroboscopic device to balance wheels on the car.

Opposite top: This machine turns the tire while a spinning cutting wheel shaves the tire to a round shape. That's one way of doing it. Some shops have machines that turn the wheel on the car's own hubs while they true it. That seems like a better idea, if you can find a shop that has that equipment.

Opposite bottom: On some problem cars, wheel balancing is best done on the car. This Hunter "Tune-In" balancer was in use in better shops for decades. Operator skill is important.

on older cars may need filling or rebuilding. When the steering wheel vibrates while applying brakes, brake drums, not tires, are the likely culprit.

Radial tires for collector cars are growing in popularity. Several companies advertise wide whitewall radials for use on collector cars. Many of these vendors are buying regular blackwall or narrow whitewall modern radial tires, grinding down the sidewall, and curing-on whitewall rubber. I'd be really cautious about 'converted' radial whitewalls. Aesthetically, there's a concern that the chemicals that give the rubber its durability can also stain whitewalls; you may be left with brownwalls. Structurally, the problem could be worse. Tire dimensions on radial tires are engineered to fine tolerances. The manufacturer did not plan for anyone to grind away at the sidewall. At a minimum, you'll void the tire manufacturer's warranty; at worst, you could be courting blowouts.

At least one manufacturer is now providing wide whitewall radial tires from the factory, in a limited range of sizes. Some collector car owners are seeking the improved handling characteristics, comfort, and longevity that radial tires can provide. Add a wide white sidewall, and it sounds like the ideal tire. It well may

A collector car tire made in a modern mold.

A new, wide-whitewall radial tire in a size to fit the collector cars of the 1950s.

be, for some applications. Still, extreme caution should be used.

Most collector cars were originally equipped with 'bias-ply tires. The cord or ply materials run from bead to bead at approximately a 45deg angle. The multiple plies of a typical 4-ply tire overlap each other. When a bias-ply tire meets a bump in the road, it tends to push the car away from the bump. On the radial tire, the cord materials are parallel to each other and run from bead to bead radially around the tire. A radial tire is more likely to "flow" over the bump because the sidewall is more able to flex.

Radial tires handle and wear as well as they do because they permit extra flex in the side-wall. This flexing creates greater stress on wheels and rims. If you plan to put radial tires on the original wheels of your collector car, I urge you to have the wheels stripped and checked for cracks by magnetic crack detection. An invisible crack that might not cause trouble with bias-ply tires is almost sure to widen under the stress placed on the wheels by radials.

Remember, too, that your collector car's suspension was matched to the characteristics of its original bias-ply tires. There have been reports of older cars whose handling deterio-rated when radial tires were installed. Seek references from others who have used them on your particular make and model.

CHAPTER ELEVEN

Thoughts on Some Chassis Components

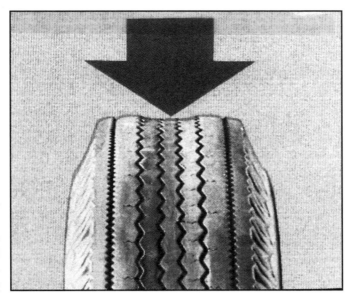

The tires on your car, after some mileage, can reveal wheel misalignment and other problems. This tire shows the results of overinflation.

Front-end Alignment

The average collector car owner will never have occasion to do his own front end work. Front-end alignment is a task best left to specialists who have the equipment and theoretical knowledge to do the job. However, it can be useful for owners to understand front end alignment basics, just to get this work done correctly.

There are good texts out there on wheel alignment. They'll illustrate that all alignment theory flows from one simple purpose: to keep a vehicle's four wheels rotating with a minimum of slipping, scuffing, and dragging, no matter by what amount the front wheels are turned. There are four angles that affect the handling, steering, and tire wear patterns in older cars. These are camber, caster, toe (toe-in or toe-out), and kingpin inclination. Not all of the first three are adjustable on every car. Kingpin inclination almost never is. Specifications for your car will appear in the car's service manual.

To these relatively simple concepts today's cars have added complications like four-wheel steering, all-independent suspensions, front-wheel drive, and four-wheel drive. Digitized, laser-emitting, beeping, and blinking alignment equipment is needed to keep track of all the variables. But we are lucky. The cars that we collect, nurture, restore, and love are far simpler, and they permit simpler solutions.

There are several obvious symptoms indicating that your car's wheels may be out of alignment, and a few that are more subtle. The obvious ones are excessive and uneven tire wear, the tendency for the car to pull to one side or the other when being driven on a flat road surface, a lack of stability that causes the car to wander about on the road, lunging into turns, the failure of the steering wheel to return to center, or a tendency to violently snap back. More subtle symptoms sometimes involve a handling feel that is just not right. All of these can be due to improper wheel alignment.

Wheel alignment is actually the final step in correcting these problems. That's because they can also be due to worn or bent steering linkage, a sloppy steering box, bad ball joints, bad shocks, worn kingpins, or worn suspension bushings. Unevenly worn tires will throw alignment settings off, too. A straight and square frame and correct spring height are also prerequisites for predictable road manners.

Underinflation makes tires wear like this.

Improper toe adjustment gives "saw-toothed" wear.

Most of our collector cars, unless they've been in a bad accident or sadly mistreated, are not heir to all the ills described above. Use your club buddies as a source for a good local shop. The shop will check these factors out as a matter of course.

Practical front end alignment is fussy work which requires both experience and a feel for the theory. An experienced front-end man, using thirty-year-old equipment by Bee-line, Bear, Hunter, or Beam can properly align the front end of your collector car. So can the operator of the digitized, laser, and diode alignment equipment in dealerships and newer shops. In every case, the key factor is a technician who understands the theory of what needs to be accomplished. Find one, then cherish him or her.

Springs

Most of our collector cars were intended as family vehicles or touring cars and were designed to ride as comfortably as possible. Truth be told, though, many of our cars ride more harshly and noisily today than they did when they were younger.

Uncovered semi-elliptic springs are probably the most common rear suspension on our cars. Ford-built cars used a single transverse leaf spring at the front and at the rear through 1948. Studebaker and some others used a transverse semi-elliptic in front as part of an independent suspension. While primitive provisions were sometimes made to lubricate these springs, most were neglected for much of their lives. Rust, and the abrasive dirt that gets in between the leaves, creates a great deal of extra interleaf friction. Since the spring leaves have to slide on each other as the spring flexes, the car's ride may be adversely affected.

In early automobiles, some interleaf friction was designed into the spring, to help damp the spring's action. As modern shock absorbers were developed, this became less necessary. In any case, it is important that interleaf friction remain constant. To accomplish this, some production cars over the years have used interleaf liners made of fabric, wax, and plastic. Others used buttons of rubber or bronze or zinc strips. Still others provided a drilled center bolt and a grease fitting, with channels in the leaves to distribute the lubricant. Studebaker, which used a transverse leaf as the front springing medium for years, ground a short channel near the ends of the leaves in which a ball-bearing rode. (Some makers covered the springs to retain a lubricant. These covers were designed to keep dirt out and lubricants in; in practice it sometimes seems like they keep water in and make it difficult to get lubricant in.)

If your original leaf springs are not sagging, you can restore the original ride quality to them. Removing springs from your car is not a job to be regarded lightly. There's a great deal of energy stored in car springs. Unless you're experienced at this, it would be best to explain what you want to a good spring shop. If you insist, they'll do it just the way you want it.

The shop will remove and dismantle the spring. You want them to clean and strip the spring leaves. For want of lubrication, the ends of some leaves may have worn a groove in the leaf below them. This groove makes the leaves "catch" when they lengthen as the spring flexes and makes the ride harsher. Have the shop carefully smooth any such grooves.

There are several ways you can maintain the original predictable action of your rebuilt springs. Both involve a reduction of interleaf

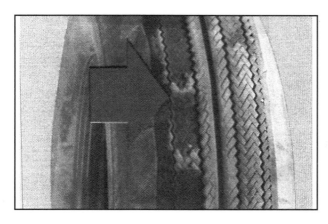

"Cupping" indicates that the tire has been run for a considerable distance in an out-of-balance condition.

friction. One method is to insert thin polyolefin plastic between the leaves of your springs. This is slippery stuff that comes in rolls of varying widths. The plastic is black; with the spring leaves painted black too, the plastic is essentially invisible on the job. Some suppliers provide buttons or tabs of similar material, for the same purpose. Street rodders use these extensively.

Another way of keeping interleaf friction predictable is to paint the spring leaves with a graphite-laced finish called Slip-Plate. This is basically a charcoal gray paint with very good adhesion to clean metal and excellent lubricating properties. It's designed for an environment with extreme pressures and slow movement, which well describes a leaf spring.

If your springs are sagging, buy new ones or have them made. You'll save time and money. Shops re-arch old leaf springs by laying each spring leaf over an anvil, then striking it mighty blows with a large hammer. The leaf spring's arch is restored while it's off the car but it doesn't last very long after you're back on the road. Forcing steel supports into sagging coil springs (another remedy) will simply reduce the spring's ability to flex.

Have the spring shop put in all new rubber bushings when they reinstall your leaf springs. This alone will often improve the ride and restore a more precise feel to the car.

The Gas Tank

One of the parts most vulnerable to corrosion on an old car is the gas tank. It's made of comparatively thin material and is attacked from both within and without. Any water that enters the tank with gasoline over the years falls to the bottom, and the tank is pelted from underneath by rocks and stones and subject to corrosion from salt mixtures in the winter. It's amazing that some of them last as long as they do.

Rust on the inside of the tank can detach itself and be drawn into the fuel line. It may

You can check some front-end conditions yourself. With the car on a jack stand placed close to the tire, grab the wheel at top and bottom and try to shake it. Any movement may indicate play in the wheel bearings.

Now hold the wheel at the sides and shake in the direction of the arrows. Movement may indicate worn steering linkage.

STEPS IN RENEWING A GAS TANK

The outside of the rusty tank is bead blasted.

owner. It's an exquisite form of automotive torture.

This problem brought gas tank sloshing sealers into the old car market. They were originally a material used in airplane fuel tanks; new automotive fuel formulations, some of which are not compatible with the old sealants, have brought new formulas especially for old cars. As often happens, the purveyor of each new formula derides the capabilities of his competitor's formula. We are told that certain colors are useless and that others are frauds. It's a frightening choice for the car owner.

None of the sealers can be properly used unless the tank is removed from the car. This done, another avenue opens. A company called

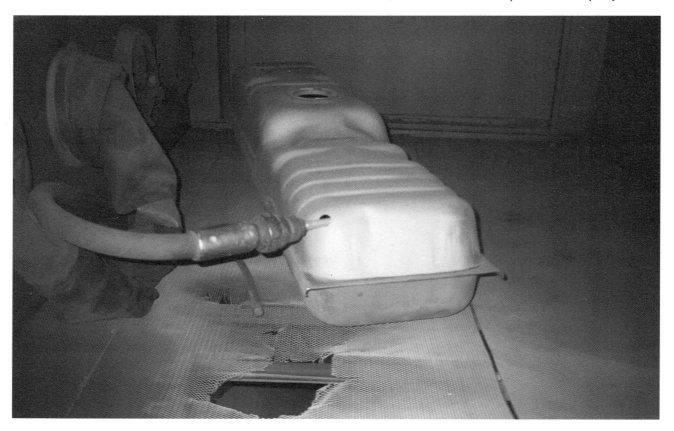

A 3/4in hole is drilled on a corner and nozzles are used to bead blast the inside. The hole is then welded up.

make its way through the line to the fuel pump, perhaps even to the carburetor, causing harm there, or it may block the line and cause fuel starvation. You don't know what misery is until you've driven a car with dirt and rust alternately blocking the fuel line, then falling back so the car runs again for a while giving brief hope to the

Gas Tank Renu now has franchises all over the country. Some do nothing but gas tanks. The process involves bead blasting the tank to bare steel. To get the inside clean, a hole is drilled in a top corner of the tank to admit the blasting nozzle. After the bead-blast cleaning, a sealer is poured in and the tank manipulated, so all inside

Left: The sealing solution is poured in, then poured out.

areas are covered. The rest of the sealer is poured out. (That part of the process is little different from the sloshing method, but the bare steel inside makes all the difference in sealer adhesion.) The outside of the tank is coated by brush with a black sealant. The tank is then baked at 350deg for ten minutes to cure the sealants. Finished tanks are guaranteed against leakage or internal sealant separation for the life of the car.

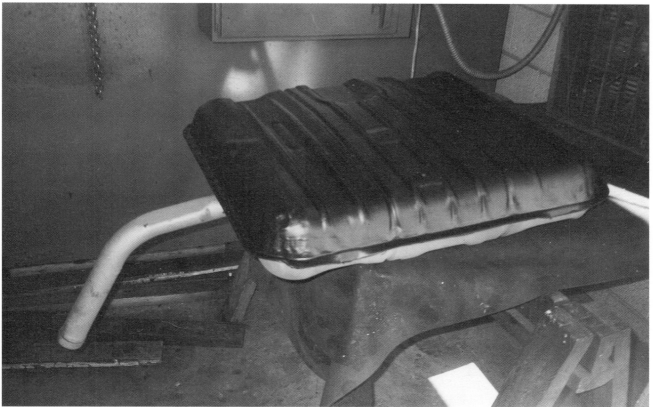

Left and above: One side of the outside is sealed, then the tank is baked. The other side is then sealed, and the tank is baked again.

The black exterior sealant has a satin finish and closely resembles the original finish on the gas tanks of many collector cars. For show buffs, the process is offered with only the interior seal, so you can put your concours finish on the outside. The guarantee is then limited to two years.

Certainly this is more expensive than buying a quantity of sloshing sealer, but it seems to me that you buy a lot of peace of mind, too.

CHAPTER TWELVE

Making it on Six Volts

This type of battery is often called a "tar-top." After the battery is assembled, the top is sealed with a mastic compound. Such batteries were original equipment in cars of the 1930s through the 1950s. They're made today by specialty companies to look like the originals.

Statistics kept by AAA and other road service organizations indicate that nearly 50 percent of calls requiring road service deal with problems electrical. Happily, an informed collector car owner can maintain his car's electrical system in a reliable state with a relatively small investment in finances and time.

Many American cars that are now collectible were built before 1954; their original electrical system carried 6V. Articles now appear regularly in magazines for street rodders and others describing how to convert the electrical system of such cars to 12V. That's a good idea for a highly modified vehicle like a street rod; the electrical conversion, after all, is probably the least of the indignities visited on the original car. If yours is an authentic early car, you'll want to retain your original system if you can.

Let no one suggest that those among us who drive cars with their original 6V system do so because it's the preferred voltage. There's good reason for the fact that every production car in the world today uses 12V power. A 12V electrical system suffers less voltage drop for equivalent wire size, provides more reserve in battery starting power, and is more forgiving of minor problems like dirty terminals. There is no reason, though, that a 6V system cannot power your car reliably. You just have to pay more attention to its maintenance and understand its potential shortcomings.

If you drive a later collectible with a stock 12V system, you'll find that some of the suggestions given in this chapter will be useful, too.

Easier starting is the reason usually given for 12V conversion. Still, most collectible cars were everyday transportation when they were new. Why do they have starting problems now that they're older? There are several reasons.

First, batteries don't always supply the full voltage that's demanded of them. The ability of a lead-acid battery to accept a full charge diminishes with time and many cycles of charge and discharge. It's also adversely affected by sitting for long periods of time without cycling at all. Also, authentic antique battery cases are often made of hard rubber and thicker than modern plastic cases. This reduces the interior space available for plates and electrolyte. The maximum current output of these batteries may suffice under the best of conditions but leaves little reserve in case of other starting problems.

Second, the cable carrying battery voltage to the starter can introduce voltage drop. Original cables were frequently sized at the smallest that the manufacturer could get away with; copper cost money. Most batteries were grounded to the chassis or to the body at a point near the battery. The body and frame were expected to supply the return route for current. This was not good practice to start with and a recipe for failure as years corroded the connections.

Third, most of us take the starter itself for granted. We assume that if it turns when voltage is applied to it, it's ready to do its job. Not necessarily so. Starters begin to crank more slowly as their components age and wear. The design of a starter requires an air gap between the armature and the field coil pole shoes. A worn bushing allows the armature to move closer to the field coils. The intense magnetism of the field tries to hold the armature, and reduces the power available. With enough bushing wear the armature can actually drag on the field coils. In addition to slowing the starter, the drag increases the current requirement, which causes the voltage to drop, which makes it more difficult for the coil to provide spark for starting! What's more, brushes wear, brush springs lose tension, internal insulation frays, and wires to commutator segments short or break.

Lastly, I think that standards have changed. It's hard to recollect accurately, but folks I talk to who were there remember that engines did indeed turn over more slowly when cars of the 1930s, 1940s, and 1950s were new. In most cases the engine started right up. But there was much less margin for error.

Nevertheless, your collectible car did usually start and run well on 6V when it was new. If you want to keep your car driveable *and* authentic, it can continue to do so. You'll have to address some potential problems and perhaps make some minor modifications.

There are fine books in print describing basic automotive electrical components and theory. Others deal with testing and repair. (See the appendix for suggested reading.) I won't repeat this material here, except as needed for clarity. With that in mind, here are some ways to put your 6V machine in Tour Trim.

Three Steps to a Super, 6V Starting System
The Battery

The major function of the battery in your

The 6V Optima battery. It's much smaller than an original battery.

car is starting the engine. That may seem elementary but not all batteries are designed for the same purpose. Traction batteries, for example, operate forklift trucks, electric wheelchairs, and electric cars. They're also known as deep-cycle batteries. They put out their energy at low rates over long periods of time. Standby batteries, as used in emergency lighting systems, are constantly being charged. Our auto batteries are actually Starter-Lighting-Ignition (S-L-I) batteries, with the emphasis on Starter. They must put out huge quantities of power for a brief period of time while maintaining high voltage. The chemistry is the same in all these batteries, but the internal construction is different.

Install the most powerful 6V battery you can find. When our collector cars were new, battery power was rated by ampere-hours. This meant that a certain current could be obtained from a battery for a certain number of hours, which could, for example, keep a lamp lit for a certain length of time. Since we're talking about *starter* batteries, this is not a very useful standard of comparison. Today's automobile S-L-I batteries are rated by a standardized SAE measure of Cold Cranking Amps (CCA). A 6V battery, fully charged, should deliver its CCA rating for thirty seconds at a temperature of 0deg Fahrenheit without falling below 3.6V. (Double that voltage for a 12V battery.) The more CCAs, the better.

The battery's ability to start your car reliably is a primary component in the enjoyment you'll get from your collector vehicle. So, since the bat-

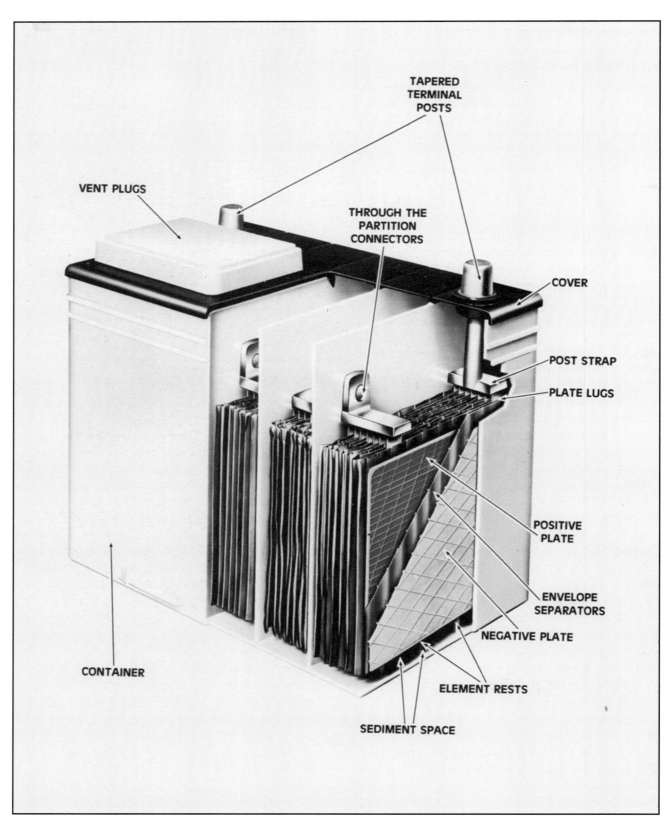

TAPERED
TERMINAL
POSTS

VENT PLUGS

THROUGH THE
PARTITION
CONNECTORS

COVER

POST STRAP

PLATE LUGS

POSITIVE
PLATE

ENVELOPE
SEPARATORS

NEGATIVE PLATE

CONTAINER

ELEMENT RESTS

SEDIMENT SPACE

How a conventional battery is constructed.

tery is a unit that's easy to replace for shows, consider equipping your collector car with the most powerful modern battery you can find and using an authentic-appearing battery for shows. If your car's battery lives under the seat or in

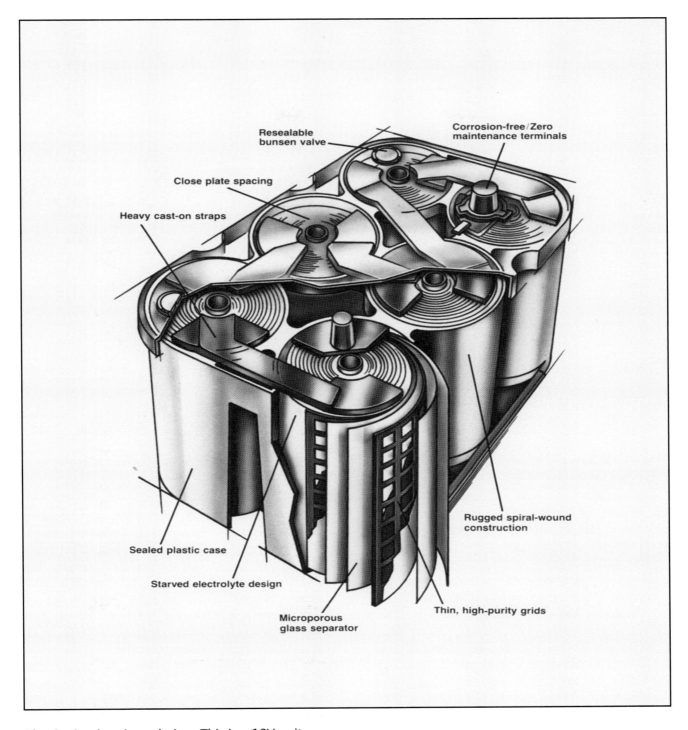

The Optima's unique design. This is a 12V unit.

another out-of-sight location, you can keep your Tour Trim battery in place permanently. If the battery in your car is visible and you want to retain the authentic look for shows, you'll seek a battery that looks right. That usually means a tar top and a black, hard rubber case.

For Tour Trim, I've had excellent results with a 6V battery that goes by the name of Optima. It's very different in appearance from the usual battery; it sort of resembles three large cylinders stuck together. That's because that's what it is, internally. The experience of other collector car owners confirms that the Optima is indeed different from other batteries, so some words on the subject might be useful.

The original research on the Optima battery was started by The Gates Rubber Company in 1973. (Among car owners, Gates is best-known

Find a local auto electrical shop with a crimper like this, or order your cables made to length by a supplier like Bob Groulx (that's him on the other end of the crimper).

for its radiator hoses and fan belts.) Gates spent eighteen years and millions of dollars developing this technology, without making a significant impact on the battery market. The battery company, now separately incorporated, was purchased in 1992 by a Swedish conglomerate.

Basically, a lead-acid battery consists of two different types of lead compounds formed into positive and negative plates, separated by insulators and immersed in a weak sulfuric acid solution. The old "open" batteries permitted oxygen and hydrogen to escape during charging. They had filler caps, so the electrolyte could be kept topped off. Newer, "maintenance-free" batteries have plates made of a purer material to reduce gassing rates. They're often filled, when they're manufactured, with more acid than open batteries were. They still lose liquid through gassing and usually can't be refilled. "Recombinant" batteries are constructed so they can convert hydrogen and oxygen back into water. They have no provision for refilling or adding water.

The Optima battery uses recombinant chemistry, but its major differences from other batteries lies in its construction. Its positive and negative plates are wrapped in a spiral in a manner resembling a condenser. The electrolyte is absorbed in the thin porous glass separators, so there is no free liquid in the battery case. (It is NOT what is commonly referred to as a gel cell.) The thin separators permit a smaller gap between the positive and negative plates, permitting the release of large quantities of current quickly.

These design differences also cause the Optima to be extremely resistant to vibration and impact. It won't crack if it freezes, and it won't leak acid if the case breaks. Perhaps more important is that the Optima neither builds up nor releases hydrogen gas, so the explosion risk is reduced.

The 6V Optima is rated at an impressive 850 CCA but is only about one-half the size of an ordinary battery of that capacity. It's completely sealed, so water never needs to be checked or added. It doesn't even have any caps to do so. That's a special virtue if your car's battery is mounted under the seat or in another less-than-accessible position.

The crimper dies close.

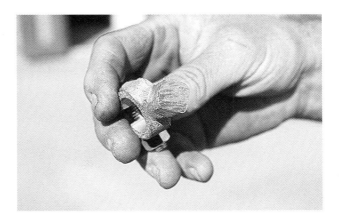

The dissected result: Wire strands and terminal squeeze solid with no voids.

After all these laudatory comments, a word of caution. The Optima is narrowly designed specifically to start engines. It would be a poor choice for electric cars or wheelchairs, or for powering the lights and accommodations in an RV or boat.

For Tour Trim choose a starter battery, Optima or any other, with the highest CCA rating that you can fit into the space available. This is vital step number one in effective 6V starting. In any case, be certain to determine the CCA

Heat-shrink tubing comes in a variety of sizes. You'll find it at electronics supply stores and flea markets.

Use this type of battery terminal only in an emergency.

The 2/0 cable you should be using.

rating and physical size specifications before you order a battery from advertisers in the collector car publications. And for convenience in switching from Tour to Show trim, look for a battery whose terminal locations match those of the authentic battery.

Battery Cables

As already noted, original battery cables were sized at the minimum the manufacturer could get by with. For long cables, like the ones to under-seat or other remotely located batteries, the temptation to skimp was even greater. Typical stock cables from the hot battery terminal to the starter solenoid ranged in gauge from #00 (sometimes labeled #2/0 and pronounced "two ought") to #2. The latter is smaller. The accompanying figure shows some comparative cross sections.

The return path, or ground, was usually provided by an uninsulated strap from the battery ground terminal to a nearby point on the chassis or body. Sometimes an additional smaller strap was used to ground the engine block to the chassis. In either case, the return path to the battery depended on metal-to-metal contact through frame and body joints.

To get reliable starting with 6V you must reduce the resistance loss in the battery cables to as near zero as practical and maintain it that way. For reliable regular use, replace your old cables and terminals. The cost isn't great, and the results of this one improvement will often surprise you.

Use #2/0 or larger *welding* cable. Welding cable needs to be flexible, so while the diameter of the copper conductor is about the same as in automotive cable of the same gauge, welding cable has many more, smaller strands. The additional flexibility makes it easier to place the wire where you want it to go. (Engineers differ on whether electron activity takes place on the surface of the conductor or through it. Welding cable has more conductor surface area and more cross-sectional area, so it wins either way.)

You can get such cable from your local welding supplier while battery terminals and cable lugs can be purchased from several mail-

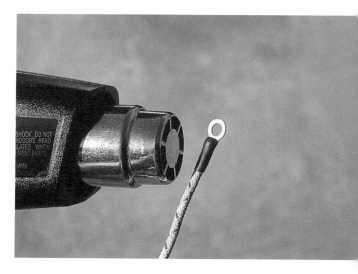

A crimped terminal covered with a bit of heat-shrink tubing. Visually, the result is very close to a soldered terminal with a rubber sleeve on it. Electrically, the modern joint is superior.

100

Alternator Versus Generator

All 6V cars were originally equipped with a generator. It's purpose, of course, is to replace the current used by the car in normal operation and to keep the battery charged. (This isn't precisely correct chemically, but it's the end result.) External regulators are required, since a typical generator will simply keep increasing its voltage output as its rotational speed increases. The goal was to limit output to about 7.2V, which would keep the battery charged to its normal 6.2V.

Generator design progressed from the third-brush designs of the late 1920s and early 1930s to the "shunt" (two-brush) designs of the mid-1930s. At the same time, regulator design progressed from simple cut-outs to two-charge regulators to vibrating voltage and current regulators. By the late 1930s most American cars were so equipped. With minor exceptions, there was really no further improvement in the basic engineering of automobile generators and regulators until their replacement by alternators beginning in 1960.

Your car's specifications will usually give the rated output of the generator in amperes. In most cases, the figure is the *maximum* that you can expect from that generator, in new condition and at its maximum permissible rpm. At highway driving speeds, expect about 75 percent of that figure.

Do the calculation. Your car's ignition system draws about 2A, mostly for the coil. Sealed beam headlights pull about 12A; add another 2A for parking and taillamps. If you play your tube-type radio, figure another 5A.

For Tour Trim, consider replacing the original generator with an alternator. There are good reasons why every new car in the world is equipped with one. An alternator's voltage curve is far more suited to the way cars are driven than is that of a generator. This becomes important in a car that may not be driven for long periods, and then only for relatively short distances. For Show Trim, removing the alternator and re-installing the authentic generator is usually a matter of less than an hour's work.

You'll see 6V alternators advertised by various suppliers. Before you buy, check the specs. You're looking for a unit that was built as a 6V alternator. Many of the less expensive ones on the market are simply stock 12V units whose output is cut in half by internal diodes. That reduces the voltage from 12 to 6 but has that effect on the amperage as well. You want an alternator with an output rating of at least 50A. Since most alternators put out about 75 percent of their rated amps at normal driving speeds, that will give you 35A to replace current draw.

I use an alternator made by Fifth Avenue Auto Supply. They offer a variety of pulley widths to adapt to your original fan belt. For some popular makes and models, they also offer brackets for direct replacement of your generator. For others, there's an adjustable universal bracket. You may have to make up an adjusting link for your particular installation.

Fifth Avenue's alternators offer "one-wire" installation. The alternator has a single terminal to which you attach the wire that goes to the ammeter on most cars. This is the lead that was originally attached to the BAT terminal of the regulator. Regulation on these alternators is provided by internal diodes, so there's no new regulator to install. Your original regulator, if it wasn't mounted on the generator itself, remains in place for quick return to Show Trim.

If the original BAT wire won't reach the alternator, make an extension with ring terminals at both ends; attach the wires together with a small machine screw and nut. Insulate the connection with tape or heat-shrink tubing, so the original wire terminal will be ready for quick conversion to Show Trim. Bend any other generator wires out of the way, insulate their ends, and secure them neatly with nylon cable ties. These are easy to clip off for re-conversions, without leaving tape residue.

The Fifth Avenue alternator is self-exciting. That means that it begins to charge at relatively low engine revolutions. It's also negative ground. The two characteristics are related. I experimented with several brands of alternators before choosing Fifth Avenue. I found that available positive ground alternators had to be kicked up to about 1500rpms before they would start to charge. Some required this every time engine rpms fell to idling speed.

If your electrical system is positive ground, you'll have to convert it to negative ground. First you'll have to reverse the low-tension wires to the coil. That's a simple job in most cars. Some early cars had the wire from the ignition lock to the coil encased in an armored conduit. Others had the coil mounted on the firewall, with one terminal on the engine side and one on the passenger side. These will need some imagination in conversion.

Reversing the polarity will cause your ammeter to read backward; it'll show charge when you turn your headlights on, for example. Aside from looking weird, this does no harm. If you convert with any regularity from Tour Trim to Show Trim and back, consider just leaving the ammeter alone. (Do remember which way it's supposed to read when you're out driving!)

The first time you reinstall your generator when you convert to Tour Trim, you'll have to re-polarize it. That needs to be done only once. Afterward, the generator will be polarized for negative ground whenever you re-install it. Some Delco regulators are polarity sensitive. You'll have to replace your original unit by seeking out one similar in appearance and specifications to the one on your car but intended for a 6V negative ground system.

If you've added an electric fuel pump to your car, it may be polarity sensitive. The 'vibrator' types, like the Bendix, don't care about polarity. Motor-driven pumps, like the Carter and AC, do. Reverse the supply and ground wires, and you're done.

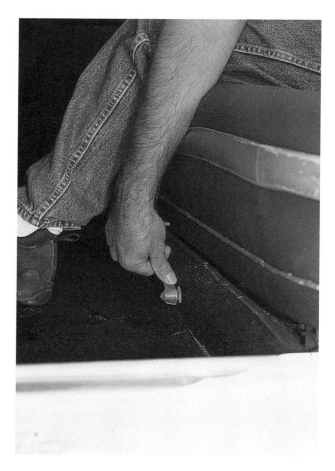

Install a master switch in a location you can reach from the driver's seat.

order sources. Putting them all together requires the use of *big* professional crimping tools. The terminals and lugs must be squeezed around the conductor, so there's no air space around them. Just filling the gap with solder will not do. (Contrary to popular assumption, solder is not a great conductor.) Find someone with the proper tools to crimp your terminals onto their cable. Heat-shrink tubing of the proper size makes a neat finished product.

Stay away from bolt-on battery terminals. They cause needless resistance even when they're brand new, and they corrode very rapidly. About the only legitimate use for one of these is if neglect finds you on the road with a cable terminal that needs replacing. Have a new terminal properly crimped on as soon as you get home.

To assure reliable low-resistance current for the starter you must run a second cable from the battery ground terminal to a mounting bolt on the starter. This is vital step number two. Use a length of mechanics wire or

stiff electrical wire to plan out the path for this cable. Since it'll be permanent and can't be removed in Show Trim, you're looking for the shortest cable path that you can conceal from normal viewing angles. The welding cable is flexible but plan carefully for any sharp, 90deg turns.

The Starter

Certain 6V starters were intended for use under conditions that required frequent starts and the ability to turn over a very powerful engine. Starters used on equipment like fork lifts were often equipped with field coil windings which, compared to automobile starters, contained fewer turns of heavier wire. These are often called high-torque windings. Their advantage is that, with the application of the same voltage, they'll make a starter motor turn faster. The flip side is that they draw greater current. Since you've now equipped your collector car with the most powerful—that means highest amperage—battery that will fit, you're ready to use high-torque windings in your starter. That's step number three for reliable starting.

One caveat. The greater current drawn by the starter will cause some drop in the voltage available to the coil. If you convert to high-torque windings, be sure that your coil is fresh and in good condition.

Specialized test equipment and tools are needed to rebuild a starter. The cost of having a knowledgeable professional do this for you is a lot cheaper than the tools. A good source for high-torque conversions and new cables is listed in the appendix.

Miscellaneous Electrical Concerns

There are other things you ought to know about that will help keep your collector car safe and sound electrically. Here's a selection:

Master Switches

A good time to install a battery master switch, if you don't already have one, is while you're making new battery cables. Such switches are intended for use as a cut-off during periods of non-operation, to reduce battery discharge. They fulfill that function admirably.

Master switches have an even more important function as emergency cut-offs. When you first sniff burning rubber or see that wisp of smoke, you want to disconnect the battery from the electrical system *now*. To do that, consider a path for the battery ground cable that permits you to install the battery master switch in a position where you can quickly reach the handle from the driver's seat. Master switches from which the handle can be removed are an effective, additional anti-theft measure when your car is untended. Just be sure that you leave the handle in the switch while you're driving. An emergency is not the time you want to be hunting for the handle.

Put the switch in the *ground* cable. That way it's fail-safe. In the unlikely event of an internal short in the switch, all you'll have is a normal ground connection. If the switch were installed in the hot cable, you might have a fire.

Incidentally, most car clubs do not deduct points in judging for neat installations of safety equipment like a battery cutoff switch.

Wiring

A loss of 1/2V in a 6V system represents about 8 percent of the total available voltage. To appreciate the effects, consider that headlights lose about 30 percent of their brightness for every 10 percent of reduced voltage.

Voltage in the system is reduced wherever resistance occurs. There is resistance in the wire leading to each load; proper sizing keeps this to a minimum. There's resistance at every connection; clean and tight are the watchwords here.

New wiring harnesses, made to factory dimensions, are available for nearly every popular collector car. The wires have color codes that are close to the original. For earlier cars they even look like the original lacquered cotton. Underneath though, they boast modern insulation. Terminals are usually crimped and soldered. Installing a new harness can be a chore, but if you're experiencing intermittent problems that are traceable to old wires, the new harness can make your driving a happier experience.

Grounds

Mentioned earlier was the need to ground the starter directly to the battery with a second cable. The grounding issue applies to every electrical circuit in your car. My friend Tom Pendergast has often lectured me on the importance of good electrical grounds, especially in older machinery that depends on potentially rusty points of connection.

Most cars were originally grounded through a single ground strap from the battery to the nearest point on the frame or body. It was expected that the steel body and frame would provide the return path from headlights, taillights, horns, and other electrical devices. Classic car collector Buck Varnon calls this "the invisible battery cable."

This arrangement worked adequately when the car was new. But both deterioration and restoration disrupt the invisible battery cable. The return electrical path must pass through body-frame connections, joints between lamp housings and fenders, and panel-to-panel connections. In many cases, rubber gaskets or anti-squeak materials are interposed between units, and the only ground path is thru bolts or sheet metal screws. As these connections corrode over time, the resistance grows. There is no difference, electrically, between resistance in the supply wire to a device and resistance in the ground path. The result is the same: flickering lights and sputtering horns.

Here's the Catch-22: restoration of the car will often make the problem worse. In our zeal to restore Plymouths and Fords to Rolls-Royce standards, we often diligently paint every surface of every part. Rust, a poor conductor, is replaced by paint, a very good insulator. Freshly installed horns may not blow if their brackets are painted. Nor may headlights light if their connections to sheetmetal are thus insulated.

The handle on some master switches can be removed as an anti-theft measure.

Left top and bottom: Ammeters as they looked in the days when cars had ammeters. Some were precision instruments, others gave vague indications. All were better than today's indicator lights.

The first part of the solution is to be certain that there's a metal-to-metal path for the ground return from each electrical device. In some cases, to get a good connection between body panels and between panels and frame, you'd have to break the paint film; that would contribute to future rust. Furthermore, current flow between adjacent metal panels is thought to contribute to accelerated electrolytic corrosion. We've already provided a direct return for the starter cable; if the wires can be concealed, consider grounding headlights and taillights directly back to the starter ground or the battery. Use a wire of the same size as the supply wire. If you're making up new harnesses, you might want to build the ground wires in. You may be pleasantly surprised by brighter lamps and more reliable operation.

Coils

A coil has no moving parts, so it would seem to be no cause for concern until it suddenly stops working. Not so. The coils made in the earlier years of our collector car era used shellac and similar substances as internal insulation. Many years ago, classic car owner Pat McCarthy tested the internal circuits and resistances of NOS coils. (NOS stands for New Old Stock, or New Original Stock. Either way, what's meant is a part manufactured during the era of the original car and never used.) Using very sensitive instruments available to him at his work, Pat found that time was breaking down these early coils, even though they had never left their boxes. The coil would still work but produced lower output voltage. When the current draw of the starter reduced the voltage available to the coil, hard starting resulted. Pass on those older NOS coils at swap meets.

Lights

Sealed beam headlamps were introduced in

New wiring harnesses look exactly like the originals—lacquered, cotton-covered wire; rubber insulators on the terminals; and braided wire loom. But all the materials are products of modern technology and will outperform and outlast the originals.

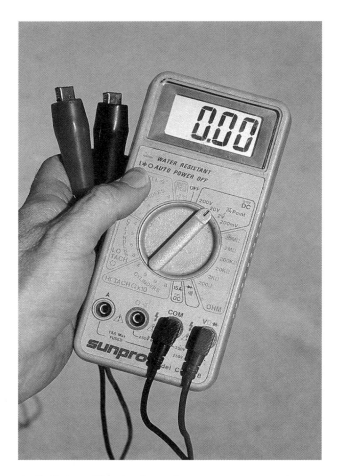

A digital multimeter is no longer very expensive, and far more useful than the test light or analog meter of the past.

the United States with the 1940 models, superseding headlights of a variety of shapes and sizes. For years afterward, motor vehicle codes restricted the shape, size, and number of headlights. Even the maximum output was regulated, for fear of blinding oncoming drivers. Those days are long gone. The lights on modern cars come in weird and wonderful shapes again, and their light output is impressive by any standard. With the fine brakes with which modern cars are equipped, today's motorist drives well within the capabilities of his lighting system.

That isn't always true for collector cars. As a general rule, the less effective your brakes, the brighter your headlights need to be; you'll want to see objects at night as far away as possible. You may not intend to drive your collector car at night. But the occasion will occur when, like Cinderella, you'll stay too long at the ball. It's for those occasions that you must pay attention to your car's lighting systems.

For adequate lighting with any kind of headlamps, you must assure that full voltage is reaching your headlights. The process of searching for voltage losses is explained in detail in the publications listed in the appendix. Tools used are simple: a digital multimeter and a selection of test probes and jumper cables. Owning them will pay dividends.

For Drivers of All Pre-1940 cars, and Some Later Ones
Adding Headlight Relays

Most cars built before 1940 did not use headlight relays. Those came into use with the advent of sealed beam headlamps. (Some makes took even more years to adopt their use.) The purpose of a relay was to shorten the length of the wire run and to reduce voltage drop. Headlight relays were widely sold by auto supply stores to enable owners of older cars to gain these advantages. If your car is of the earlier era and you may ever get caught driving at night, consider installing a headlight relay. If you're installing a sealed beam conversion, a relay is imperative. Six volt single or double headlight relays aren't made anymore but can still be found at automotive swap meets and from some mail order vendors. Installing a relay does more than just reduce the effective length of the wire run, it also saves the headlight switch. Many older switches were barely capable of handling the full load of the headlights when they were

Six-volt headlight relays can still be found at swap meets. The cover is usually attached with one screw, so open it up and check the relay contacts inside.

UVIRA-coated reflectors are as reflective as silver, and stay that way for years.

new. Age and wear have further reduced this ability. Feel the switch after you've had the headlights on for a few minutes; you may be surprised by how warm it is. An aging switch also contributes substantially to voltage drop to the headlights. Bulb brightness is very dependent on voltage; a drop of only 10 percent in voltage will reduce candlepower by nearly 30 percent! Using a relay means that the switch only needs to handle the load of a relay coil, greatly prolonging the life of the switch. The relay also eliminates that voltage drop through the switch.

Typically, the relay is intended to be installed close to the headlights. Considerations of authenticity may force you to seek alternatives. Wherever you put the relay, run a #10 wire directly from the battery or ammeter to supply power.

Brighter Headlamps

For cars with round headlamps, sealed-beam conversions are available from vendors specializing in the various makes. In addition to the relay, consider increasing your headlamp

A 6/12V "automatic" battery. The Orpin switch on top supplies 12V to the starter when energized.

Above and below: Conversion kits give your car a halogen taillight that can be seen by modern drivers. There are some precautions to be observed (see the text).

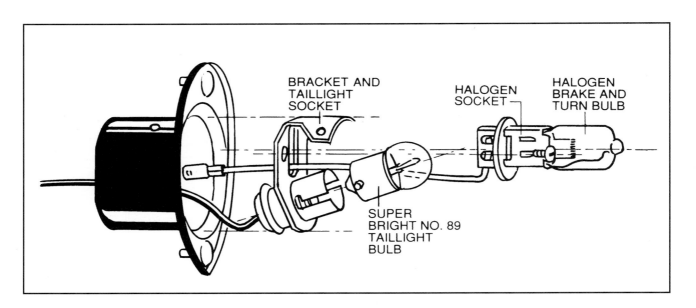

BRACKET AND TAILLIGHT SOCKET

HALOGEN SOCKET

HALOGEN BRAKE AND TURN BULB

SUPER BRIGHT NO. 89 TAILLIGHT BULB

output by conversion to sealed beams. These are fine for Tour Trim but are not very easy to convert back.

If you choose not to convert to sealed beams, you'll have to make sure that your original headlamps give you everything they've got.

Headlamps in the thirties included three basic elements: a lens, a reflector, and a bulb. Like those of today, headlamps had to be adjusted to determine where the beam pointed.

(Before 1934, the bulb also had to be "focused" to place the filaments at the most effective point in relation to the reflector. With the introduction of the prefocused bulb, this variable was removed.) While the bulbs were standardized after this date, lenses and their accompanying reflectors came in a variety of shapes.

It should be noted that the reason for the introduction of sealed beam lamps in 1940 was not necessarily an inability of the lens-reflector-bulb arrangement to put enough light on the road. The main problem was the difficulty of keeping the light output consistent, with the reflector being the worst culprit. The coating which gives the highest reflectance is silver; about 94 percent of the light gathered from the bulb is returned. Despite efforts to seal the unit with gaskets, the silvered reflector tarnished quickly; light output began dropping at the same time. It was not unusual for light output to diminish by half within six months of the installation of new reflectors. (The silver surface is so delicate that fingerprints accelerate the tarnishing process, and ordinary silver polishes are too harsh

to use on it.) By contrast, the disposable sealed beam unit had a reflector that lasted the life of the bulb and was renewed each time the bulb was changed.

The reflectors are key to the successful use of original headlamps. To effectively concentrate the available light from the bulb, the reflectors must be free of dents, and round. Most reflectors are badly tarnished. In an attempt to solve this problem some owners chrome plate the reflectors. True, they don't tarnish anymore, but they don't reflect much light, either. Shiny as chrome looks, it's dark compared to silver. Its reflectance is only about 65 percent, compared to new silver's 94 percent.

Space technology has come to our rescue. The proprietor of a company called UVIRA is a car collector. His company makes mirrors that are used to reflect laser beams; he's adapted this process to our reflectors. After the old reflectors are buffed down to the brass, a vacuum process deposits a pure aluminum coating, with a micro-thin layer of glass over it to protect it. *Voila:* a modern reflector

Above and next page: Taillights on cars of the 1950s were tiny compared to today's beacons.

The Battery Tender is a long leap forward from the old trickle charger.

with a reflectance of 92 percent that's guaranteed not to fall below 90 percent for five years.

If you still choose to have your reflectors silver plated and you have to store them for a while before they're installed in the car, here's a tip: seal them up in a box with unscented mothballs (pure paradichlorbenzene). The evaporating mothballs turn to a heavier-than-air gas which drives out air and keeps the reflectors from tarnishing.

Newly refinished reflectors deserve new sockets. Brand new units are available. They're of more modern designs but are identical in appearance and function where it counts—on the reflector side.

The original headlight bulb in most pre-war cars was rated 32-32; that's 32 candlepower on the high beam and 32 on the low. (All that's different is the focus and direction of each beam.) Replacements are available with 50 candlepower on the high beam, 32 on the low. (K-D used to make a "lamp bulb glove" to aid in headlight bulb removal and replacement. It looked like a soft rubber crutch tip and had gripping ribs on the inside for the bulb and the outside for your hand. They still turn up at flea markets.)

Adapters are made to permit the installation of 6V quartz-halogen bulbs in early cars. Be cautious about these. Although the bulb is much brighter, if the filament is not located at exactly the original point with relation to the reflector, the light output will be scattered. Also, halogen bulbs are much hotter, and most of the old headlight lenses were not Pyrex. The possibility of cracking exists.

Don't even consider a halogen conversion unless you're using new wiring harnesses, direct grounds, and a headlight relay. An H-4 halogen bulb draws 10A on high beam; that's nearly double the current draw of a sealed beam. Any wiring problems can be quickly turned into disasters.

Taillamp Improvements

Taillights in cars before 1950 were often small and usually dim. Drivers today expect more and might not notice your taillights or brake lights until too late.

Many taillamp housings used painted interiors as reflectors. As the paint rusted, the output got dimmer and dimmer. Try lining the inside of the lamp housing with heavy duty aluminum foil, molded to shape.

One place where halogen lamps are a good idea on old cars is as brake lights. Drivers today just ignore the dim glow that comes from the taillights of many collector cars when you apply the brakes. Street rod suppliers sell brackets designed to replace the original in many Ford and Chevrolet taillamps. They carry a double socket; one for a single filament taillight bulb and one for a small halogen brake light. There are enough different combinations that you may be able to fit one to your car of a different make. As a last resort, there's a bulb that will fit many 6V sockets that includes two bulbs—one incandescent and one halogen on a single base.

Two safety precautions. Halogen bulbs draw much more current than do the incandescent filaments you're replacing. So even though brake or directional lamps are not usually on for long periods, more heat will be produced. Be sure your brake light wires are in good condition. Also be prepared for the possibility of more frequent brake switch replacement. And I wouldn't use halogen bulbs on a taillamp that's fitted with plastic lenses.

One of the vendors who sells halogen conversions also supplies a "third brake light" that mounts in the rear window of your collector car. It's quite slim, so it doesn't affect vision, and it puts a brake light where modern drivers are accustomed to seeing one. You'll have to add the wiring, but with some ingenuity the device can be made removable for Show Trim. This seems like an attractive alternative.

Alternatives to the 6V System

The major perceived problem with 6V systems is their starting ability. Some makeshift arrangements have been used to deal with these. One is the use of an 8V battery. In my opinion, this brute force response creates more problems than it solves. You'll need to install solid-state voltage-dropping devices or dropping resistors to avoid damage to voltage-sensitive instruments, radios, and other accessories. There aren't any 8V accessories available, and 6V equipment used on 8V will have a short life. Headlights especially will be brighter, but very short-lived.

Another solution to the problem of starting on 6V is the "automatic 6/12V battery." Basically, this is a 6-cell battery divided into two 6V sections of three cells each. A solenoid-operated series-parallel switch is mounted on specially cast terminals on the battery. All car wiring is supplied from a

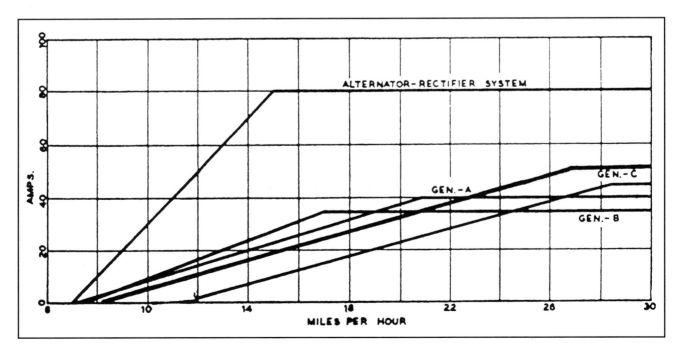

A comparison done in the 1950s of the output of an automotive alternator and several contemporary generators.

Left: Terminals on some electrical devices are hard to reach. When you're chasing a short or an open circuit, it can be very useful to be able to to test wires anywhere along their length. This test probe neatly enters any wire up to about 14 gauge without damaging it. Shielded banana plugs on the other end fit neatly into your multimeter. They're professional quality, so they're a bit pricey, but they'll be priceless when you need them.

center tap on the switch, so only 6V goes to the car wiring regardless of the position of the switch.

This switch was originally patented and manufactured by the Orpin Company and still bears their name. (The Orpin switch can also be mounted remotely, and used to connect two ordinary 6V batteries.) In its normal position, the Orpin switch connects the two batteries in parallel, creating one large 6V battery. When energized by the car's starter button, the Orpin switch reconnects the two 6V batteries in series, creating a single 12V battery. Twelve volts goes only to the starter; 6V goes to every other circuit from the center tap.

As far as starting goes, this works very well.

Below: A 6V alternator installed in a 1930s classic car in Tour Trim.

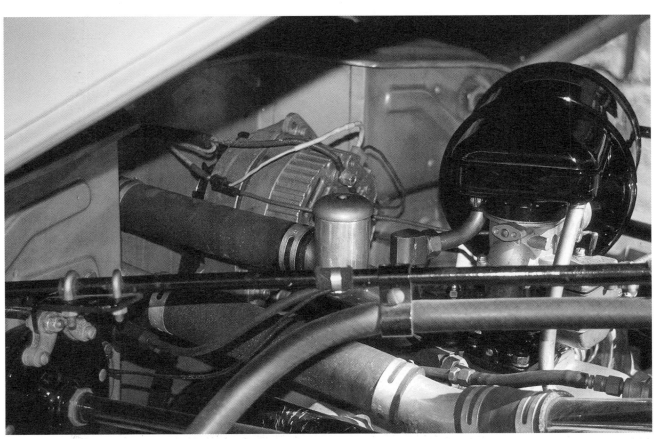

Above and left: Front and rear of a typical halogen headlight conversion, in an original reflector

The 6V starter spins merrily on 12V and starting is usually quick. My friend Matt Joseph refers to the use of 12V to spin 6V starters as "mugging the starter." I used Orpin-switched batteries for many years and never burned out a starter. When I recently examined the Bendix drive in my car, though, I found that the pinion was becoming loose. I'm not positive that the substantially greater impact of the pinion hitting the flywheel ring gear was responsible, but it certainly seems possible.

The solenoid in the Orpin switch has a heavy amperage draw. If your battery is not fully charged, the switch's contacts may not close. In that case, you'll get only 6V at the starter, just when you most need 12. If you put your 6V starting system into tiptop condition and still don't have reliable starting and you don't want to convert your car's entire electrical system to 12V, the Orpin switch may be your last resort.

If you use a 6/12V battery with an Orpin series/parallel switch, you'll need *two* battery cut-off switches. Strange as it may seem, lights and horn will work just fine with one terminal of the battery disconnected! The electrical system is still connected through the other terminal and the center tap on the battery. You have to disconnect both terminals to be safe.

If You Insist on 12V

If you're not comfortable driving a collector car operating on 6V, then convert the car's entire electrical system to 12V. No, that won't make you beloved by the purists (I suspect that I won't be either, for even suggesting this alternative), but if the greater reliability of a more modern electrical system is an important factor for you in your regular use of your collector car, then perhaps it's the right thing for you to do. A 12V electrical system may be no more inauthentic than the use of modern paints or gas tank sealants or stainless steel fasteners, or modern wire disguised by a cotton-braided cover. Does such a conversion do violence to another small piece of auto history? It's your call.

Instructions for converting your 6V system to 12V have been offered in several books and magazines. I'll try to condense here the advantage of 12V over 6V in one paragraph, without diagrams.

Given the same amount of work to do, like turning a starter, the current (amperage) in a 12V system will be one-half that in a 6V system. Professor Ohm's well known law says that voltage is equal to current times resistance. As a result, the same resistance loss in a 12V system will result in only half the voltage loss experienced by a 6V system—halving the current halves the voltage loss, too. Since we're dealing with very small voltages, that makes a big difference.

So higher voltages are more efficient simply because of our inability to completely control resistance. Wires have resistance; corrosion increases resistance in switch contacts; fuse holders corrode; starter brushes glaze; ground paths deteriorate. The effect of all of these cumulative resistances is far less in a 12V system than in a 6V one.

Twelve-volt systems arrived in cars long after they did in heavy equipment, railroad cars, and trucks. The reason was that until the 1950s, 12V batteries were about twice the physical size and weight of 6V batteries. There just wasn't enough room for them under the hood. In the 1950s, plastic began to be used for plate separators and battery cases, saving size and weight. Increased knowledge about the chemistry of lead acid batteries permitted the use of smaller components. Twelve-volt batteries shrank to a practical size. By the end of the 1950s, nearly every vehicle used on land, sea, or air used voltages of 12 and higher.

To convert your electrical system to 12V, you will *not* have to change wires, fuses, lamp sockets, or switches. Indeed, some of these components will be subjected to less load and heat than they were with 6V. You will have to change the battery, generator, voltage regulator, starter solenoid, coil, light bulbs, and turn signal flasher. You'll also have to reduce the voltage to the radio, the heater motor, and to other accessories. Certain gauges will require voltage-reducers too. Many collector cars used vacuum windshield wiper motors. If yours used electric motors, you'll have to reduce the voltage to them too. Starter concerns will be the same as those described for the Orpin switch.

CHAPTER THIRTEEN

Exterior and Interior Maintenance

A soft rubber squeegee gets wash water off quickly.

There are a number of good books on the subject of cleaning and maintaining the exterior and interior of your collector car. The subject is usually referred to as detailing. Some of these volumes do indeed go into excruciating detail on keeping the visible surfaces of your collector car beautiful and protected. I list some of my favorites in the bibliography. This chapter gives an overview of this subject.

As with other tasks you set for yourself in the maintenance of your collector car, the level of effort will be determined by how you use your car. Keeping your car clean and its surfaces protected are important components in its long-term survival. Specifics like the color of the tire rubber after treatment are more related to Show Trim than to preservation.

Grayson Walker maintains the finishes on his own vintage Ferraris. What follows are mostly his suggestions, tested by time. The products mentioned are those he has used successfully.

Here are a few simple rules that apply to all car-cleaning situations:

1. Use the most gentle product that will do the job.

2. Read the instructions of whatever product you select. Improperly used, some can be dangerous to your car's finishes. Many can be dangerous to your eyes, your skin, your respiratory system. Take appropriate precautions.

3. Before you prepare the car, prepare yourself. Take off rings, watches, buckles, or anything else on your body, clothing, or shoes that could scratch the finish of your car. Think of it this way: Is there anything I'm wearing, or plan to bring within 1ft of the car, that I wouldn't want to drag across the hood? Look at the rivets on your jeans and at the zippers on your coveralls. If the answer is yes, then don't come near your car with that item! Murphy will sooner or later scratch the finish with it. (I wear cheap sweat clothes to work on or clean my car.)

4. When possible, make sure that the car and its parts are cool and in the shade. Washing a hot car will cause the wash water to dry on the finish, causing water spots.

Now select your tools. You'll need a hose with shut-off. While trigger spray nozzles are convenient, the best way to rinse is to flow the water on in sheets, rather than blasting it into thousands or millions of droplets. A plastic shut

Many prefer a soft brush to a sponge. This one is made of boar's hair.

off valve and a short section of hose with the end cutoff is an ideal way to control the water.

You'll also need a bucket and cleaning products, and an assortment of detailing brushes. Many collectors use a lamb's wool mitt to apply cleaning solution. Others will use nothing but a one-hundred percent natural boar's hair car wash brush. These brushes are expensive, but many swear by them.

Add your favorite car wash concentrate to your bucket. Reams have been written on the virtues of various dishwashing and clotheswashing detergents. All are powerful dirt-removers. Some will remove wax. Others leave a residue. I prefer to stay safe with a product made for washing cars, by a reputable supplier.

Agitate the solution enough to get about 20 percent suds by volume. More suds do not mean more cleaning power; they'll just increase the rinsing chore. And, since more suds in the bucket means less room for water, you'll be rinsing and refilling your bucket more often. If the weather is cool, your hands will appreciate warm (never hot) water in the bucket. Your car doesn't care much either way.

Wheels, Wells, and Tires

Wash the wheel wells first. They and the wheels and tires are the dirtiest parts of your car

and may require (relatively) harsh cleaning products. You don't want to splash the dirt and chemicals from the wheels onto your nicely cleaned car body.

The wheel wells should be washed using an old wash mitt and a stiff brush. Work to loosen any dried mud, salt, tar or bird nests from the wheel wells. Inspect each wheel well carefully. Some manufacturers create nasty little pockets that can hold dirt and moisture, creating a starting point for rust. Keep any pockets or crevices clean. (Make note of missing undercoating, for later touch-up.)

Different types of wheels require different types of cleaners. Your collector car may have wire wheels or disk wheels made of steel or aluminum or magnesium alloy. Wire wheels may have painted, polished, or chromed alloy or steel rims; the spokes may be painted, chromed, or stainless steel. Steel wheels may be painted or chromed. Alloy wheels may be painted, chromed, anodized, polished, machined, or have an "as cast" finish.

Newly relined brakes shoes use a non-asbestos material. As this material wears, it deposits a nasty adhesive and corrosive black powder on the wheels and tires—with the front wheels receiving the brunt of the punishment. This black dust can permanently damage the finish of painted or clear coated alloy wheels. Grayson Walker calls it the "black peril." It must be carefully removed on a regular basis.

Remember the rule about using the most gentle product that will do the job. Simple Green is a fine cleaner. The fluorine-based QuickSilver by Armor-All is excellent and not too expensive if you get the pump bottle. It will remove years of caked on black dust.

Do not clean the wheels while they are hot. Wheels become heated by driving and braking, and hot surfaces will rapidly accelerate the chemical action of the cleaners. An otherwise safe product can now cause damage. Let the wheels cool to ambient temperature.

Some owners, especially those whose cars have wire wheels, have a collection of pointed, rounded and otherwise shaped brushes for cleaning wheels. The major parts chains and discount stores offer a wide variety of detailing brushes, or prowl the houseware sections of your local supermarkets and home products stores. The bristles of any brush you buy should be soft enough not to scratch the wheel's finish.

Clean one wheel at a time. Spray your chosen product on the wheel according to the directions on the label. Use your brushes to clean every nook and cranny; take your time and do a thorough job. Sit down on the job. Sit on the ground, sit on a bucket, or sit on a stool. Your back will thank you.

Make sure that the cleaning product does not dry on the wheel; this will only make a difficult job harder. When you have finished a wheel, rinse it thoroughly with clear water. Inspect your work and repeat the cleaning process if necessary.

Tire sidewalls, black and white, should be washed thoroughly whenever you wash your car. 'Dead' rubber dulls the appearance of the tire, just as 'dead' paint does to the finish. If you plan to spray cleaners and protectants on your tires, make up or buy a mask to protect the newly-cleaned wheels.

Owners differ on the final shade of black they prefer for the black rubber of tires. Different dressings and protectants give different hues; you'll have to experiment. Most people agree, though, that too shiny an appearance is undesirable on either black or white rubber.

If you use a bleach-type cleaner for your whitewalls (and they do give excellent results), be aware that they will dull the black rubber around the whitewalls. After cleaning the whites, you'll have to scrub the black rubber with cleaner and fine steel wool. Apply the black tire dressing of your choice with a small brush afterward.

Convertible Tops

Convertible tops (and vinyl tops) require special care. The "Hartz" brand woven fabric on older American cars and on newer European ones is treated differently from the vinyl later used by domestic manufacturers. The key to deep cleaning is to use a brush. The brush should be stiff enough to clean the texture of the fabric, but not so stiff that it abrades the thread of the fabric.

Vinyl convertible tops can be safely cleaned with a brush and car wash solution. For embedded dirt, soak the area and go over it with the brush several times. Do not make the mistake of rubbing harder or using some sort of scouring powder.

Washing the Car Body

The paint film on your car is *very* thin. On a typical collector car, paint thickness on the vertical areas is between 90 and 125 microns; on the horizontal areas slightly more, perhaps 110 to 130 microns (a micron is one-millionth of a meter). If your repaint job has been clearcoated, the new paint and the clearcoat will each be a bit thinner than the older paint was. Putting this into perspective, the average human hair is about 100 microns in diameter. Keep this in mind when you wash your car—the protective paint film is about as thick as one of the hairs on your head.

Heavily oxidized paint film may have scratches and roughness that are half the thickness of the paint film. Restoring such an oxidized paint may remove more than half of the paint; on contour lines and panel edges, it may remove all of the color, exposing the primer. Be very careful when rubbing these areas, whether with soapy water, cleaners, or polishes.

Begin by getting the entire car wet. Use the hose to rinse off as much surface dirt and dust as possible, starting at the bottom, especially if your car is very dirty or dusty. Rinse water will cut paths through dirty areas below, and the streaks will be difficult to remove. The problem

A very useful hose nozzle. It's all rubber, so it won't hurt the car when you accidentally hit it. Bend it and it turns on the water; release and the flow stops.

is diminished if you've rinsed off the dirty lower areas first.

Keep the entire car wet all through the washing process. Start washing at the top of the wet, pre-rinsed car. Don't let the washing solution dry on the car. Wash a small section and rinse. Keep going back with your hose to keep the cleaned and rinsed sections wet until you are ready to dry the entire car. Go over the wheels and tires again with your wash mitt.

Open the hood, the trunk, and all the doors. Carefully wash inside these areas, paying particular attention to the areas around the rubber moldings. If you find greasy dirt in these

This little foam mitt gets into the nooks, where dirt abounds.

areas, don't contaminate your nice new lambs wool mitt. Use a shop towel or paper towel and some grease-and-tar remover to get rid of any greasy dirt. Hinge posts, striker plates, and latches may have excessive grease. Get rid of it.

Drying the Car

Never allow either the wash or rinse water to dry on the car; if the water stands in beads in bright sunlight and dries, you will get water spots. If the water simply evaporates in the shade, all of the minerals in the water will be deposited as water spots.

There is a good deal of question about the merits of drying your car with an expensive chamois. The consensus appears to be a single word: don't. Chamois' can pick up and hold grit, which will leave fine scratches on your paint. The same is true for the cheaper chamois-like thin sponges. Instead, buy a half-dozen 100 percent cotton towels. Don't get the jumbo bath size; they are too heavy when wet. Don't get the small tea towels. Choose small bath towels, about 24 by 36in. Color coordinate your drying towels—if you dry your dark blue Chrysler with a dark blue towel, any lint left by the towel will be much less noticeable.

Before you let them touch your car, run the towels through at least six wash cycles. Use a fabric softener in the washer or the dryer; the former seems more effective. (Softeners work by attaching a waxy coating to the fabric strands. Years ago this diminished the towel's absorbency. According to consumer magazines, the manufacturers appear to have licked this problem.)

When you start to dry, there will be large areas of standing water on your car, including the windows. There are several ways to quickly remove lots of water. The simple way is to drive around the block. A second way is to use a soft rubber squeegee (make sure it is soft rubber and not vinyl). Rubber tends to harden with age, so check the squeegee's rubber each time before you use it on your car. If you have a compressor in your shop, a third way is to use compressed air, though I'd be really careful about this method.

When using towels, technique matters. Your goal is to dry the car with a minimum of rubbing. Think of your towel as a blotting device rather than one for rubbing. You will find the squeegee comes in very handy on the windows. Don't try to remove all of the water with the squeegee. In fact, leave a little, so that when you finish up with the towel, you won't have any water spots.

Open the hood, the trunk, and all the doors. After you have dried the windows and painted areas of the car, turn your attention to the nooks and crannies. If you have access to compressed air, use the air to dry out any pockets holding water; if you don't have the air, just use your towels to blot up all water.

At this point, you should have a clean car and several towels that range from being very wet to damp. Use the damp towels to clean the inside of all windows. If necessary, supplement the damp towels with an automotive glass cleaning product. If you do this regularly, you will find that you do not need anything more than the damp towel.

Last, dry the wheels and tires. You now have a spotlessly washed and dried car.

Protectants

This is the time to apply rubber/vinyl protectants. There are a number of good products on the market, along with some not-so-good ones. I have used Meguiar's #42 with success. Whichever brand you use, read and follow the manufacturer's directions.

Remember that most protectants contain silicones. If you plan to apply silicones to painted surfaces, you'll need special treatment to remove it when the time comes for repainting or touching up.

You should apply the protectant of your choice to each square inch of rubber and vinyl on your car, including all of the sealing gaskets on the doors, hood, and trunk. The rubber around the side windows and the tires should also be treated.

Whatever you do, do not simply spray the protectant at your car; you will make a mess of the car that you just spent several hours washing and drying. (And, you'll get silicones all over it.) For treating larger areas, a disposable foam paint brush does an excellent job; it gives you excellent control and saves you money by not wasting the protectant. For small areas, my favorite is a cotton swab; easy to control and economical.

If this is the first application of protectant, you may notice that the rubber or vinyl soaks it up quickly. If this is the case, give it a second coat. Older tires, in particular, may soak up the protectant like a dry sponge. (More on treating tires in Chapter 10.)

Polishes, Glazes, and Waxes

A polish is an abrasive. It's designed to remove oxidized paint. Think of it as extraordinarily fine sandpaper, but remember that it's still sanding off paint. Since we are dealing with a paint film thickness approximating the diameter of a human hair, we want to avoid sanding off what little paint we may have left.

A glaze is a clear coating that will fill minor paint surface imperfections. Glazes usually contain resins and/or oils that give the paint a wet look.

A wax is a protectant. Waxes are complex hydrocarbons that may be organic or inorganic in origin.

Polish

A polish is designed to deal with oxidized paint. When your paint was new, the paint film was (relatively) smooth and even, and there would have been no oxidation. Paint in this condition does not need to be polished, but it does need to be protected. The highest gloss will come from an application of glaze followed by an application of wax. The purpose of the wax is to protect the paint.

The KOZAK drywash cloth. Used as directed, it cleans without damage to the paint.

A "California" duster. They're effective and easy to use, but a bit clumsy to carry on a trip.

The rule with polishes is to use the least abrasive product that will do the job. Meguiar's makes an excellent line of products. Comparable products are available from 3M, Eagle One, and others.

The so-called one-step cleaner-waxes that mix abrasives, resins, and wax. They are not the products for an important car; avoid them. If the claims for a product seem too good to be true, they probably are! Avoid the miracle products, and the overpriced ones.

Glaze

A glaze is a clear coating, containing oils and resins to make the paint look wet. These are often called gloss enhancers.

Keep in mind that if you have a clear-coated finish on your car, there is nothing you can do to enhance the gloss. You are working on the clear, transparent protective paint film.

Wax

For our collector cars, I divide waxes into two categories: carnauba and synthetics. The carnauba palm grows in the hot countryside of South America. Carnauba wax is harvested from large carnauba plantations. There are a number of uses for carnauba wax, including as a food additive. The raw carnauba wax must be dissolved with solvents in order to be usable on our cars. Carnauba wax is not soluble in water, so other solvents must be used.

Carnauba wax products can give excellent gloss but tend to be rather short lived. Excellent carnauba-based products include those by Meguiar's and Eagle One. Expect to reapply a carnauba wax at least four times a year.

Synthetic waxes are similar to carnauba, except they are created on the designer chemist's bench. They are logically similar to synthetic oil. Just as a good synthetic oil has a number of advantages, so too does the synthetic wax. Among these advantages are better durability, higher gloss, and better protection. Meguiar's Medallion and Liquid Glass are excellent synthetic products that can outperform and outlast any carnauba based product. Some of these synthetics will last twelve months or more.

Chrome

Like other steel parts, chromed parts are subject to electrolytic corrosion. The conducting electrolyte can be as subtle as water absorbed from the air by the dirt on the surface of the parts. Despite its hard appearance and reputation, chrome plating is quite porous. And very thin. Protect it with wax, and you will lengthen its life dramatically.

The back sides of bumpers are chromed too; they're just not polished. Wax them too, wherever you can reach.

Leather Care and Maintenance

Most automotive leather uses a flexible dye. Don't think of the dye as something that has penetrated the leather; instead, compare it to the painted surface of your car. Except for vat-dyed leathers, most leathers today use acrylic based dyes. The flexibility and softness of the leather come from the leather structure itself, and from the tanning process. Sometimes improvements are possible.

Connolly Brothers make a leather cleaning soap that includes ammonia. If the Connolly soap is not available, saddle soap can be found at tack shops and shoe repair shops. Step one is to clean the leather with one of these soaps. Read the directions. Get the leather *damp*, not *wet*. It is best to do this on a sunny, warm day. Unlike waxing your car, the warmth of the sun helps.

Step two is done while the leather is still damp from step one. Connolly makes what they call Resurrection Oil. If you can't get this, neatsfoot oil seems close. Heat the oil very carefully. You don't have to boil it, just get it uncomfortably warm to the touch. Use a small paint brush and paint the damp leather with heated oil. Leave the windows up with the car in the sun. Check the leather every ten or fifteen minutes. Any spots that look dry are areas where the oil has been absorbed by the leather; paint another coat of heated oil on these areas. Finally, the leather will be unable to absorb any more of the oil. Let it sit (overnight if possible).

A nice warm and sunny day is just what you need for step three. Let the sun warm the leather. Wipe off the excess oil that you applied in step two, using a clean, 100 percent terry towel. (Poly blend cloths can scratch the leather finish, just as they can scratch a painted finish.) Connolly has another excellent product called Hide Food. The key ingredient is lanolin, a naturally occurring fat found in and extracted from wool. There are a number of similar products on the market by Lexol, Zymol, Eagle-One, and others. Following the directions, apply it to the leather. Wipe off any excess.

You may notice that the leather is softer and more supple after this routine. This treatment has produced significant improvements on the leather upholstery of some cars and minimal results on others.

If it works for you, routine maintenance should be done every two to three months. That consists of steps one and three. Step two should be viewed as an annual treatment.

Dusting

Don't wipe the dust from the painted surface of your car with an ordinary dry towel or cloth. There are two tested methods for dusting a car dry. "California" car dusters are now sold by several mail order vendors. They look like large shaggy brushes. Their strands are twisted cotton, mounted in a wood block with a long handle. The strands are treated with paraffin or creosote to cause dust to stick to them. The strands have a loose weave, so the dirt is trapped in them and doesn't act as an abrasive to damage the paint. Handle lengths vary from brand to brand. If your collector car is a sedan or other large vehicle, go for the longest handle you can find to ease reaching across the car.

Car dusters may be the latest dusting method, but they're no better than a much older tool, the KOZAK drywash cloth. I mention it by name because that's how its best known. After nearly seventy years of manufacture, it still appears to have no direct competition. The KOZAK is a heavy, flannel dusting cloth with a deep nap. It's used folded in a pad, passing it lightly over the surface first to collect dust, then a second time more firmly to polish. (Polishing is something the car duster can't do.) The pad is unfolded and snapped periodically to release the entrapped dust. The cloth comes with a mild perfume that's very distinctive. You'll remember it years later if you smell one again.

Neither dusting method should be used if there is any moisture, even dew, on the car. All you'll get is a mess. If the car is dewy and dusty and you can't wash it, you'll have to wait for it to dry.

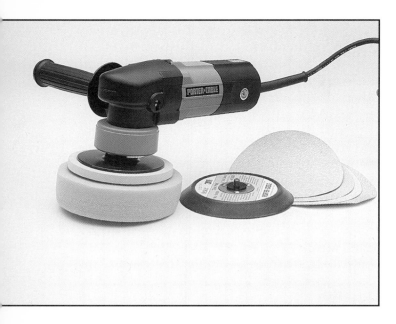

A professional orbital polisher. They turn slowly so the risk of damage is low, and it won't stall under load like discount store models. Learn how to use one before you tackle your precious collector car.

Odor

Odors can build up in older cars, especially closed vehicles. Cigarettes, mildew, food, and young children can all leave their characteristic signatures. Here's a trick shared by enthusiast John Schoepke. If your car has an objectionable odor inside, sprinkle fresh ground coffee on the problem area, or over the carpet and upholstery. Leave it for twenty-four hours, then vacuum it up. I have used this method many times, with surprisingly effective results. Commercial odor absorbents are available too, but try the ground coffee first.

Lubrication

After you've carefully cleaned grease and oil off all the visible parts of your car, now go back and apply oil and grease to many of those same parts, including door latches and strikers, hinges, hood latches and other parts that move against each other. Apply clean grease to replace the dirty and contaminated stuff that you removed. Use a grease stick or oil gun neatly, and wipe off any excess. Eventually this fresh grease will be old and dirty and will have found its way onto parts where you never put it originally. Then it'll be time to clean it off and do it again.

CHAPTER FOURTEEN

Rust

According to many car collectors, rust is caused by the "tinworm." According to my dictionary, rust is "an electrochemical reaction that occurs as iron reverts to its natural state as iron oxide." Iron, and the steel that's made from it, are always trying to do that. All that's required is oxygen and water. Both are present in abundance in the air around us. So the coatings we put on car parts are an attempt to keep the air away from the iron.

Cars are particularly vulnerable to rust. They're made of thin sheets of steel. They travel on roads on which more than 12 million tons of salt are poured every winter. Their shape includes pockets and crevices where dirt and salt can hold water against the steel for long periods. Some cars, sad experience has revealed, have shapes that lend themselves to trapping corrosive materials. Neither Chevrolet nor Mercedes is immune to such design flaws.

Modern cars make use of the latest in anti-corrosion technology. Sheet steel may be galvanized on one or both surfaces. Galvanizing applies a sacrificial coating of zinc—since zinc is a more vulnerable metal than steel, any corrosion attacks the zinc coating first. Trim fasteners are made of plastic, so as not to encourage corrosion between dissimilar metals. Parts are attached with adhesives rather than by welding. Sheet metal parts, and connecting seams, are designed not to trap water. More components are made of plastic and aluminum, which don't rust.

Bottoms First

Your collector car lacks most of these protections, so it depends on you to help protect it from rust. Regular washing is your most important defense.

One area you may forget to wash is the one that is most in danger—the underside. Besides the fact that the frame and floorboards are constantly attacked by the debris thrown up when you drive, they have the most irregular sheet metal surfaces, which can hold and conceal moisture and the dreaded road salt, and are also the most difficult to inspect.

Many cars of the 1940s and 1950s were factory undercoated. Some had this done as an extra-cost procedure. These older undercoated cars are in particular danger today. The undercoating material was a rubberized material applied about 1/8in thick, with sound-deadening, not rust protection, as its major function. Decades later, this material is peeling and flaking away from the sheetmetal of the car floor. In addition, typical undercoating spray patterns created pockets which did not entirely cover the metal but provided ideal traps for moisture. About half the states in the country use salt on their roads in the winter months to melt ice. If your car was ever used in the wintertime in any of these states, chances are good that a mixture of salt and water remained trapped in some of these pockets.

So, inspect the bottom of your car at least once a year. If you have access to a lift, that's the best way; if not, use jack stands or ramps. You'll probably find that some areas of the underbody are entirely rust-free. These are usually the frame members or mechanical parts that are covered with any one of the fluids that tend to leak from our old cars — motor oil, transmission fluid, grease. (That's a clue to one way we can help prevent rust.)

Examine the sheet metal floorpans, looking for flaking and peeling undercoating. Peel off large pieces and scrape off loose ones. A putty knife is a good tool for this. Look for where undercoating may still be intact but sagging away from the sheet metal. Cut such areas open and scrape them clean. Check drain holes in the door bottoms and in rocker panels. Stick an ice pick carefully through any that are clogged; try not to scratch the sheet metal, leaving a scar that is vulnerable to rust. Then run a pipe cleaner back and forth to finish cleaning the hole.

Exhaust Systems

Your exhaust system is probably rusty. Console yourself; as rusty as it may look on the outside, its probably even rustier on the inside. Not much you can do here. While there are heat-resistant coatings that can be applied to exhaust pipes, all of them require a clean, rust-free surface for initial application. The time to make your exhaust system less vulnerable is the next time you replace the pipes. Here's how.

First, consider stainless steel exhaust pipes. They can be expensive but not enough to require a second mortgage. 304 stainless steel is more difficult for the fabricator to bend into the convoluted shapes of many stock pipes but is far more corrosion resistant than the less expensive 409. If you're comparing prices, be sure to determine from each vendor which material was used. Some vendors also offer stainless steel mufflers to complete the system.

Exhaust pipe rust is a greater threat to collector cars than to an everyday vehicle because the water that's created by combustion must be burned away by the heat of a fully warmed-up engine. Consider the inevitable disintegration of these pipes, the fact that prices will go up as the years go by, the potential hazard of driving a car with any leakage of exhaust fumes, and the effort or expense of complete replacement. Those stainless steel pipes may not sound so expensive anymore.

Dissimilar Materials

Where two different (dissimilar) metals are in contact with each other and moisture is pre-sent, the point where they meet will corrode faster than would a connecting point of two similar metals. Look at the Vulnerability Index below. The wider apart metals are on the index, the greater will be the galvanic corrosive action when they're in contact and damp. Most of the corrosion will attack the more vulnerable metal. For this reason, it's best to avoid placing metals with widely different vulnerabilities next to each other.

Comparative Vulnerability

Gold	1
Platinum	4
Silver	17
Stainless Steel	21
Bronze & Copper	27
Brass	29
Tin	32
Nickel	36
Cadmium	41
Iron & Steel	44
Chromium	50
Zinc	57
Aluminum	64
Magnesium	67

Some of us want our collector cars to last forever, so we treat them to materials that were not used in the originals. Our good intentions can have exactly the opposite effect. Here's an example. You drill a hole in a sheet steel panel to mount a headlight relay. You've now created a bare steel edge in that hole. Your car deserves only the best, so you mount the relay with stainless steel cap screws and nuts. Not only will the joint corrode faster than it would have had you used carbon steel hardware, but it's the more vulnerable steel panel that will corrode fastest, not the nuts and bolts!

Defending Your Car

You've noticed, of course, that parts of your car's frame that are covered with oil from a leaky engine or transmission don't rust. Oil and grease seal the metal parts away from air and moisture, denying rust one of its necessary ingredients. Spraying oil over the undercarriage of your car, and into all its crevices, is just not a practical long-term rust-preventing solution. It's also very messy.

There is a method of covering parts with oil that's more practical. It's been used in England for some years, in both military and civilian applications; it's also used on North Sea oil rigs. Essentially, it's oil and a corrosion inhibitor in a waxy carrier. It's called, understandably, Waxoyl.

Waxoyl is applied by spray and dries to a clear, thin film. It works by displacing moisture, preventing air from reaching the car's steel parts. You can spray it on the entire underbody of the car and on suspension and springs. Waxoyl claims that it won't harm rubber parts. You can coat steel brake lines to keep them from rusting on the outside. You can spray it over cracking undercoating that you have not yet had the opportunity to remove and replace.

If you can gain access to the insides of your car's rocker panels, Waxoyl is excellent for sealing this hidden area. Spray it into the drain holes of door panels too, if you can avoid aiming the nozzle of the sprayer at the inside of the upholstery panels.

Waxoyl is available only by mail-order in the U.S., to my knowledge. It's commonplace in Canada. Many service stations will spray your car.

Rust-Resistant Finishes.

Terry Cowan of H.C. Fastener Company characterizes rust as light, mild, and heavy. Light rust is what a piece of cleaned steel will acquire overnight. It's soft, transparent, and does not pit the surface. Mild rust is not transparent and causes some pitting. Heavy rust involves deep pitting and substantial weight loss to the metal. In the late 1980s, restorer and author Matt Joseph did some extensive testing of finishes claimed to prevent or neutralize rust; his results were published in a series in *Skinned Knuckles* magazine. Though Matt later agreed that his tests lacked some sophisticated enhancements that might have been provided by a research laboratory, they nevertheless provided for restorers some guidelines that had not been previously available.

Rust being such a universal problem, the hype machines of the vendors of rust cures are always in full voice. Basically, though, there are only a few ways to combat rust chemically. Most of them attempt to establish a barrier between the metal and the oxygen and electrolyte needed for corrosion to occur. The finishes described here are intended for use on areas other than the visible body, and on frames, undercarriages and mechanical parts.

Matt tested three general types of products. Rust converters attempt to convert rust to a more stable material like magnetite. Examples of these are Ospho (manufactured by Skybrite), Rust Reformer (Rust-Oleum), and Extend (Loctite). Anti-rust fortified slow-dry enamels include Corroless and the original Rust-Oleum. The best-known example of moisture-cured urethanes is POR-15. Matt's tests over two years came to several conclusions. First, no product by itself will stop rust forever. Second, within categories there are some products that are more effective than others. *At the time of those tests*, Matt gave high marks to Corroless, POR-15, and Rust-Oleum.

Cathodic Rust Protection

This impressive-sounding gadget surfaces regularly, each time with claims of having improved capabilities over the previous version. Car owners are reminded that ship hulls and oil pipelines are protected by a device which impresses a low-voltage current on the vulnerable steel. Owners are told that they can now protect their precious car with a device that uses the same principle, at a cost of only a few hundred dollars.

The principle is simple. A negative voltage is applied to the car itself, making it a "cathode." A positive voltage is applied to one or more terminals, called "anodes," that are attached to the car. Because the process of corrosion is electrical, the current that flows from cathode to anode is supposed to interfere with the galvanic corrosion process. (That's what makes the fastener in a sheet metal panel corrode. This process doesn't claim to prevent oxidation, like the rusting of a sheet metal panel.)

It should be noted that cathodic protection does work on ships and pipelines because an electrolyte is required to make this process work. Ships float in conductive salt water. Pipelines lie in moisture-soaked soil. For application to a car on dry land, the principle is flawed.

Cathodic protection might protect your car if it were completely immersed in salt water or if a grid of anodes spaced only a few inches apart covered the entire vehicle. Neither is practical. Save your money.

CHAPTER FIFTEEN

Safety

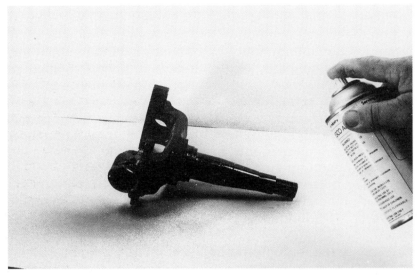

First step in dye penetrant inspection is applying the dye. This process can be performed with the part still on the car if it's accessible.

A Safety Checklist

We spend countless hours primping our cars and many others adjusting and repairing. Most of us spend only a fraction of that time on safety checks. We have much to learn here from the antique airplane folks. It's true that they have farther to fall in the event of catastrophic failure, but we can get killed just as dead while sitting only 18in above the ground.

I suggest that we each put together a safety checklist to be performed at least once a year. Here's my list to start you off. Knowing your car as you do, you'll no doubt have items to add.

At least once a year, preferably in the spring, get the car up on a lift. If you don't have a friend at a local service station, try and rent some time. It's inconvenient and expensive, but an accident is much more so. Use a good light. The new fluorescent work lights are far better than the old dusty 75W incandescent drop lights. A magnifying glass will be useful too.

1. Remove all four wheels with a lug wrench. While you're turning, feel for crossthreads or burrs or stripped threads on the studs, nuts, or lug bolts.

2. Check the wheels as described in Chapter 10.

3. Inspect the tires for tread wear and cracks. Look especially at the inside sidewalls; they're the ones you never get to see. Look for separations or bubbles. Check the spare too.

4. Look for any leakage at brake line fittings and at any hydraulic brake switch.

5. Bend all the brake hoses. Look for cracks that might signal the beginning of deterioration. Check to see that hoses aren't rubbing on any part of the suspension or frame. Swing the front wheels from lock to lock and check this again on each side.

6. Examine the full length of every brake line. If the metal line is dirty, wash it clean with solvent, so you can see it clearly. Watch for shiny spots where a line may be touching a moving part. Be sure clamps are tight. Look for kinks or dents in lines that may have been caused by rocks or by careless use of jacks or stands. Try to wiggle every line at its end fittings.

Before you take the next step, *learn the proper procedures for working around asbestos dust.* For decades we have received often-contradictory health warnings from our government and from a parade of "scientific" institutes. We've since discovered that drinking a cyclamate-sweetened diet cola did not mean instant death;

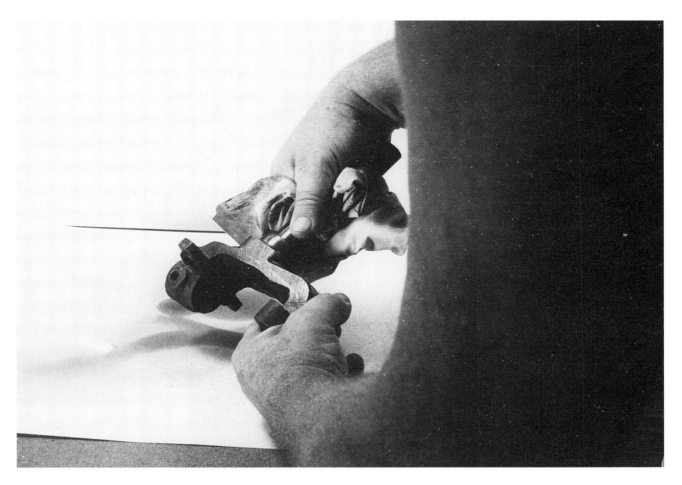

The excess dye is removed with a clean cloth and special cleaning solution.

neither does working with asbestos brake lining. The stuff *is* hazardous though, and you must learn the proper procedures for working with it. You respect your welding torch and poisonous cleaning solvents and the potential violence of your grinding wheel. Do the same for asbestos.

7. Remove all four brake drums. Be sure there's safe remaining lining thickness.

8. Turn back all eight wheel-cylinder boots and look for any leakage. Examine springs, anchor pins, cams, and retaining devices. Be sure everything is tight and in place.

9. Check the brake pedal linkage for free play. Be sure there is a cotter pin in every clevis pin.

10. Look for frayed wires in the parking brake cables. These can cause sticking and make the brake inoperative. The parking brake should be adjusted, so there's just a little slack in the cable with the brakes released.

11. While the brake drum is off, carefully examine the spindles on which the wheel bearings turn. (That will be on the front wheels,

except for front-wheel drive cars like Cords, Citroens, and others.) Clean the spindles carefully and use your magnifying glass. If there is any question in your mind about a possible crack, use one of the crack detection methods described later in this chapter.

12. Shake every pipe in the exhaust system. Look for loose joints or for pipes that don't nest together properly. Be sure that all hangars are present and tight and that rubber mounting insulators aren't deteriorated. Examine every pipe and muffler for holes; poke at suspicious areas with an ice pick. Use a mirror to check the top sides.

13. Examine the fuel line from gas tank to carburetor. Look for oozing at fittings and joints.

14. Go over the frame from end to end. From your marque club, you may have learned of potential weak spots or likely rust sites on your particular car. Pay special attention to these.

15. Wires and harnesses run through holes in the firewall and frame and are often located

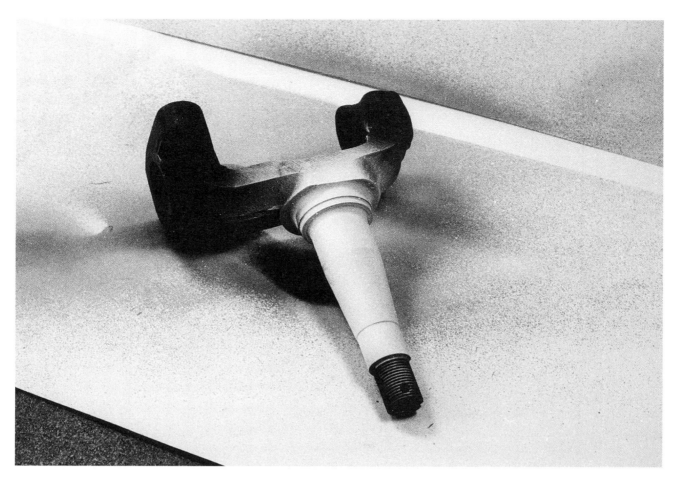

A uniform coat of developer is applied. It dries quickly to a translucent white film. Cracks will begin to show up quickly as red lines. Very small cracks may take some minutes to appear.

near moving parts, so look for frayed loom or insulation. Be sure there are grommets where they are supposed to be.

16. Look for looseness in the steering linkage and kingpins. Push and pull on pitman arm, drag link, idler and steering arms, and tie rods.

With the car back on the ground, do a top-side check.

17. Blow the horn.

18. Wet the windshield to avoid scratching the glass, then turn on the windshield wipers. Be sure the wipers clean the glass smoothly.

19. Turn the parking lights on. Be sure that they and the taillights and license lights are burning. Turn the headlights on and try both beams. (Check the taillights again; old switches can do funny tricks!)

20. Check the headlight aim. If your car uses sealed beam headlamps, the units come with aligning pins molded into the face of the lens. An inexpensive tool is available from most auto supply stores that enables you to align sealed beam headlights yourself. It's easy to use, and even compensates for slope in your garage or driveway. The tool assists only with vertical alignment; you'll have to aim side-to-side by eye.

If your car is pre-1940, most repair shops can check the aim for you. Because so many of the newest headlights are of sizes and shapes that defy the mechanical aimers, free-standing units are now used to aim them. They'll work just as well on your Graham Sharknose as on a new Lexus. (If you want to be traditional and you have the space, you can create an aiming grid on your garage door or on a fence. But unless you have the grade and distances just right, that won't do the job as well as the shop's new gadget. It's cheaper, though.) *Now*, you're ready to enjoy your collector car on the road!

Finding Cracks Early

Steel fatigues, so cyclic stress can result in tiny cracks that become bigger cracks that cause the part to fail. A failure in a transmission gear may result in a stalled car and perhaps an unhappy end to a tour; a failure of a front wheel spindle can have far more disastrous consequences. Try to anticipate failure before it happens. If your safety inspection turns up a questionable part, you may be able to determine whether it is about to fail by the use of one of several methods of crack detection.

Race cars and other highly stressed machinery are checked regularly for the beginning of cracks that could cause disaster on the track. Racers often use the expression "Magnafluxing" as a generic term for magnetic crack detection—that's one of the prices paid for being the first or a leader in your field. The Magnaflux Corporation—along with Xerox, Vaseline, and Frigidaire—continues to fight the good fight for the protection of its trademark. In deference to their efforts, we'll employ the correct generic term here.

The process of magnetic crack detection goes back at least to the early years of the twentieth century. It's based on the principle that magnetic lines of flux induced in a part made of a ferrous material will be distorted by any flaw on, or just below, the surface of a part. Several different methods are used to induce those lines of flux. Large parts like artillery gun barrels may have large currents passed through them. Smaller parts may be placed inside an induction coil carrying a heavy current. Or, a magnetic field may be induced by placing parts between the poles of a large permanent magnet or electromagnet. That's the method most applicable to our car parts.

The simplest way of using the magnetic field to identify cracks is to use the field to attract magnetic particles which collect around the sites of defects in the test piece. This makes the flaws visible. The magnetic detection powder, containing iron particles, may be applied to the test piece in dry or wet form.

Most machine shops routinely use magnetic crack detection to check engine blocks and cylinder heads before rebuilding. These shops can test other parts too. If you're rebuilding your collector car, consider having critical parts tested for cracks before reinstalling them. A list would include steering linkage, spindles, steering knuckles, brake parts, and axle shafts. Include in this list any other parts whose failure could threaten injury to car, driver, or passengers.

It is possible for an adept amateur to build magnetic detection equipment, but it's probably more practical for most of us to bring components to a local shop. Look in your Yellow Pages under "Magnetic Inspection Service" or "Non-destructive Testing."

There is, however, another effective method of crack detection that can be used in your own garage very effectively and inexpensively. Its called dye penetrant inspection. It has an advantage over magnetic crack detection in that it can be used on non-ferrous metals like aluminum. The limitation is that it must be used on smooth, preferably machined surfaces, but that describes many of the parts that we might want to test.

Dye penetrant inspection can be performed using fluorescent dyes under ultraviolet light or under visible light using a red dye. The second method will be usable by most collector car owners and is the simplest.

Briefly, these are the steps in conducting dye penetrant inspection of a metal part. First, clean the part scrupulously. Then spray a red dye, which comes in an aerosol can, on the surface of the part. Allow a few minutes for the dye to penetrate any cracks. Then use a clean cloth and solvent to remove excess dye from the surface. Next, spray a 'developer' onto the surface of the part. This dries quickly to a fine, powdery, absorbent film that draws up the dye that seeped down into any cracks or pores. The result is a clear

Here's a cracked brass part with the dye showing the cracks. (The spindle in earlier photos tested out fine.)

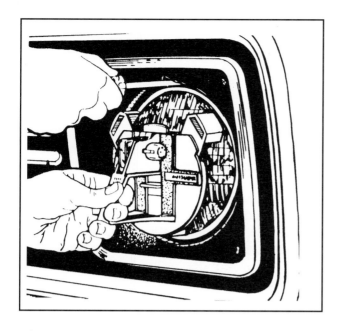

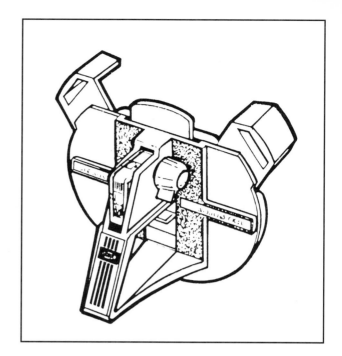

Above and right: The Hoppy aiming device can be used to check your headlights regularly for up-and-down aim.

marking on the surface of the part showing the flaw. Modestly priced dye penetrant kits contain all the materials needed for inspecting dozens of parts.

Whether you do your crack detection in your own shop or take it out, it's important to know of this technology. Use it as one of the preventive weapons in your safety arsenal.

CHAPTER SIXTEEN

The Open Road

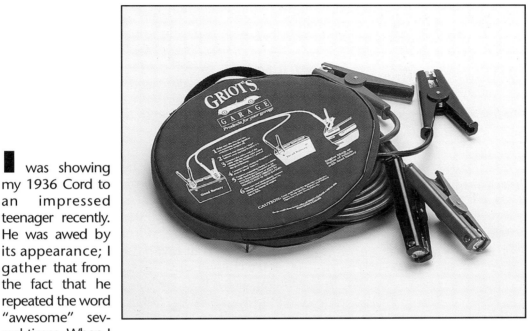

Jumper cables and bag.

I was showing my 1936 Cord to an impressed teenager recently. He was awed by its appearance; I gather that from the fact that he repeated the word "awesome" several times. When I mentioned driving it on California freeways, though, he was shocked.

Many of today's drivers are surprised to discover that our collector cars can comfortably exceed today's speed limits. Moreover, they can travel at those speeds for hour upon hour, with no harm to themselves. Some of our cars are so comfortable at touring speeds that we actually forget that we're not driving modern iron. And therein lies a danger.

Today's drivers expect all cars on the road to be able to accelerate and brake at the rate that they do. Many of them, to boot, don't have the foggiest notion of how long it takes to bring a car to a stop from 70mph, from the moment that the brain sends the STOP signal. Perhaps that's why they so often drive only 5ft behind other cars at 70. When entering a highway behind us, they expect us to move smartly out of their way. They make no allowances for the slight drop in speed as we shift our cars; you'll see them suddenly grow larger in your rear view mirror.

If they won't drive safely, we must drive even more defensively and deal with some of our cars' potential short-comings too.

Directional Signals

Many collector cars were equipped with directional signals when new, or were built in an era when retrofitting was common. Put them on, and use them. If your 1930s car has no provision for directionals, consider modifying existing lights. Taillight lamps already have the necessary two filaments. At the front, a change of sockets can put double-filament bulbs in parking lights. If that's not feasible, abandon the parking lights altogether (when does one use them?) and use the fixture as a directional signal. Fog lamps can be pressed into this service too. Wiring diagrams for switches that can be installed unobtrusively have appeared in car collector magazines over the years.

Driving in the Rain

Today's tires have treads designed by computers, with grooves and slots and who-knows-what-else. Their rubber composition is carefully calculated to provide a reasonable balance of dry

Safety switch can be installed on your existing jumper cables.

traction, wet traction, and wear life. Our handsome collector car whitewalls are innocent of such sophistication. Their tread designs, in most cases, are simplistic replicas of those of bygone years. Bear this in mind if it starts to rain while you're out driving your collector car. Studies have shown that highways are actually more slippery when they're a little wet than a lot. Slow down a bit, even more than in your everyday car.

The Ammeter

One of the nice things about older cars is that they rarely used mere lights to indicate a malfunction. Most had meters to show engine temperature, charging rate, and oil pressure. (Actually, a combination of gauge *and* warning light would be the best arrangement!) In the 1930s the gauges carried numerical markings, even though many could not be precisely relied upon. By the 1950s most gauges had lost their numbers entirely, so the pointer positions became largely symbolic. Still, they were far better diagnostic tools than are lights.

An excellent diagnostic gauge is the ammeter. Its scale has zero at the center; the scale to the right of zero shows the amount of "charge," to the left the amount of "discharge." The ammeter is wired into the car's electric circuit in a position where any electrical load except the starter must pass through it. Current from the generator to the battery goes through the ammeter too. As a result, if the current draw is greater than the amount of current being restored by the generator, the ammeter will show a discharge. If the current draw is less than generator output, the needle will be on the charge side.

When a car is started, the battery is depleted. Whether a little or a lot will depend on the amount of starter cranking you had to do. Once running, the generator will begin to recharge the battery, so the needle should be well up on the charge side of the scale. If it isn't, have the generator and regulator checked. As the battery recharges, the regulator will reduce generator output, and the ammeter needle should begin to fall back toward zero. If the ammeter remains high after a long period of highway driving, there's a possible regulator problem.

Keep an occasional eye on your ammeter. For most driving the needle should be just to the charge side. Zero is usually OK too. If the needle shows a slight discharge, the generator may not be charging. The small current draw is the coil and ignition system; if you're playing the radio or running the heater, the discharge will be greater. If the ammeter suddenly shows full discharge, that indicates a short circuit. Pull to the side of the road (if the car is still running), and turn off your battery master switch.

The short may reveal itself by smoke or odor or both. Use your eyes and ears. If the shorted circuit is not immediately evident, use the elimination process. What you'll be doing is disconnecting one circuit at a time until the short disappears. Removing fuses is the easiest way to do this. A central fuse location makes this chore more convenient. If your car isn't so equipped, there'll be fuses located somewhere in most circuits—on a headlight switch, in line with the radio power wire, in a headlight relay. To disconnect those circuits or accessories that aren't fused you'll have to remove the wire that feeds each component. Disconnect one circuit; the radio, for example. Eyes glued to the ammeter, turn the battery master switch back on. Full discharge means that this isn't the shorted circuit. Go on to the next one. When the ammeter doesn't move, you've found the bad circuit.

If you can get along without the affected circuit until you get home, or to help, just leave the fuse out. If the shorted wire powered the coil, you'll have to make a temporary repair. Look for worn insulation. If you can't find the problem, try wiring around it. Note where the ends of the wire to the coil attach at the coil and at the ignition switch or terminal block. Disconnect both ends of this wire. Now attach jumper cable in its place. If there's no short now, this will get you home.

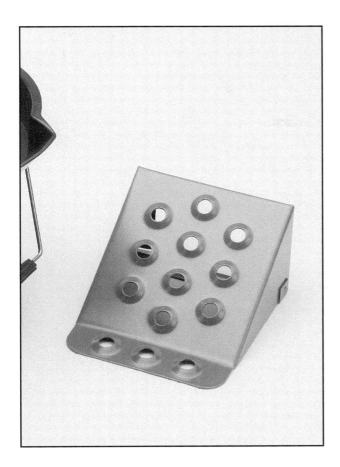

Wheel chocks will be a lifesaver if you ever have to change a tire on an incline. Or if your parking brake fails while on a trip!

Axle Ratios

The rear axle ratio indicates how many turns of the driveshaft result in one turn of the rear wheels. A low ratio improves acceleration, but the engine will have to turn faster at high speeds. A high ratio offers easier cruising, but reduces acceleration somewhat.

Before WWII, and immediately afterward, most family cars had relatively low rear axle ratios. Cars were rarely driven long distances, and fast superhighways were decades in the future. Even in the 1950s, rear axle ratios were kept on the low side to improve acceleration performance, a major selling point during the beginning years of the horsepower race.

The effect of these low ratios is that some collector cars' engines strain more than necessary to maintain comfortable highway speeds. If your car's engine seems to be turning very fast at highway speeds, the rear axle ratio may be the problem. Find out if optional ratios were available for your car. In many cases, the rear axle ratio for a car with automatic transmission was higher than for the same model with stick shift. (A "higher" ratio has a "lower" number. For example, 4.3:1 is a higher ratio than 4.7:1.) Since few of us engage in drag races with our collector cars anymore, the improvement in cruising performance by installing "taller" gears may be well worth the effort.

Daytime Running Lights

DRLs are front lamps that go on with the ignition and stay on all the time. They're required in Canada, Sweden, and Norway. Finland requires them outside of urban areas; they're now working their way into the U.S. practice. On some cars they're separate dedicated lamps, on others they're reduced-output headlights.

Canada's DRL laws date back to 1990. In 1992, the Canadian Bureau of Standards did a study of daytime accidents. The results showed a drop of about 4–6 percent in multiple vehicle collisions. Skeptical? Do your own study. On a day that is anything less than totally sunny, see how many oncoming cars you can spot with their headlights on. Now notice how those cars stand out of the pack in which they're traveling.

Its true that the countries that now mandate DRLs are all closer to the Arctic Circle than any of our lower forty-eight states and so have special concerns regarding visibility during much of the year. Still, we should learn our lessons wherever we can, and there *is* one to be learned here.

In less-than-sunny weather, most cars tend to look gray. Since many of our collector cars are painted in dark colors to boot, they tend to be even more difficult to see. Do yourself and your precious car a favor; *drive with your headlight low beams on all the time.* You'll be visible much earlier to oncoming cars. Since your taillights will also be on, you'll gain an additional measure of visibility from that angle. Think this is extreme? Then at least keep the headlights on when driving on highways or roads without a center median strip or barrier.

It's true that your bulbs or sealed beams will burn out more often, but they're a small expense to exchange for a major safety benefit. (You'll also have to be certain that your charging system can handle the higher load created by the headlights.)

Your major problem with DRLs may come from other drivers flashing their lights to let you know that you've got your lights on in the daytime. Two blinks back says, "I know."

Put your car on dollies and you won't have to start it to move it a few inches—even sideways.

Test Your Brakes

Get in the habit of testing the brakes on your collector car *every time* you take it out of the garage. In the safety of your own driveway, *stand on it with everything you've got.* We usually treat our favorite cars gingerly and try not to stress any component more than we have to. Brakes are the exception. When that little kid chases a ball into the street, you're not going to worry about your forty-year-old components. You're going to stand on the brake pedal! If anything is going to fail, better it should do so in your driveway. A brake system worth driving with will not be damaged or start to leak as a result of such a test. If it does, it needed rebuilding anyway, and you may have saved yourself lots of aggravation, or even a life.

Starting and Stopping Your Engine

Starting your engine is a not a terrible thing to do. *Starting your engine and then not keeping it running is.* Engines begin to produce water as soon as they start. We've all seen water actually dripping from the exhaust pipe of a cold engine. It's this water that combines with sulfur compounds in the engine to produce sulfuric acid in the oil. Corrosion from acids is a major cause of engine wear, particularly affecting cylinder walls and combustion chambers. To minimize this, make acid-reduction your primary concern in engine startup. So . . .

1. Warm your engine up as quickly as possible. Don't idle a cold engine. Give it up to a minute for oil pressure to stabilize and the intake manifold to begin to warm, then drive off slowly. Yes, the cold engine may stumble and run rough, but the light driving load is vital to rapidly bringing engine temperature up to full operating level.

2. Don't stop the engine until it has

reached full operating temperature. The time and distance it takes to do this will, of course, vary from car to car. Don't run the old girl over to the supermarket and back thinking that this exercise is good for it. It isn't.

3. If you must move your car in and out of your garage and you can't give it the warm-up drive, consider pushing it. This is clearly not a practical proposal if your car is a mid-1960s Cadillac convertible. If your family doesn't include several brawny teenagers, try a set of the widely-advertised roller-skates-type dollies.

There's a suggested routine for shutting-down, too. I learned it years ago from engine rebuilder John M. Sico and have been using it since. He developed it after observation of corrosion in combustion chambers and the upper part of the cylinders. The corrosion, John felt, was the result of rust. Exhaust gases condense into acidic products when the engine cools; light rust develops. Enough rusting, and there's metal loss. And this happens in the upper part of the cylinder wall, the very area where lubrication is least adequate. I have never torn down the engine in my collector car, so I can't personally prove the usefulness of this technique. But it makes sense. Here are the steps.

1. We've been through this before: Be sure the engine is up to operating temperature before you shut it down for the day.

2. Gun it a few times to blow any accumulated liquid out of the combustion chambers.

3. Increase rpms to about 1/3 of the safe maximum and hold it there for a couple of seconds. This throws more oil up on the cylinders. Higher vacuum draws some oil past the rings and valve guides.

4. With the engine running at that speed, turn off the key.

5. Release the throttle only after the engine comes to a stop. John feels that its better to leave fresh fuel mixture in the cylinders than exhaust gases. And while there may be room for theoretical arguments, his are supported by examination of many engines.

Hot starts

Nearly every collector car driver experiences just a bit of anxiety when the finger approaches the starter button after the car has been standing all day under a hot summer sun. It *is* harder to start many collector cars when they and the weather are hot. What's the best way to do it?

The starting problem is often a result of percolation—in effect a flooded carburetor. There are several accelerator-handling techniques that can help. Slowly depress the accelerator and hold it down, then crank the engine without releasing the pedal. The engine should pump out the over-rich mixture and start with a roar. This works every time with many cars. An alternate method is to crank the engine for about ten seconds without touching the gas pedal. Then depress the pedal about halfway. The engine should start. In either case, run the engine at fast idle for about a minute to refill the carburetor bowl with fresh, cooler gasoline. If neither of these methods work, stop. If you keep cranking until the battery is dead, you may not get home that day. Leave the car's hood up. Go sit in the shade, read a bit, indulge in an ice cream. When the engine is cool, the car will start.

Don't Leave Home Without Them

You can't very well take with you every spare part you own. You know your car best, so you know which items might be most likely to need a spare. Besides, spares are like umbrellas; you'll never need them if you have them with you.

Here's a list of items that I carry on long trips in my collector car. If you don't have a list of your own yet, use this one and add or subtract to suit your own needs and those of your car.

1. Fluids: any special fluids that may not be easy to find or match on the road. Include your favorite motor oil, transmission lube, steering box lube, brake fluid.

2. Tire changing equipment: Jack, lug wrench, special hub cap tools. I carry a torque wrench to tighten up wheel nuts accurately. For safety, bring wheel chocks. Carry an extra inner tube, too.

3. If you have to stop for an emergency, you'll need to protect your own rear end. Set out reflective triangles. They're much safer than flares, and tests have proven that they can be seen from a further distance.

4. A copy of your car club's directory. You may need specialized help from a local club member.

5. Spare bulbs and fuses.

6. Owner's Manual and service manual.

7. Your tool kit or box. I risked a hernia getting mine in and out of the trunk until I discovered that half the weight was the steel box itself. Modern plastic tool boxes may

not last long enough to become heirlooms, but they're light and amazingly strong. And inexpensive.

8. Flashlight. Consider a magnetic or clamp-type holder too, for when there's no-one to hold the light.

9. A 1gal jug of the coolant you use.

10. Jumper cables. I installed a switch in mine that advises if the polarity hookup is correct and permits you to switch them on far away from the danger of battery explosion. I carry them in a neat circular bag.

11. Tow rope. Polyethelene ones are light, and don't rust or clank around like chains do.

12. Fire extinguisher. I know that you never even leave your driveway without this. Check the gauge regularly. Incidentally, they're of little use in the trunk—I mounted mine to a wood block and keep it on the floor on the passenger side.

13. First aid kit.

14. A spare set of keys: ignition, door, glove box, spare tire locks, gas cap lock.

15. Hand cleaner. Some of the new citrus-based ones work well, smell great, and are biodegradable.

16. Coveralls. Disposable ones made of Tyvek are now available. (Tyvek is the paper-like material that tearproof envelopes are made from.)

17. Latex gloves.

18. Funnels: For water, motor oil and gear lubes, and brake fluid. Don't mix. I use a brand that comes with a screw-on cover. They take more space, but they don't drip on anything or collect dirt after I've used them.

19. Paper towels.

20. Tire pressure gauge.

21. Ground cloth.

22. Rain-X, both exterior and anti-fog. These products are very valuable for cars with less-than-perfect wipers and defrosters.

23. Duster. A KOZAK takes less space than a brush-type duster. If you should have to wash your car, the hotel's plastic waste basket and shampoo should work fine.

24. Local and state maps.

25. Distilled water, battery filler and hydrometer, if your battery has removable caps.

26. Battery carrier.

27. Emergency Link belt. These clever devices sure beat trying to install a new fan belt

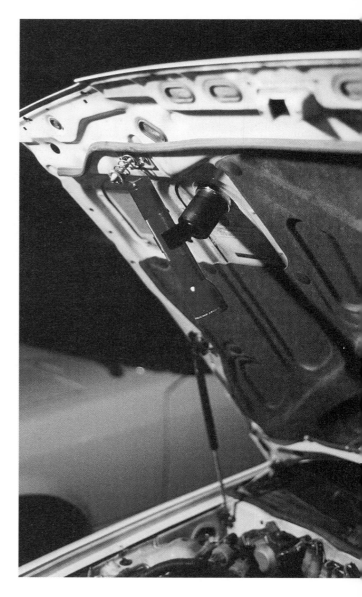

This magnetic flashlight holder is a wonderful third hand if you're ever under the hood alone on a dark night. It comes in several sizes to fit the classic Mag-Lites.

at the side of an interstate while the 18-wheelers roar by. One size fits all. Practice putting them together at home first.

28. Wiper blades.

29. Gasket material, in several thicknesses.

30. Lengths of #14 wire with fork terminals at each end. These can be used to wire around shorted circuits.

31. Small tubes of anaerobic adhesives. I carry Loctite 242, Gasket Eliminator 515 and 518, and PST pipe sealant.

CHAPTER SEVENTEEN

Storage, Short and Long

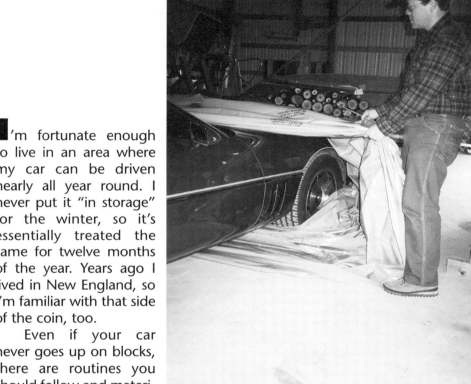

I'm fortunate enough to live in an area where my car can be driven nearly all year round. I never put it "in storage" for the winter, so it's essentially treated the same for twelve months of the year. Years ago I lived in New England, so I'm familiar with that side of the coin, too.

Even if your car never goes up on blocks, there are routines you should follow and materials you should consider that may help increase its aesthetic and mechanical longevity. Some of these

Above and next page: Two people can stow a car for the winter in an Omnibag.

techniques even apply to the short "storage" period between drives.

Your car's enemies are sun, air, and dirt. The ultraviolet rays of the sun fade or dull paint and cloth upholstery and dry the oils out of leather. Humidity is in the air everywhere, even in Arizona these days. Dirt on the car helps absorb water from the air and holds it close against paint and chrome. It's the humidity in the air that permits electrolytic corrosion to happen. That reinforces the oxidation of your paint and helps make chrome rust.

So keep your car clean. Wash it regularly during the months that you use it. Dry it carefully to

eliminate moisture. Store it indoors and keep it covered to protect it from sunlight and dirt. If a day or more has elapsed since the wash or if you've driven any distance from the car wash to your home, go over the car with a duster before you put the cover on. Just lowering your garage door can shake abrasive dirt onto the car. While your soft car cover will not scratch the paint, the dirt on the surface, propelled by the cover as you move it across the body, surely will. This is especially true of flannel covers; they're great when they're clean, but they can also hold more finish-destroying dirt.

I've never found any measurable difference among the vaunted 100 percent cotton car covers. Many of the cotton-polyester blends are of high quality too. I have found, though, a large difference in price from brand to brand, each extolling its own material and workmanship. To choose a new cover, get swatches from the several mail-order companies. Look at the weight of each fabric. Examine each weave with an inexpensive 8X jeweler's loupe (you can find these at a camera supply store, and they're useful for all kinds of things).

You'll discover that some fabrics have a tighter weave than others and more threads to the inch. Those are usually better quality and should last longer.

While fabrics may differ from brand to brand, you may find as I did that the patterns, pattern numbers, and stitching are identical. Notice how every vendor offers "thousands of patterns." It doesn't seem cost-effective for every vendor to keep a pattern in stock to fit the unusual body style of a rare classic. It isn't.

Two or three companies sew nearly all the car covers offered by the heaviest advertisers in the hobby magazines. (Some of these purchase their least expensive covers off-shore.) For their biggest customers, the manufacturers dye the cloth in the vendor's special colors. So check out the weave to find the cover you'll like best.

I prefer a cover with a flannel surface next to the car. That's because my car is a sedan. If yours is a convertible with a fabric top, avoid flannel; flannel lints, and you'll be picking fuzzballs off your top forever. If you want the soft flannel next to your paint, plan to throw a cotton sheet over the car's top before you put the car cover on. To manufacture flannel, the fabric is uniformly abraded on one or both sides to give the fibers that fuzzy feel. Some car covers are advertised as flannel-lined. Actually, there's no lining; it just means that the material is "flanneled" on the inside. (Your pajamas, on their other hand, are flanneled on both sides.) To prevent the abrasion from resulting in a too-weak fabric, material to be processed as flannel starts out much thicker. When you lift a flannel car cover for a large car, you'll feel the significant difference in weight.

Most companies offer a car cover made with a fabric by Kimberly-Clark called Evolution. Each vendor gives it his own unique name, but the fine print will mention Evolution. It's a multi-layer fabric-like plastic that has water-repellent qualities. (Each time Kimberly-Clark improves the material or construction, the series number increments upward.)

Wash your car cover at least several times a year. Be sure to follow the manufacturer's instructions, particularly for specialty fabrics like Evolution. After the winter snooze and before putting the car away again are logical intervals. The easiest way is to use the commercial washer at your local coin laundry; they have large dryers to match, too. Don't ever put your Kimberly-Clark Evolution cover in a dryer, though—it will melt.

Moisture is the major car-killer. It encourages mold growth on fabric and leather. The ever-present humidity in the air will condense on the surface of your car under the right atmospheric conditions. Here's how that happens. The amount of water that air can hold depends, among other things, on the air's temperature; warmer air can hold more moisture than cool air. Warm moist air can occur on many fall and spring days, and on an occasional winter day. When that air comes in contact with a large cool object like your car, the temperature of the air is lowered. Now it can't hold as much water, so it releases it onto the cool object. That's condensation, less politely known as sweating. That's how the lovely vehicle that you never took out on a rainy day during the summer months comes to be bathed several times a year in wet, corrosion-encouraging condensation.

How to prevent this? One way is to modify the environment. You could make certain that the temperature in your garage never changes. That requires an expensive heating system. You could attempt to keep the humidity very low, but this requires an expensive ventilating and dehumidification system.

Actually, the only environment you're really concerned about is that of the car itself, not the rest of the garage. So the practical way to go is to create an environment for the car that seals it off from moisture-producing condensation. First get the car indoors: a garage, a barn, a warehouse, or a plastic shelter. Then bag it.

There several types of products that are designed to do this. I'll define them as "storage bags" and "zippered coveralls." A storage bag may be described as a huge plastic bag, roughly 6ft tall, 9ft wide, and 25ft long. The pioneer in this field was Omnibag. A zippered coverall is a cover that encloses the car on all sides, including the bottom, and is zippered shut to seal it. Car/Jacket is the only representative of this category with which I'm familiar. Omnibag and Car/Jacket are both made and sold by the same family of car enthusiasts.

The plastic film of which storage bags are made is rated by its water vapor transmission factor. While it seems waterproof, all plastic will eventually let some water vapor through. High density film is usually strong, tough, and brittle, and has a low water vapor transmission rate. Low density plastic is less strong but more pliable and has a higher water vapor transmission rate. A combination of the two gains some of the virtues of each. Omnibag, for example, is made of a three-ply laminated film of low and high density material. That provides strength while keeping weight and bulk down.

Do not plan to bag a freshly painted car. Allow at least three months for the paint to cure and for vapors to evaporate. That's a conservative recommendation, but better safe than sorry.

Wash your car at least a day before you bag it. Time will be needed for all the nooks and crannies to dry completely. Leave doors half-latched so water can drain out. Be sure the car is cool; don't put it in a bag while the engine or exhaust are hot. Correct leaks in the cooling system or air conditioner. If there are oil leaks that can't be fixed at this time, then place absorbent mats or trays under the car after it's in the bag. Oil and grease inside the bag will make cleaning it for reuse a most unpleasant chore. *If the leak is gasoline, do not bag your car until the leak is completely repaired.*

Bag your car during a low humidity period, if possible. That will reduce the amount of moisture that you seal into the bag. Mid-afternoon on a dry day is best.

Bagging your car in a storage bag is a two-person job. If you don't have that second person available, consider building a frame out of 1in diameter PVC pipe. The material, including corner fittings, is inexpensive and available at home supply stores. Make the frame about 1ft larger than your car on all sides. Use end caps at the bottom of the frame legs to protect the plastic bag as you install it. After the car is in place, put plastic coffee can lids under each

Some air and moisture will be trapped with your car when you seal the bag. It's important to enclose the desiccant pouches that are supplied with the bag. Desiccants absorb moisture out of air; silica gel is a well-known one. (That's what's in those little bags packed with your Japanese camera, to keep it dry during its long sea voyage.) The desiccant will eventually become saturated with water, so before you use it the next season, dry it out in a conventional oven. Follow the instructions that come with the desiccant; it loses effectiveness if overheated. You can also buy additional desiccant from several suppliers.

Bags help in other ways, too. The opaque ones keep out sunlight and its ultraviolet rays, protecting your paint and upholstery. Ozone, which deteriorates rubber, is excluded too. And, since you can't get at your car, it'll spare you the temptation of starting up the engine for a few minutes every so often and causing acid damage!

Above, below and opposite: Putting your car into a Car/Jacket needs a bit of room around the car, but this is exaggerated! Putting on this zippered coverall can be done by one person. A car cover should go on first.

A zippered coverall is a different concept. Car/Jacket is the premier example. It's different from the typical storage bag in several important ways. Most important is its zipper closure. That makes it practical to bag a car that you use only on weekends, or only for shows and tours.

leg for further protection against tearing. Inspect the bag when you're finished. The material of which storage bags are made can be torn if you're not careful. If you find any tears, repair them with vinyl or duct tape.

Since the bag opens up completely, the car can be driven on to it under its own power. One person can then zip the bag shut in about five minutes. Because the bag opens completely, any spills or leaks during storage can be cleaned up relatively simply. Disadvantages? A zippered coverall requires several feet of free space on one side of the car while the car is being bagged or unbagged. It also costs considerably more than a storage bag. That must be balanced against the reusability of the zippered coverall. While storage bags are designed for use for a limited number of winters, you can use a zippered coverall over and over. The material of which it's made is a rip-stop plastic and very difficult to tear.

It should go without saying, but neither a car cover nor a bag is a substitute for a garage. During the more pleasant months of the year, some cover materials can defend against the elements better than others. Evolution is one of these. And certainly there are situations where a car cannot spend the inclement months in a garage, but be aware that it will suffer some. If you leave a car all winter under any car cover, the cover won't mildew, but the car's paint may.

Some brands of "instant garages" can do a creditable job of protecting a car through the winter. Be aware that if you pitch one of these heavy plastic/canvas tents on grass or dirt, you're courting serious corrosion from the moisture coming up from the ground that will attack the car's surfaces for all those months. Several layers of heavy-gauge plastic must go down before the car rolls inside. Even better, protect your car with a storage bag or zippered coverall inside the temporary garage. The combination is an effective winter storage measure.

One of the most intriguing devices for keeping mice from using your original upholstery for nest material is the application of ultrasonic technology. In brief, this involves installing in your garage a small transmitter which emits sound waves in the range above that which human beings can hear. The theory is that animals *can* hear them. The further claim is that the frequency of the waves is such that they cause pain to rodents, who will now avoid your garage and car like, pardon the pun, the plague. The deluxe versions of these devices change frequencies at random, and remain silent for random intervals. The idea is apparently to keep the mice off balance.

The scientific concept here apparently has validity. And we're all attracted by the idea of using the newest of technologies to stave off the oldest of pests. Unfortunately, the machines advertised for use by the homeowner to protect the collector car in your garage are simply inadequate as a stand-alone pest control method.

Comprehensive tests have been conducted by government agencies in the United States and Denmark, by the Department of Defense and by universities around the country. None of the groups concluded that the concept of ultrasonics as pest control is an out-and-out scam. It isn't. Mice are easily frightened creatures and will avoid unfamiliar sounds, or sounds coming from new locations. The problem is that the remedy is short-lived and haphazard. Each test has shown a similar result. In those cases where an initial ultrasonics installation has caused rodents to leave an area or dissuaded them from entering, a short time later they were back again, this time to stay. Without accepted standards for the effectiveness and marketing of ultrasonic pest control devices, this is just too risky a solution for you to spend your money on or to trust with the welfare of your precious upholstery.

When ultrasonics are advocated for pest control, it's almost always "in conjunction with other pest control methods." These other methods are the ones that actually work. They're the traditional steps including rodent inspections, sanitation (removing food and nesting materials), rodent proofing (keeping the critters out), and population reduction (a pretty name for trapping and poisoning). Competent consultants are just a phone call away at most state extension services or local health departments. And while they don't necessarily claim to be rodent-proof, the sturdier plastic bags can be a deterrent to Mickey and his friends.

Desiccant comes in bags like this. When the bag turns a dark color, its time to dry it (carefully) in the oven.

For a confident start when you next want to use your car, make sure that the battery remains fully charged. Each time you put the car away, wipe off the top of the battery to be certain that electrolyte mist and dirt haven't combined to provide a leakage path for a tiny bit of current. That's enough to reduce the battery's cranking power next time you're ready to go.

Whenever you return your car to its garage, turn off the battery master switch. That will effectively eliminate any current leakage from any device that you forgot about and that may draw current. It also reduces to near zero the likelihood of a fire in the car started by a short circuit.

Over the years many of us kept our batteries at maximum charge during storage periods by the use of a trickle charger. These crude devices were, essentially, very small battery chargers. When the battery approached full charge, a trickle charger diminished the charging current, but not the voltage. A 6V battery 'gases' at about 6.9V, and the trickle charger sometimes exceeded that voltage.

The modern way to go is by use of a device called the SuperSmart Battery Tender. It charges your battery at 1.25A, until the battery is accepting only 0.5A. At that point the charger switches to a "float" or maintenance mode. Current drops to very close to zero (actually 10MA). Voltage drops to 6.8V, just below the battery's gassing point. This clever device has solid state controls that periodically permit some battery gassing to mix the electrolyte. It indicates if you've hooked the polarity up backwards and protects itself

from damage. In case of brownouts or power surges, it maintains constant voltage to the battery. The Battery Tender also compensates for ambient temperatures, lowering the voltage if it gets hotter in your garage.

There are other brands of chargers that work similarly to The Battery Tender, but this is the only one I know of that's available for 6V.

The Battery Tender comes with a two-prong polarized female miniplug attached to the battery wires. A choice of two harnesses is provided, each of which has a male miniplug. One ends in two clamps, for temporary hookups; the other has ring terminals for permanent attachment to the battery. I recommend this latter for Touring Trim. When you return from a drive, just plug the Battery Tender cable into the battery harness. The red light will go on, indicating charging. After a few hours the green light will come on. When you next want to enjoy your car, all of your mighty 6V will await the turn of your ignition key.

If you're using a zippered coverall, the battery will remain in your car. You'll want to be able to connect your Battery Tender to the battery while the car is in the bag. Make up an extension cord for your battery harness, with a male miniplug at one end and a female at the other. For wire you can use the zipcord sold in hardware stores for use in table and floor lamps. Radio Shack carries miniature connectors that match the ones on the Battery Tender. Open the zipper just enough to pass the mini-plug. Put the extension cord through the opening. Then close the zipper up tight, with the extension cord in place.

If you're planning to store your car for the long cold winter, some simple steps will make the spring startup more pleasant.

• Make a list now of the things you'll need to do in the spring, especially if you've drained fluids or taken other storage steps that will affect the car's driveability. It may easily slip your mind in April that you emptied the radiator in October. Place the list on the driver's seat so you can't miss it in the spring.

• Overinflate the tires by 10–15psi. This helps reduce flat spots. If you have a slow leak, chances are the tire will still have some air in the spring.

• Fill your gas tank just before you put the car away. Modern gasolines include a short-term stabilizer to counteract the gumming tendencies of some of their components. To be safe rather than sorry, add additional stabilizer in this last tankful. Sta-bil is a widely available brand. Run the car for about 10 miles, so the stabilizer gets all the way up to the carburetor.

• Remove the windshield wiper blades. Store them in a cool dark place. Pad the ends of the arms and secure with a nylon tie.

• Consider having the oiling system flushed. See Chapter 18.

• Change your engine oil. You don't want to leave that acid-contaminated oil in there all winter. Do this just before you fill the gas tank for the last time. The same short drive that brings the fuel stabilizer to the carburetor will circulate the clean oil through the engine.

• Now is the time too for some of those annual pain-in-the-neck chores. Drain the cooling system and refill with fresh antifreeze. If it's time to replace your DOT 3 brake fluid, do it now and bleed the brakes. This way, when you're impatient to get going in the spring, everything will be ready.

• If you're using a storage bag, remove the battery. Wipe the top with a rag dampened in a solution of baking soda, then dry it carefully. Connect the battery to your Battery Tender.

• Cover the car with its newly-washed, dry car cover.

• If you're using a bag, put the car in now. Place pans or absorbent mats under the engine or anywhere you know leaks occur. Be sure the desiccants are regenerated and in place. Seal the bag.

In the spring:

• If you used a bag, be careful when you reopen it. Crack it open a bit and sniff. (This goes for all bag storage, short or long.) Be alert for gas fumes. Do not open the bag while smoking or near an open flame.

• If you find a flat tire when you're ready to bring your car out of a storage bag, cut a small opening in the bag next to the tire valve stem. Inflate the tire so you can roll the car out. Repair the hole with tape. (Since a zippered coverall opens up entirely, you can inflate the tire without doing surgery on the bag.)

• Check your list on the driver's seat for anything that needs to be done before starting or driving the car. Do these now.

• Unless you flushed the engine's oil system in the fall, change the engine oil again. This will assure that any internal condensation that

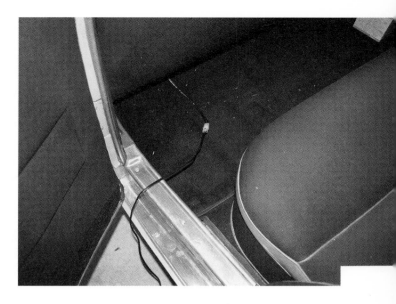

An underseat battery is easily charged by Connecting the Battery Tender's harness permanently to the battery. For underhood batteries, a harness with battery clamps also comes with the unit.

occurred during the winter sleep is removed.

• Check all fluid levels: oil, transmission, differential, water, brake fluid. Top off if needed.

• Look for any leaks that may have begun during the lay-up period.

• Check coolant hoses for condition.

• Check belts for condition and adjustment.

• Check tire pressure and adjust to normal.

• Clean the battery terminal posts with a terminal tool or a medium abrasive. Clean the inside of the terminals on the cable the same way. Then install the battery if you removed it in the fall.

• Turn on the battery master switch and check the ammeter for a significant discharge that might indicate a short circuit. Check again after you turn on the ignition switch.

• Install wiper blades. If yours are easily available, replace them each year.

• Do your safety check routine.

• Start the car engine. If the car has a manual transmission, engage the clutch slowly. Move the shift lever through all the gears. Move an automatic shift lever through all its positions.

• Move the car into the driveway. Listen for unusual noises. There are bound to be some that you hadn't heard before, but most of these will go away by themselves. Idle valves may stick a bit for a few minutes. Fan belts will be stiff until they've run for a while.

This large, plastic shelter will keep the rain and snow off two cars. They're available in smaller sizes. Be sure to cover the ground. A storage bag is advised.

Some noises are of more concern. Water pump noises may go away, but they may not. Make notes.

• Take the car on a short local trip. Bring along a friend to follow you or carry a portable phone. Don't get too far from home and stay off interstates. Apply the brakes with increasing force. Try to leave room on both sides for the possible pull to one side.

• Keep an eye on your temperature gauge, oil pressure gauge, and ammeter. Be alert for unusual smells and how the car 'feels'. If you smell burning or see smoke, reach for the battery master switch. If you haven't installed one yet, be sure to have a wrench of the correct size on the seat next to you, so you can leap from the car and disconnect the battery terminal. Yes, all this sounds like Caspar Milquetoast's description of how to drive a car. But if this routine saves you just once from a small or large disaster, it'll have paid you back manyfold.

CHAPTER EIGHTEEN

Afterthoughts

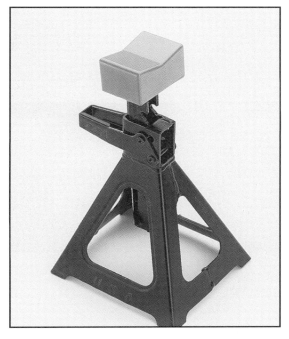

Look for jack stands with a wide base like these. The pad on top helps keeps the stands from scratching your car's nicely painted undercarriage.

Sometimes useful thoughts don't fall into the neat category of a particular chapter. I've collected them here. If nothing else, it reminds us that our collector car hobby exposes us to an amazing variety of skills and bodies of knowledge.

Paper Tools

The most important tools in the maintenance of your collector car are made of paper, not steel. They're the car's original factory service manual, supplemented by the publications of companies like Motor and Chilton. For an older car, and especially for orphan makes, mail order book vendors, like Classic Motorbooks, and automotive swap meets are your best sources. Books are usually available at reasonable prices. Buy everything you can find that pertains to your car. You never know when you'll need the information.

Cores

Commercial rebuilders of auto components usually don't rebuild your part. They send you a rebuilt unit and require that you exchange your old part for the newly rebuilt one. Typically this is true of brake cylinders, generators, carburetors, water pumps, and similar assemblies. To assure the return, rebuilders assess a deposit for the "core," which is how they refer to your old, rebuildable unit.

My advice is to let them keep the "core charge" while you retain your old unit. Several reasons. First, although the exchange unit may work exactly like the original, there is often a difference in external appearance. Someday you may want to restore your car to perfect authenticity, and you'll have a spare. What may now seem like a high core charge is a fraction of what you will pay for that same part ten years from now when it's rare or unavailable.

Lifting Your Car

I don't know about you, but it just isn't as easy for me to slide under my car and slither around as it used to be. Must be that the car is sagging closer to the ground. I also find that I can't see things that are only 3in from my nose as easily as I used to. Maybe its getting darker under there.

The answer, my friends, is to get the car off the ground a bit. Not that difficult to do, but a few safety admonitions may be in order.

You've heard it before, so hear it once more. Never (that means NEVER) get under a

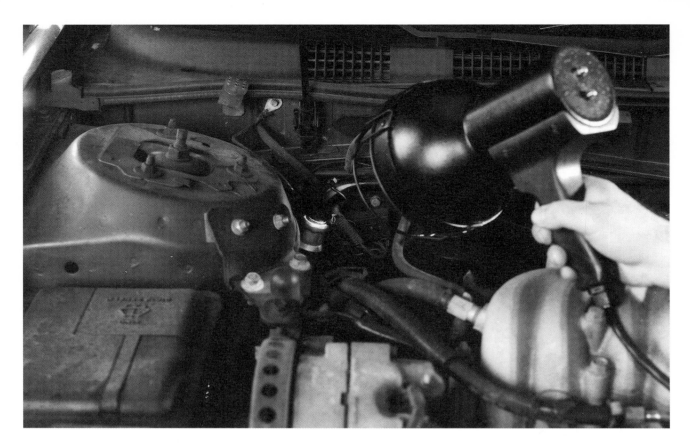

This high-powered ultraviolet light lets you see those fluorescent leak-detector dyes with the garage lights on.

car that's supported only by a hydraulic jack. We do not have so many collector car enthusiasts that we can afford to lose any. Every time I'm tempted just to take a quick dive under the car without setting the jack stands, I use a technique that works for me. By neglecting the jack stands I can save about two minutes, right? Now how long would it take, after the car falls on me, to have it lifted off, wait for the paramedics, ride to the ER in the ambulance, lie on a gurney in the corridor till they get to me . . . anyway, you get the idea. I do the same when I'm too lazy to walk over get my safety goggles before getting underneath to look up at a dirty frame crossmember. It works for me.

Jack stands are an indispensable item for the collector car owner. Look carefully at the unit itself before you buy. Check workmanship; neat welds usually indicate greater potential strength than sloppy ones do. Examine the latching mechanism. Remember that the weight capacity advertised is for *both* stands. Get stands with the highest weight-carrying ability you can afford. Spring for three-ton units

in preference to two-ton ones; five-tonners are best of all. Stands with these weight-carrying capacities all have about the same range of maximum and minimum heights. Heavier stands have a safer, wider base and give more margin of protection. Quality mail-order tool companies sell quality jack stands. The price difference is very small—consider that your life is on the line.

Never let your car stand on more than two jack stands at a time. They tip easily that way. When the stand is at maximum height, be certain that the bottom of the post remains enclosed by the full length of the tube of the base.

If you'll be working under the car for a full weekend and the job does not require the removal of the wheels, the safest way to provide more working clearance is with ramps. Some new ramps are made of high-strength plastic. They're lighter to carry around and light enough to hang on the wall for easy storage. And, they won't rust. Typically, a plastic ramp will lift your car about 6in. That's a bit less height than you can get with most jack stands.

But you *can* put a car on four ramps, and that will give you full clearance from front to back of the car. Need a bit more height? A steel ramp will go about 8in, but they're much heavier and harder to store. I don't drive my car up on ramps. I prefer to lift the car with a hydraulic jack, then lower it onto the ramps.

The ultimate way to lift your car is with an electric or air-operated lift. The new twin post lifts require no excavation. But, while prices have come down, they're still pretty expensive for most hobbyists. A worse problem is garage height. To be able to lift the car to a height where you can walk underneath it, you need a clear ceiling or rafter height of about 12ft. That's rare in home garages.

Consider a compromise. The lifts used by some tire shops only lift the car, using pads under the frame, about 3ft. As tire shops expand into other service areas, they're purchasing twin post asymmetrical lifts. The old tire lifts are sold off cheap. Ask any shops in your area that have these lifts to let you know if they upgrade. What's obsolete to them may be just right for you. Call some local lift suppliers, too, and ask about used lifts.

Check out the design of the lift you're interested in. You're looking for a "medium-rise" lift. "Low-rise" lifts only raise the car about 20in from the ground, not enough to make them worthwhile. Since the lifts are intended to be used from the side for tire work, some have a jungle of braces on the inside that make them useless for work under the car. But if you find one that works for you and the price is right, its much easier to work sitting up than flat on your back!

Looking for Liquid Leaks

There's a booming industry in pads and pans to place beneath your collector car when it's standing in the garage. That's because everyone knows that old cars leak. They really don't have to. But sometimes the biggest part of the problem isn't fixing the leak; its determining from where *exactly* the motor oil or transmission lube or coolant is leaking. Oil pans, transmissions, and rear ends can wind up covered with escaping lubricant. Coolant sometimes drips off a frame crossmember some distance from where its coming out of a radiator hose. Eyes alone often aren't sufficient.

There's a tested method of finding leaks that's non-invasive and relatively modest in cost. The latest equipment can get expensive, but earlier versions often wind up on the used market. I bought mine cheap at an automotive swap meet.

The method is ultraviolet or black-light leak detection. For such an effective diagnostic tool, the process is remarkably simple. To find a motor oil leak, for example, you pour about an ounce of a fluorescent tracer dye into the crankcase through the oil filler cap. Let the engine run for fifteen minutes or take the car for a drive—you need to allow sufficient time for the dye to mix thoroughly with the oil and to start leaking out. Then stop the engine and look underneath with your ultraviolet light. (If the gook on your engine is really thick, you may want to wipe and scrape much of it off). Modern 120–150W ultraviolet spotlights can be used in a lighted garage. If you're using an older 15W fluorescent tube, as I do, you'd best darken the garage as much as you can. The leak will leap out at you in bright yellow. (If you don't see it immediately, wait a while. It'll show up eventually.)

Eyes are *much* more difficult to replace than any part of your car, so protect your eyes from the ultraviolet. The spotlights are quite safe because they're easy to aim away from your eyes. I'm not so comfortable with the fluorescent

The older fluorescent UV lamps require that you turn out the lights to get a good view of the dyes.

tubes, which spray black light in all directions. You also get closer to them, because they're dimmer. I always wear UV-blocking safety glasses when I use my fluorescent black light. You won't find them at the discount store, but a good tool

Above and right: Apply an air hose to this fitting, and listen for leaks at your leisure.

find out. But, if you have a source of compressed air, there's a simpler way.

You need a fitting that will permit you to apply air pressure to a cylinder. Your local tool supply store carries these adapters, for use with leakdown testers. (You can make one, if you choose, by breaking and drilling the insulator and center electrode out of an old spark plug, then brazing on an air hose fitting.)

Screw the adapter into the spark plug hole of the offending cylinder. Bring that cylinder to top dead center on the firing stroke. Both valves should now be closed. Transmission in high gear and parking brake on. That should keep the engine from turning. (If your car has an automatic transmission, you'll have to find some way to keep the flywheel from turning.)

Now apply pressure to the fitting. If there's a leak, the air has to go someplace. Listen at the oil filler opening; if the leak is past the rings, you'll hear it hiss. If the exhaust valve is bad, you'll hear it at the tailpipe. If it's the intake valve, you'll hear it at the carburetor. If a head gasket is bad, you'll see the bubbles when you remove the cap and look into the radiator. Leak finding this way can be almost fun!

shop will order them for you. Or, you can order a set from the maker of the test equipment.

The detection principle is the same for transmission fluid and for coolant. Dyes are made that are compatible with fuel and automatic transmission fluid too, only the colors are different for each. Happily, the dyes do no harm and may be left in until you next change the lubricant or coolant. When you wash off the outside of the dirty engine or transmission, the dye will wash off, too.

Listening for Compression Leaks

Most collector car owners have used the traditional compression gauge to check the compression of the engine's cylinders. They know that the important issue is relative uniformity between the cylinders, rather than the absolute compression pressure in each.

When you've found a cylinder or two with low pressures, you know that pressure is leaking out. But is it from a leaky valve? Which one? Worn rings? A bad head gasket? There's a fancy tool called a leakdown tester that can help you

Anaerobic Adhesives

The files of the US Patent Office are filled with devices intended to keep a nut from loosening on a screw. Who knew that the ultimate answer would come in a tiny bottle? The word "anaerobic" means "without air." It refers to a liquid that hardens only in the absence of air. This type of threadlocker was first marketed in 1953 by a father-son team—Professor Vernon Krieble and his son Robert. Their trade name, Loctite, was contributed by the professor's wife Nancy. Loctite has since become a huge worldwide enterprise, swallowing up previous household names like Permatex.

Loctite's great contribution is that, unlike lock washers, a properly assembled threaded part will never loosen in use. Race car builders love it. So should collector car drivers.

Most of Loctite's thread sealers are liquids that harden into a thermoplastic when deprived of air. They come in various strengths, usually color-coded. For most of us, the little bottle that dispenses a drop of blue liquid is the most common use. A fastener sealed with this can be removed with ordinary wrench pressure.

There is a wide range of Loctite threadlockers, adhesives, and other chemicals. Their catalog describes them all. Here are a few that I use regularly. Threadlocker 242: This is the blue stuff, a medium strength adhesive. Threadlocker 271: Red, and for use when you don't ever expect to take it off again. Threadlocker 290: This one is green. It's very thin and wicks its way into already assembled fasteners. Porosity sealer 290: Same stuff; it's used to seal cracks in castings and welds. Brush it on and wipe it off. I used it to seal some hairline cracks on the outside of a rare aluminum cylinder head.

There are other items in the Loctite line. My favorites include Gasket Eliminator 515, the all-purpose gasket replacement. Gasket Eliminator 518 is intended for use as a gasket replacement for aluminum flanges, but it's also a fine gasket dressing. Loctite also sells the same product as Master Gasket.

I seal pipe threads with PST Pipe Sealant with Teflon. It's anaerobic, so it seals well but never quite hardens, so you can move the fitting a bit to match it up to a line.

Anaerobic sealants are not magic. You have to properly prepare surfaces and understand how each product is best used. So get catalogs and read instructions. Also, Loctite is no longer the only game in town. Anaerobic technology is well understood and no longer protected by Loctite's original patents. But Loctite and other suppliers keep improving their products. One of them may help you solve that fastener problem.

Hand Protection

Car maintenance involves work with many toxic substances. Few of them will kill you unless you drink them, but they're capable of making your life very unpleasant if you're careless with them. So we're usually very careful not to spray brake cleaner in our eyes, and we've learned to be more careful with asbestos and gasoline.

We sometimes don't pay enough attention to our body's largest organ—the skin. It's got

I carry most of this array of anaerobic adhesives on trips. It's amazing what they'll stick together!

immense self-protective ability, or it wouldn't survive the things we do to it every day, but it still can use all the help we can give it.

I use latex gloves whenever I work on my car. They're they same as the ones used by surgeons, but they're non-sterile, so they cost less. They fit tight enough, so I lose very little feel, and they're inexpensive enough to be discarded after every use. Strong solvents dissolve them, so you may have to change them during a cleaning job. They come in large, medium, and small sizes. I've bought latex gloves in several places, at varying prices; some were stronger than others. Keep trying till you find a source you like. You'll find that they extend your car hobby time too. With less time needed to scrub your hands and nails, you can work until closer to dinnertime.

There are also hand lotions especially made to protect your skin from harsh chemicals. One I've begun using is Skin Coat, and I find it effective. It claims to even protect from acids long

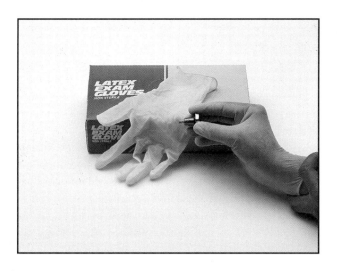

Wear latex gloves. Your hands will love you for it.

enough to wash them off, but happily I have not had the occasion to test this.

Engine Oil System Flushing

This is a technique that's been through several incarnations over past decades, with only so-so reviews. The current offering, though, is marketed by Bilstein, a German company with a reputation for quality products (best known for its shock absorbers.) The process itself is far more sophisticated than earlier attempts. The patents are held by The Perix Group, headquartered in San Diego.

The rationale for this procedure is that even after you drain the oil from your car, about half a quart of dirty oil remains in the engine's oil galleries and in the bottom of the pan. Water, acid, wear particles, and other contaminants remain behind with it. These contaminants go right back into circulation as soon as you start the engine with its crankcase full of fresh oil.

Bilstein offers some impressive statistics. Particulates five microns in size can damage engine bearings. In a typical test, 16,046 parts per million (ppm) of particulates this size were found in a Thunderbird's oil before it was changed. In the fresh oil immediately after a typical oil change, the count was still 3,149ppm. Only 276ppm remained when the engine was flushed before the oil change. Old oil in a Ford Taurus contained 38ppm of sulfur. After an oil change, the amount of sulfur was the same! The flush removed it all.

The machine goes through six cycles. It injects a warm flushing solvent which back-flushes engine passages. Then it leaves six

quarts of solution in the engine to soak and dissolve contaminants. Cleaning solutions and dirt are then extracted from the engine, and the three steps are repeated. Warm air is blown through the engine's oil galleys and bearings, before fresh oil is poured in. (Sounds a bit like a dishwasher!) The designers had hoped to back-flush the oil pump and strainer as well but found that the solvent wouldn't push past the pump gears. Therefore the soak.

Bilstein calls their flushing machine the R-2000. (The marketing department at work, no doubt.) It's intended to be used only on cars with full-flow filtration, because the adapter through which it injects the cleaning solvent screws on in place of the oil filter cartridge. If your car has a by-pass filter and you want to have it flushed, contact Perix.

I've seen the R-2000 in use at several dealers in expensive new cars. I felt that collector car owners might want to know about the existence of this process. I've seen the test results, and they appear to bear out Bilstein's claims. Time will tell whether the market will agree. If you're interested, contact Bilstein for a brochure and the name of a nearby provider.

Insurance

If your collector car is driven every day, you'll have to insure it as you would any other car. Your regular agent can handle that transaction. Be aware that you'll have difficulty getting collision, fire, and theft coverage that will reimburse you for the real value in the event of total loss to a forty-year-old vehicle. There's also likely to be a deductible on these coverages.

If your collector car meets certain standards, you're eligible for one of the great bargains in auto insurance—collector car insurance. Your car must be at least twenty-five years old and stored in a garage. There must have been no modifications to the car's engine; street rods aren't covered. The car must be driven fewer than 2,500 miles per year, primarily to meets and shows, and you may not use it to commute to work. Cars only twenty years old can be covered, but the premium is double that for the older cars.

Available from several sources who specialize in this coverage, collector car insurance sets a fixed price for liability, no-fault property damage, uninsured motorist coverage, and medical insurance. These rates are filed by the companies for

occur if the car's value appears to have been mis-represented. I have not heard of this being a serious problem. In two accidents—one major, one minor—in forty years of driving classic cars, I've received excellent service from my company.

"Year of Manufacture" Plates

A continuing bow to America's love affair with cars, YOM plates are available in most states. In essence, your collector car is permitted to drive on the public way wearing a set of license plates issued in the year that the car was manufactured. Different states have different names for this arrangement.

YOM plates enable the casual admirer to determine the year of your car. They add a historic touch. And, for those who drive a car of which fiberglass replicas have been made, they identify your car as the real thing.

In most states cars over twenty-five years of age are eligible for YOM plates. (In one state the law has the cut-off year fixed at 1968.) Here's the typical procedure.

You need a set of license plates of the year shown on your current registration and title. If your

Above and below: The Bilstein Engine Flush may have merit for engines of any type. It should certainly be strongly considered for engines with no oil filters or with by-pass filtration only. Just before the car is put away for the winter would be a good time to have the flush performed.

approval by each state. The minimum dollar coverage in each category is also set by each state.

The ads for collector car insurance usually list rather low coverage limits, by today's standards, for liability insurance. The companies will provide higher levels of coverage. Just ask. If you want even more coverage, your own insurance agent can provide an umbrella policy that sits over the regular automobile policy.

Comprehensive and collision coverages are based on an *agreed value*. You set the value on your car. If it's over $20,000, the company will ask for an appraisal and a photo of the car. They sometimes ask for these when you increase the coverage amount too.

If your car is totally destroyed, the company will pay the agreed amount. If there's a partial loss, the company will usually pay the repair costs approved by their adjuster. Hitches only

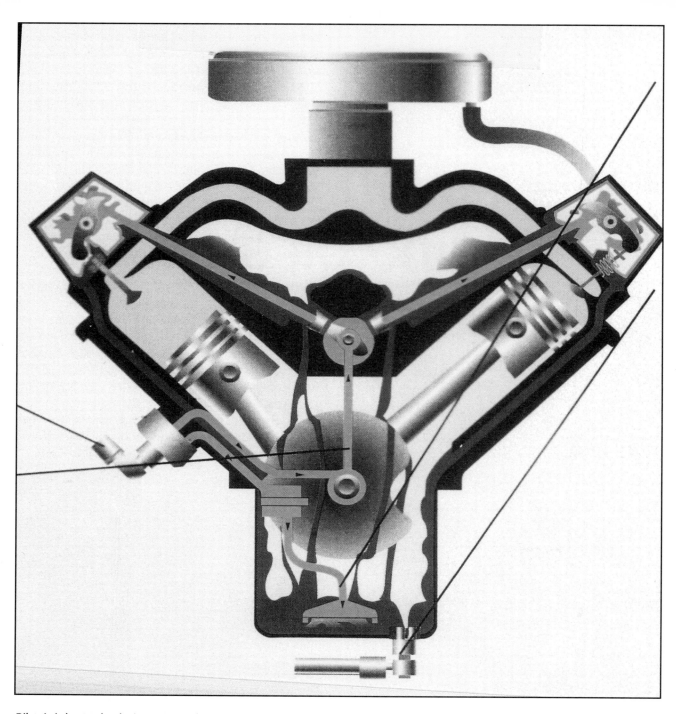

Bilstein's heated solution enters the engine on the left and exits through the oil pan drain at the bottom.

state only required a rear plate in that year, then you only need one plate. You can get plates from vendors at most of the larger swap meets. There are also vendors who buy and sell plates listed in Hemmings Motor News and other publications.

The plates you purchase may not be in condition good enough to use or to put on your beautiful car. (Some states require that the plates be in original and good condition, that is, unre-

stored. I've never seen this provision enforced.) License plate restoration is a mini-hobby in itself. It's important that the colors of background and numbers be accurate. There are *many* shades of orange, and no two states chose the same one. Restoration techniques vary, too. Some restorers use stencils, others use a roller method. Most will fix dents and small holes. Ask for references before you entrust your valuable plates.

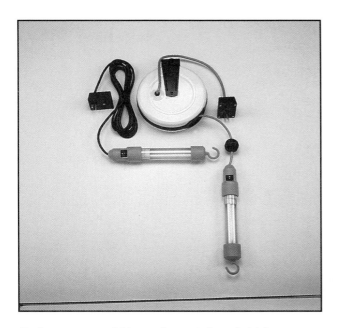

Exchange your old incandescent drop-light for a new fluorescent unit. They're brighter. Most important, you'll never burn yourself again when you turn your head without looking. Some brands come with a reel.

In some states the YOM procedure can be conducted by mail. In others you'll have to bring your title and registration to the local office of your state's Department of Motor Vehicles. In the latter case, be aware that the regulations regarding YOM plates are not invoked often, and you may find that the clerks you deal with are not aware of them. If your locality has more than one office, it's worth some time on the phone to identify a clerk who is familiar with the regulations before you make the trip. No matter how its done, you can be sure that there will be a form to fill out.

Some states require that you bring the actual plates to the Motor Vehicle Department office to verify that they exist and are legible. The local office may access the state's main computer database to determine whether the number on the plates you submit are currently in use.

There are fees to be paid. (In at least one state the small fee is permanent, and you never need pay again. A car hobbyist legislator tacked this provision onto some bill many years ago, God bless him.) Some time later you'll receive your new registration. A prefix to the number indicates that these are vintage plates, for the benefit of the highway patrolman who stops you looking for a current registration. In Califor-

A Year-of-Manufacture plate on a 1936 classic.

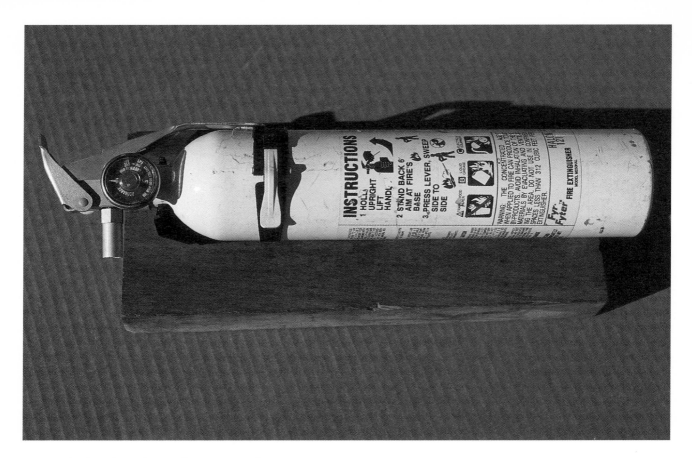

Screw the bracket of your fire extinguisher to a block of wood. It will be portable while not rolling around.

nia, the registration is accompanied by a small metal tab that's to be mounted at the top of the plate, to provide a place to stick the annual validation stickers.

Most states also offer "historic" plates to cars more than twenty-five years old. These special plates often carry a lower fee than the regular registration fee. They may also have restrictions on use.

Appendix

The products and services listed below are those I have used or am personally familiar with. For some of these items, there are other sources whose products may be equally useful.

Sources for Products in Chapter 2

Lubricants
Lubriplate Division
Fiske Brothers Refining Company
129 Lockwood Street
Newark, NJ 07105

Steering box lubricant
Penrite Lubricants
The Classic Oil Company
1330 Galaxy Way
Concord, CA 94520

Oil Hypo pre-luber
Hagen Enterprises
684 Terra Drive
Corona, CA 91719

Ultra-Lube pre-luber
SOS Automotive Specialties Company
PO Box 608
LaPlace, LA 70069

Master Luber pre-luber
Bob Sullivan Restorations
2260 Orchard Home Drive
Medford, OR 97501

Sources for Products in Chapter 4

Oil analysis

Herguth Petroleum Laboratories
101 Corporate Place
Vallejo, CA 94590

SmartCheck
275 Market Street Suite 1001
Minneapolis, MN 55405

Oil pan drain valve
Sterling Specialties
RD #4 Box
291 Lakes Road
Monroe, NY 10950

Sources for Products in Chapter 5

Air and oil filters
Wix Filters
1301 E. Ozark Avenue
Gastonia, NC 28053-1967

Amsoil, Inc.
Amsoil Building
Superior, WI 54880

Magnetic drain plugs
Lisle Corporation
Clarinda, IA 51632

Sources for Products in Chapter 8

Coolant filter
Gano Filter
1205 Sandalwood Lane
Los Altos, CA 94024

Water

Black Mountain Spring Water
San Carlos, CA 94070

Coatings
Swain Tech Coatings, Inc.
35 Main Street
Scottsville, NY 14546

Needle valve substitute
Grose-Jet
D & G Valve Manufacturing Company, Inc.
8 Mt. Vernon Street
Stoneham, MA 02180

Hoses
The Gates Rubber Company
990 South Broadway
Denver, CO 80217-5887

Propylene Glycol anti-freeze (Sta-Clean brand)
Restoration Supply Company
2060 Palisade Drive
Reno, NV 89509

Sources for Products in Chapter 10

Tires
Coker Tire
1317 Chestnut Street
Chattanooga, TN 37402

Lucas Automotive
2850 Temple Avenue
Long Beach, CA 90806

Sources for Products in Chapter 11

Gas tank renovation
Gas Tank Renu - USA
12727 Greenfield
Detroit, MI 48227

Gas tank sealers
Bill Hirsch Automotive
396 Littleton Avenue
Newark, NJ 07103

POR-15 Inc.
RestoMotive Laboratories Division
PO Box 1235
Morristown, NJ 07962-1235

Slip-Plate
Superior Graphite Company
120 South Riverside Plaza
Chicago, IL 60606

Sources for Products in Chapter 12

6V alternators
Fifth Avenue Auto Parts
502 Arthur Avenue
Clay Center, KS 67432

Starter, generator, speedometer repair, and battery cables
Bob Groulx
1970 Buena Vista
Livermore, CA 94550

Batteries
Optima Batteries, Inc.
9 E. Mississippi Avenue
Denver, CO 80210

Master Switches
Bathurst, Inc.
Box 27
Tyrone, PA 16686

Headlight reflector renovation
UVIRA
310 Pleasant Valley Road
Merlin, OR 97532

6-12 volt battery
Antique Auto Battery Manufacturing Company
2320 Old Mill Road
Hudson, OH 44236

Sources for Products in Chapter 13

Squeegee
First Pass
PO Box 31121
Cleveland, OH 44131

Sources for Products in Chapter 14

Waxoyl
Brit-Tek
6 Londonderry Commons Suite 111
Londonderry, NH 03053

Sources for Products in Chapter 15

Dye penetrant kit
URESCO, Inc.
10603 Midway Avenue
Cerritos, CA 90701

Headlamp adjusting tool

Hopkins Manufacturing Corporation
428 Peyton
Emporia, KS 66801-1157

Sources for Products in Chapter 16

Drywash cloth

KOZAK
Auto DryWash, Inc.
6 S. Lyon Street
Batavia, NY 14021

Sources for Products in Chapter 17

Omnibag storage bag
Car/Jacket storage bag

Pine Ridge Enterprise
13165 Center Road
Bath, MI 48808

Car covers

A.P.A. Industries (Covercraft brand)
PO Box 7722
Mission Hills, CA 91346

Battery Tender

Deltran, Inc.
DeLand, FL 32720

Sources for Products in Chapter 18

Leak Detection

Tracer Products
956 Brush Hollow Road
Westbury, NY 11590

Anaerobic adhesives

Loctite North America
1001 Trout Brook Crossing
Rocky Hill, CT 06111

Skin protection

Skin Coat North America, Inc.
Verdugo City, CA 91406

Engine Flushing

Bilstein Corporation of America
8845 Rehco Road
San Diego, CA 92121

Ramps

Rhino Ramps
99 South Cameron Street
Harrisburg, PA 17101

Insurance

J.C. Taylor Antique Auto Insurance Agency, Inc.
320 South 69th Street
Upper Darby, PA 19082

Index